Documents on the
Israeli-Palestinian Conflict, 1967–1983

Documents on the Israeli-Palestinian Conflict, 1967–1983

edited by
Yehuda Lukacs

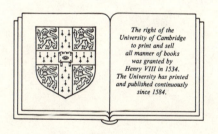

The right of the University of Cambridge to print and sell all manner of books was granted by Henry VIII in 1534. The University has printed and published continuously since 1584.

CAMBRIDGE UNIVERSITY PRESS
Cambridge
London   New York   New Rochelle
Melbourne   Sydney

Published by the Press Syndicate of the University of Cambridge
The Pitt Building, Trumpington Street, Cambridge CB2 1RP
32 East 57th Street, New York, NY 10022, USA
296 Beaconsfield Parade, Middle Park, Melbourne 3206, Australia

© The International Center for Peace in the Middle East,
107 Hahashmonaim St, Tel Aviv 67011, Israel 1984

First published 1984

Printed in Great Britain at the University Press, Cambridge

Library of Congress catalogue card number: 84–7664

British Library Cataloguing in Publication Data

Documents on the Israeli-Palestinian conflict
1967–1983.
1. Israel-Arab Border Conflicts, 1949–
– Sources
I. Lukacs, Yehuda
956′.046   DS119.7

ISBN 0 521 26795 1

Contents

Acknowledgements

My thanks to Prof. Yehoshua Porath and Dr Amnon Kapeliuk for their advice; to Cecile Panzer and the library staff of Hebrew University's Truman Institute for their patience and goodhumoured assistance; to Gary Feingold for his tireless research efforts, and Sam Boshes for his meticulous proofreading; to Laura Blum for her invaluable help and suggestions; and to my colleagues Beatrice McCartney for her occasional elucidation of the mysteries of English syntax and idiom, and David Shaham, for curbing what at times threatened to be my over-enthusiasm when faced with a deluge of material from which a selection had to be made.

This collection is dedicated to my mother and the memory of my father.

Yehuda Lukacs
October 1983, Tel Aviv

Yehuda Lukacs completed his graduate studies in International Relations at the School of International Service, the American University, Washington, D.C. He is at present working as Projects Co-ordinator for the International Center for Peace in the Middle East.

Introduction

In addition to blood, much ink has flowed in the three-and-half decades since the United Nations first turned its attention to the question of Palestine. Since then the Arab-Israeli-Palestinian conflict has generated a myriad of documents and a plethora of suggestions for its resolution. No comparable regional conflict has been subjected to such scrutiny or given rise to such radically different interpretations of the same basic facts.

This book came about as a result of a seminar on the Palestinian problem conducted by the International Center for Peace in the Middle East for members of the Israeli Knesset. At that time, a need was expressed by the legislators for the publication of the essentials of the documentary history of the conflict which could serve as a reference for policy-makers, academics, and moulders of public opinion.

The present compendium consists of key documents and statements of position of the parties to the conflict, focusing on the period 1967-1983. It begins with U.N. Security Council Resolution 242 which coined the formula 'return of territories in exchange for peace', and ends with the joint Jordanian — P.L.O. statement of 10 April, 1983 which rejected Jordanian participation in negotiations as proposed in the September 1982 Reagan Peace Plan.

My intention was not to present all the documents pertaining to the conflict (which would have been impossible in one volume), but rather to publish those documents most frequently cited by both protagonists and scholars, as well as those which best reflect the trends and vicissitudes of the parties involved. The documents speak for themselves; they reflect the deep schism separating the parties and testify to the complexity of the issues involved. Any serious analysis of the conflict demands a thorough familiarity with its documentary history, a history which for a long time has been colored by emotionalism and blind partisanship.

The book consists of seven chapters. The first chapter presents U.N., European and Soviet positions; the second, American proposals; the third pertains to the late President Sadat's historic visit to Jerusalem and the autonomy negotiations which followed in the wake of the Israeli-Egyptian Peace Treaty; The fourth chapter documents Israeli positions; the fifth chapter is composed of platforms of all the Israeli parties represented in the Knesset, dealing with the Palestinian problem and of platforms of extra-parliamentary groups such as Peace Now, Gush Emunim and the Israel Council for Israeli-Palestinian Peace. The last two chapters consist of Palestinian and Arab documents respectively.

International Documents

1. Security Council Resolution 242 Concerning Principles for a Just and Lasting Peace in the Middle East, 22 November, 1967

The Security Council

Expressing its continuing concern with the grave situation in the Middle East,

Emphasizing the inadmissibility of the acquisition of territory by war and the need to work for a just and lasting peace in which every State in the area can live in security,

Emphasizing further that all Member States in their acceptance of the Charter of the United Nations have undertaken a commitment to act in accordance with Article 2 of the Charter,

1. *Affirms* that the fulfillment of Charter principles requires the establishment of a just and lasting peace in the Middle East which should include the application of both the following principles:

(i)   Withdrawal of Israel armed forces from territories occupied in the recent conflict;

(ii)   Termination of all claims or states of belligerency and respect for and acknowledgement of the sovereignty, territorial integrity and political independence of every State in the area and their right to live in peace within secure and recognized boundaries free from threats or acts of force;

2. *Affirms further* the necessity

(a)   For guaranteeing freedom of navigation through international waterways in the area;

(b)   For achieving a just settlement of the refugee problem;

(c)   For guaranteeing the territorial inviolability and political independence of every State in the area, through measures including the establishment of demilitarized zones;

3. *Requests* the Secretary-General to designate a Special Representative to proceed to the Middle East to establish and maintain contacts with the States

concerned in order to promote agreement and assist efforts to achieve a peaceful and accepted settlement in accordance with the provisions and principles in this resolution;

4.   *Requests* the Secretary-General to report to the Security Council on the progress of the efforts of the Special Representative as soon as possible.

2. Security Council Resolution 338, Concerning the October War, 22 October, 1973

The Security Council

1.   *Calls upon* all parties to the present fighting to cease all firing and terminate all military activity immediately, no later than 12 hours after the moment of the adoption of this decision, in the positions they now occupy;

2.   *Calls upon* the parties concerned to start immediately after the cease-fire the implementation of Security Council resolution 242 (1967) in all of its parts:

3.   *Decides* that, immediately and concurrently with the cease-fire, negotiations start between the parties concerned under appropriate auspices aimed at establishing a just and durable peace in the Middle East.

3. Security Council Resolution 339, 23 October, 1973

The Security Council

Referring to its resolution 338 (1973) of 22 October 1973,

1.   *Confirms* its decision on an immediate cessation of all kinds of firing and of all military action, and urges that the forces of the two sides be returned to the positions they occupied at the moment the cease-fire became effective:

2.   *Requests* the Secretary-General to take measures for immediate dispatch of United Nations observers to supervise the observance of the cease-fire between the forces of Israel and the Arab Republic of Egypt, using for this purpose the personnel of the United Nations now in the Middle East and first of all the personnel now in Cairo.

4. The Jarring Questionnaire and Replies, January 1971

The Questionnaire. (Jarring's questions to the four ME states and the answers he received were published in January 1971 in a report drawn up by SG of the UN, U. Thant. Incomplete versions of the questions and replies were published before this report. Specific lists of questions submitted to the four ME countries were based on the following general list:)

1. Does Israel (Jordan, Lebanon, the UAR) accept Res. 242 for implementation for achieving a peaceful and accepted settlement of the ME question in accordance with the provision and principles contained in the resolution?

2. Does Israel (Jordan, Lebanon, the UAR) agree to pledge termination of all claims or states of belligerency with Jordan, Lebanon, the UAR (Israel)?

3. Does Israel (Jordan, Lebanon, the UAR) agree to pledge respect for and acknowledgement of the sovereignty, territorial integrity and political independence of Jordan, Lebanon and the UAR (Israel)?

4. Does Israel (Jordan, Lebanon, the UAR) accept the right of Jordan, Lebanon, and the UAR (Israel) to live in peace within secure and recognized boundaries free from threats or acts of force?

5. If so, what is the conception of secure and recognized boundaries held by Israel (Jordan, Lebanon, the UAR)?

6. Does Israel agree to withdraw its armed forces from territories occupied by it in the recent conflict?

7. Does the UAR agree to guarantee freedom of navigation for Israel through international waterways in the area, in particular (a) through the Straits of Tiran; and (b) through the Suez Canal?

8. Does Israel (Jordan, Lebanon, the UAR) agree that if a plan for the just settlement of the refugee problem is worked out and presented to the parties for their consideration, the acceptance in principle of such a plan by the parties and the declaration of their intention to implement it in good faith constitute sufficient implementation of this provision of Res. 242 to justify the implementation of the other provisions?

9. Does Israel (Jordan, Lebanon, the UAR) agree that the territorial inviolability and political independence of the states in the area should be guaranteed: (a) by the establishment of demilitarized zones; and (b) through additional measures?

10. Does Israel agree that such demilitarized zones should include areas on its side of the boundaries?

11. Does Jordan agree that a demilitarized zone should be established in Jordanian territory from which Israel's armed forces have been withdrawn?

12. Does the UAR agree that a demilitarized zone should be established: (a) at Sharm el-Sheikh and (b) in other parts of the Sinai Peninsula?

13. Does Israel (Jordan, Lebanon, the UAR) agree that demilitarization of such zones should be supervised and maintained by the UN?

14. Would Israel (Jordan, Lebanon, the UAR) accept as a final act of agreement on all provisions a mutually signed, multilateral document which would incorporate the agreed conditions for a just and lasting peace?

Egypt's Replies. On 27 March, Jarring again visited Cairo, where he received from Riyad the Egyptian replies to his questionnaire.

In the preamble to its replies, the UAR reiterated the contents of its memorandum of 5 March, noting Israel's "plans for annexation of Arab lands" through war; its "flagrant violation and clear rejection" of Res. 242 "and of a peaceful settlement". The preamble concluded by saying that the UAR re-affirmed its acceptance of Res. 242 and its readiness to carry out its requirements; it demanded that Israel do likewise, in particular with respect to withdrawal from "all Arab territories it occupied".

The answers to Jarring's questions were as follows:

Question (1). The UAR accepted Res. 242 and was ready to implement it in order to achieve a peaceful and accepted settlement in accordance with its provisions and principles.

Question (2). The UAR agreed to pledge termination of all claims or states of belligerency. Such a pledge would become effective upon withdrawal of Israel's forces from all the Arab territories occupied in June 1967.

A declaration by Israel terminating the state of belligerency would be meaningful only when Israel withdrew its forces from all these territories.

Question (3). Acceptance by the UAR to pledge respect for and acknowledgement of the sovereignty, territorial integrity, and political independence of every state in the area required the termination by Israel of its occupation and the withdrawal of its forces from all Arab territories it occupied in June 1967, and full implementation of Res. 242.

Question (4). The UAR accepted the right of every state in the area to live in peace with secure and recognized boundaries free from threats or acts of force, provided that Israel withdrew from all Arab territories occupied in June 1967 and implemented Res. 242.

Question (5). Israel's boundaries were defined by GA Res. 181 (II) of 29 Nov. 1947.

Question (7). The UAR declared its readiness to implement all the provisions of Res. 242, covering, *inter alia,* the freedom of navigation in international waterways in the area; providing that Israel likewise implemented all provisions of the resolution.

Question (8). The UAR had always held that the just settlement of the refugee problem was embodied in Para 11 of GA Res. 194 (III) of Dec. 1948. If a plan on the basis of that paragraph were presented for consideration to the parties concerned, its acceptance by the parties, with adequate guarantees for its full implementation, would justify the implementation of the other provisions of Res. 242.

Question (9) and (12). The UAR did not believe that the establishment of demilitarized zones was a necessity. However, it would not oppose the establishment of such zones if they were astride the boundaries.

Question (13). The UAR accepted that if such demilitarized zones were established, they would be supervised and maintained by the UN.

Question (14). In view of past experience with Israel and its "denunciation of four agreements signed by her with Arab states", the UAR considered that the instrument it would sign engaging it to carry out its obligations should be addressed to the SC. Israel should likewise sign and address to the SC an instrument engaging it to carry out its obligations emanating from Res. 242. The endorsement by the SC of these documents would constitute the final multilateral document. *(Source below).*

Jordan's Replies. (The Jordanian replies were received by Jarring at Nicosia on 24 March. They were identical with those of the UAR.)

Lebanon's Replies. The Lebanese reply to the questionnaire was received by Jarring in Moscow on 21 Apr. (The reply did not relate to each question individually, but took the form of a letter written by F.M. Salim, stating Lebanon's position on the Arab-Israeli conflict and its solution.

Lebanon, Salim wrote, was "essentially involved in the general context" of the Arab-Israeli conflict, and therefore in the consequences of the June 1967 war, because of its "brotherly solidarity" with the Arab States and the "threats... constantly directed at it" by Israel.

Lebanon considered that the armistice agreement with Israel of 23 March 1949 remained valid, as confirmed by SG of the UN, U. Thant in his report of 15 Sept. 1967 (see *MER 1967,* p. 86). The armistice lines, Salim noted, had never been altered, and "correspond to the frontiers of Lebanon which have always been internationally recognized". It was appropriate to state this fact "more particularly with a view to explaining the nature and character of the only reply which we are in a position to give to the questionnaire". This reply proclaimed Lebanon's support of the position of the Arab States "whose territory has been occupied by Israel and which have accepted Res. 242". *(Source below).*

Israel's Replies. On 2 Apr., FM Eban presented Jarring with the Israeli replies in Jerusalem. In an accompanying letter, Eban expressed Israel's willingness to continue to co-operate with Jarring, and that after the Arab governments' replies were received, Israel would join in Jarring's expected effort to obtain additional clarifications from the Arab governments. Israel was ready to carry out the suggestion which Jarring had made "some weeks ago" to convene a FMs' meeting "soon, at a suitable place, to pursue the promotion of agreement". Eban also said that the Four-Power meetings had weakened attention that should have been concentrated on the efforts of the parties themselves to move towards agreement. Israel recognized the Jarring mission as the "authoritative international framework" within which peace should be promoted. He added that Israel's statements of its position, including its replies to Jarring's questions, had taken into account speeches by Abdul Nasser and other Arab leaders, which had expressed the "specific and emphatic" refusal by the Arab States "to make peace with Israel, to recognize Israel, to negotiate with Israel, to cease terrorist attacks on Israel or to admit to the possibility of sovereign co-existence in any field."

The specific Israeli replies were the following:

Question (1). Israel accepted Res. 242 for the promotion of agreement on the establishment of a just and lasting peace, to be reached by negotiation and agreements between the governments concerned. Implementation of agreements should begin when agreement had been concluded on all their provisions.

Question (2). The Arab States, not Israel, had claimed and originated states of belligerency. For two decades they had unilaterally declared themselves to be in a state of war with Israel. It was therefore primarily incumbent upon them to terminate the state of war with Israel.

On the establishment of peace with her Arab neighbours, Israel would agree to the termination, on a reciprocal basis, of all claims of states of belligerency with each state with which peace was established. A declaration specifying each state by name would be made by Israel in each case.

The corresponding statement by any Arab State must specifically renounce belligerency "with Israel" and not merely "with any state in the area". Legal obligations must be specific in regard to those by whom they are bound.

Renunciation of belligerency included: the cessation of all maritime interference; the cessation of boycott measures involving third parties; the annulment of reservations made by Arab States on the applicability to Israel of their obligations under international conventions to which they adhered; nonadherence to political and military alliances and pacts directed against Israel or including states unwilling to renounce claims or states of belligerency with Israel and to maintain peaceful relations with it; the refusal to station the armed forces of such other states on the territory of the contracting states and the prohibition and prevention in the territory of Arab States of all preparations, actions or expeditions, by irregular or paramilitary groups or by individuals, against the lives, security or property of Israel in any part of the world.

Question (3). Israel agreed to respect and acknowledge the "sovereignty, territorial integrity and political independence" of neighbouring Arab States; this principle would be embodied in peace treaties establishing agreed boundaries.

Question (4). Israel accepted the right of Jordan, Lebanon, the UAR and other neighbouring states to live in peace "within secure and recognized boundaries, free from threats or acts of force... Explicit and unequivocal reciprocity" was Israel's only condition for this acceptance. "Acts of force" included those committed by "irregular or paramilitary groups or by individuals directed against the life, security or property of Israel in any part of the world."

Question (5). Secure and recognized boundaries had never yet existed between Israel and the Arab States; these should now be established as part of the peace-making process. The cease-fire should be replaced by peace treaties "establishing permanent, secure and recognized boundaries as agreed upon through negotiation between the governments concerned."

Question (6). When permanent, secure and recognized boundaries were agreed upon and established between Israel and each of the neighbouring Arab States, the disposition of forces would be carried out in full accordance with the boundaries determined in the peace treaties.

Question (8). The refugee problem had been caused by the wars against Israel launched by the Arab States, and had been perpetuated by them. Israel was willing to give priority to the attainment of a solution to the problem "through regional and international co-operation". Agreement should be sought even in advance of peace negotiations. Israel suggested that a conference of ME States should be convened, together with governments contributing to refugee relief and the specialized agencies of the UN, to chart a "five-year plan" for the solution of the refugee problem.

Joint refugee integration and rehabilitation commissions should be established by the governments concerned in order to work out agreed projects for refugee integration on a regional basis with international assistance. In view of the "humanitarian nature" of this issue, Israel did not make agreement on plans for a solution to the refugee problem contingent on agreement on any other aspect of the ME problem. Nor should it be invoked by Arab States to obstruct agreement on other problems.

Question (9). The effective guarantee for territorial inviolability and political independence of states lay in the observance by governments of the treaty obligations. In the context of peace providing for full respect for the sovereignty of states and the establishment of agreed boundaries, other security measures may be discussed by the contracting governments.

Question (10) through (13). Without prejudice to what was stated in answer to question (9), it was pointed out that experience had shown that the measures mentioned in questions (10) and (13) had not prevented the preparation and carrying out of aggression against Israel.

Question (14). Peace had to be juridically expressed, contractually defined and reciprocally binding in accordance with established norms of international law and practice. Accordingly, Israel's position was that the peace should be embodied in bilateral peace treaties between Israel and each Arab

State incorporating all the agreed conditions for a just and lasting peace. The treaties, once signed and ratified, should be registered with the Secretariat of the UN in accordance with the UN Charter.

5. Statement by European Community Foreign Ministers, Brussels, 6 November, 1973.

On 6 November the Foreign Ministers of the nine States of the European Community met to discuss the situation in the Middle East. At the conclusion of their meeting they issued a statement of policy.

Statement by European Community Foreign Ministers

The nine Governments of the European Community have continued their exchange of views on the situation in the Middle East. While emphasizing that the views set out below are only a first contribution on their part to the search for a comprehensive solution to the problem they have agreed on the following:

They strongly urge that the forces of both sides in the Middle East conflict should return immediately to the positions they occupied on 22 October in accordance with resolutions 339 and 340 of the Security Council. They believe that a return to these positions will facilitate a solution to other pressing problems concerning prisoners-of-war and the Egyptian Third Army.

They have the firm hope that, following the adoption by the Security Council of resolution No. 338 on 22 October, negotiations will at last begin for the restoration in the Middle East of a just and lasting peace through the application of Security Council resolution No. 242 in all its parts.

They declare themselves ready to do all in their power to contribute to that peace. They believe that those negotiations must take place in the framework of the United Nations. They recall that the Charter has entrusted to the Security Council the principal responsibility in the making and keeping of peace through the application of council resolutions Nos. 242 and 338.

They consider that a peace agreement should be based particularly on the following points:

1.   The inadmissibility of the acquisition of territory by force.

2.   The need for Israel to end the territorial occupation which it has maintained since the conflict of 1967.

3.   Respect for the sovereignty, territorial integrity and independence of every State in the area and their right to live in peace within secure and recognized boundaries.

4.   Recognition that in the establishment of a just and lasting peace account must be taken of the legitimate rights of the Palestinians.

They recall that according to resolution No. 242 the peace settlement must be the object of international guarantees.

They consider that such guarantees must be reinforced, among other means, by the dispatch of peace-keeping forces to the demilitarized zones envisaged in article 2(C) of resolution No. 242. They are agreed that such guarantees are of primary importance in settling the overall situation in the Middle East in conformity with resolution No. 242 to which the Council refers in resolution No. 338. They reserve the right to make proposals in this connection.

They recall on this occasion the ties of all kinds which have long linked them to the littoral States of the South and East of the Mediterranean. In this connection they reaffirm the terms of the declaration of the Paris summit of 2 October 1972 and recall that the Community has decided, in the framework of a global and balanced approach, to negotiate agreements with these countries.

6. General Assembly Resolution 3236 Concerning the Question of Palestine, 22 November, 1974

The Generaly Assembly,

Having considered the question of Palestine,

Having heard the statement of the Palestine Liberation Organization, the representative of the Palestinian people,

Having also héard other statements made during the debate,

Deeply concerned that no just solution to the problem of Palestine has yet been achieved and recognizing that the problem of Palestine continues to endanger international peace and security,

Recognizing that the Palestinian people is entitled to self-determination in accordance with the Charter of the United Nations,

Expressing its grave concern that the Palestinian people has been prevented from enjoying its inalienable rights, in particular its right to self-determination,

Guided by the purposes and principles of the Charter,

Recalling its relevant resolutions which affirm the right of the Palestinian people to self-determination,

1. *Reaffirms* the inalienable rights of the Palestinian people in Palestine, including:

   (a) The right to self-determination without external interference;

   (b) The right to national independence and sovereignty;

2. *Reaffirms* also the inalienable right of the Palestinians to return to their homes and property from which they have been displaced and uprooted, and calls for their return;

3.   *Emphasizes* that full respect for and the realization of these inalienable rights of the Palestinian people are indispensable for the solution of the question of Palestine;

4.   *Recognizes* that the Palestinian people is a principal party in the establishment of a just and durable peace in the Middle East;

5.   *Further recognizes* the right of the Palestinian people to regain its rights by all means in accordance with the purposes and principles of the Charter of the United Nations;

6.   *Appeals* to all States and international organizations to extend their support to the Palestinian people in its struggle to restore its rights, in accordance with the Charter;

7.   *Requests* the Secretary-General to establish contacts with the Palestine Liberation Organization on all matters concerning the question of Palestine;

8.   *Requests* the Secretary-General to report to the General Assembly at its thirtieth session on the implementation of the present resolution;

9.   *Decides* to include the item entitled "Question of Palestine" in the provisional agenda of its thirtieth session.

2296th plenary meeting

7.   Joint Statement Issued by the Governments of the U.S. and the U.S.S.R. New York, 1 October, 1977

Having exchanged views regarding the unsafe situation which remains in the Middle East, U.S. Secretary of State Cyrus Vance and Member of the Politbureau of the Central Committee of the CPSU, Minister of Foreign Affairs of the USSR A.A. Gromyko have the following statement to make on behalf of their countries, which are co-chairmen of the Geneva Peace Conference on the Middle East.

1.   Both governments are convinced that vital interests of the peoples of this area, as well as the interests of strengthening peace and international security in general, urgently dictate the necessity of achieving, as soon as possible, a just and lasting settlement of the Arab-Israeli conflict. This settlement should be comprehensive, incorporating all parties concerned and all questions. The United States and the Soviet Union believe that, within the framework of a comprehensive settlement of the Middle East problem, all specific questions of the settlement should be resolved, including such key issues as withdrawal of Israeli Armed Forces from territories occupied in the 1967 conflict; the resolution of the Palestinian question, including ensuring the legitimate rights of the Palestinian people; termination of the state of war and

establishment of normal peaceful relations on the basis of mutual recognition of the principles of sovereignty, territorial integrity, and political independence. The two governments believe that, in addition to such measures for insuring the security of the borders between Israel and the neighboring Arab States as the establishment of demilitarized zones and the agreed stationing in them of U.N. troops or observers, international guarantees of such borders as well as of the observance of the terms of the settlement can also be established should the contracting parties so desire. The United States and the Soviet Union are ready to participate in these guarantees, subject to their constitutional processes.

2.   The United States and the Soviet Union believe that the only right and effective way for achieving a fundamental solution to all aspects of the Middle East problem in its entirety is negotiations within the framework of the Geneva Peace Conference, specially convened for these purposes, with participation in its work of the representatives of all the parties involved in the conflict including those of the Palestinian people, and legal and contractual formalization of the decisions reached at the conference. In their capacity as co-chairmen of the Geneva conference, the United States and the USSR affirm their intention, through joint efforts and in their contacts with the parties concerned, to facilitate in every way the resumption of the work of the conference not later than December 1977. The co-chairmen note that there still exist several questions of a procedural and organizational nature which remain to be agreed upon by the participants to the conference.

3.   Guided by the goal of achieving a just political settlement in the Middle East and of eliminating the explosive situation in this area of the world, the United States and the USSR appeal to all the parties in the conflict to understand the necessity for careful consideration of each other's legitimate rights and interests and to demonstrate mutual readiness to act accordingly.

8.   Statement on the Problem in the Middle East, Soviet Foreign Minister Gromyko at the U.N. General Assembly, 25 September, 1979

The Middle East problem, if divested of the immaterial, boils down to the following — either the consequences of the aggression against the Arab states and peoples are eliminated or the invaders get a reward by appropriating lands that belong to others.

A just settlement and the establishment of durable peace in the Middle East requires that Israel should end its occupation of all the Arab lands it seized in 1967, that the legitimate rights of the Arab people of Palestine including the right to create their own state be safeguarded and that the right of all states in the Middle East, including Israel, to independent existence under conditions of peace be effectively guaranteed.

The separate deal between Egypt and Israel resolves nothing. It is a means designed to lull the vigilance of peoples. It is a way of piling up on a still greater scale explosive material capable of producing a new conflagration in the Middle East. Moreover, added to the tense political atmosphere in this and the adjacent areas is the heavy smell of oil.

It is high time that all states represented in the United Nations realized how vast is the tragedy of the Arab people of Palestine. What is the worth of declarations in defence of humanism and human rights — whether for refugees or not — if before the eyes of the entire world the inalienable rights of an entire people driven from its land and deprived of a livelihood are grossly trampled upon?

The Soviet policy with respect to the Middle East problem is one of principle. We are in favour of a comprehensive and just settlement, of the establishment of durable peace in the Middle East, a region not far from our borders. The Soviet Union sides firmly with Arab peoples who resolutely reject deals at the expense of their legitimate interests.

9. Soviet Chairman Brezhnev, Position on Peace, 23 February, 1981
Address before the 26th Congress of the CPSU

Now about the Middle East problem. In its bid for dominance in the Middle East, the United States has taken the path of the Camp David policy, dividing the Arab world and organizing a separate deal between Israel and Egypt. U.S. diplomacy has failed to turn this separate anti-Arab deal into a broader agreement of a capitulationist type. But it has succeeded in another way: A new deterioration of the situation has occurred in the region. A Middle East settlement was cast back.

What now? As we see it, it is high time to get matters off the ground. It is time to go back to an honest collective search for an all-embracing just and realistic settlement. In the circumstances, this could be done, say, in the framework of a specially convened international conference.

The Soviet Union is prepared to participate in such work in a constructive spirit and with good will. We are prepared to do so jointly with the other interested parties — the Arabs (naturally including the Palestine Liberation Organization) and Israel. We are prepared for such a search jointly with the United States — and I may remind you that we had some experience in this regard some years ago. We are prepared to cooperate with the European countries and with all those who are showing a sincere striving to secure a just and durable peace in the Middle East.

The UN, too, could evidently continue to play a useful role in all this.

As for the substance of the matter, we are still convinced that if there is to be real peace in the Middle East, the Israeli occupation of all Arab territories captured in 1967 must be ended. The inalienable rights of the Arab people of Palestine must be secured, up to and including the establishment of their own state. It is essential to ensure the security and sovereignty of all the states of the region, including those of Israel. Those are the basic principles. As for the details, they could naturally be considered at the negotiations.

10. The Venice European Declaration, 13 June, 1981

Following is the text of the declaration on the Middle East by the European Economic Community issued at the conclusion of a two-day summit in Venice,

1. The heads of state and government and the ministers of foreign affairs held a comprehensive exchange of views on all aspects of the present situation in the Middle East, including the state of negotiations resulting from the agreements signed between Egypt and Israel in March 1979. They agreed that growing tensions affecting this region constitute a serious danger and render a comprehensive solution to the Israeli-Arab conflict more necessary and pressing than ever.

2. The nine member states of the European Community consider that the traditional ties and common interests which link Europe to the Middle East oblige them to play a special role and now require them to work in a more concrete way toward peace.

3. In this regard the nine countries of the Community base on Security Council Resolutions 242 and 338 and the positions which they have expressed on several occasions, notably in their declarations of 29 June 1977, 19 September 1978, 26 March and 18 June 1979, as well as the speech made on their behalf on 25 September 1979 by the Irish Minister of Foreign Affairs at the 34th United Nations General Assembly.

4. On the bases thus set out, the time has come to promote the recognition and implementation of the two principles universally accepted by the international community: the right to existence and to security of all the states in the region, including Israel, and justice for all the peoples, which implies the recognition of the legitimate rights of the Palestinian people.

5. All of the countries in the area are entitled to live in peace within secure, recognized and guaranteed borders. The necessary guarantees for a peace settlement should be provided by the United Nations by a decision of the Security Council and, if necessary, on the basis of other mutually agreed procedures. The Nine declare that they are prepared to participate within the

framework of a comprehensive settlement in a system of concrete and binding international guarantees, including guarantees on the ground.

6.   A just solution must finally be found to the Palestinian problem, which is not simply one of refugees. The Palestinian people, which is conscious of existing as such, must be placed in a position, by an appropriate process defined within the framework of the comprehensive peace settlement, to exercise fully its right to self-determination.

7.   The achievement of these objectives requires the involvement and support of all the parties concerned in the peace settlement which the Nine are endeavoring to promote in keeping with the principles formulated in the declaration referred to above. These principles apply to all the parties concerned, and thus the Palestinian people, and to the Palestine Liberation Organization, which will have to be associated with the negotiations.

8.   The Nine recognize the special importance of the role played by the question of Jerusalem for all the parties concerned. The Nine stress that they will not accept any unilateral initiative designed to change the status of Jerusalem and that any agreement on the city's status should guarantee freedom of access of everyone to the holy places.

9.   The Nine stress the need for Israel to put an end to the territorial occupation which it has maintained since the conflict of 1967, as it has done for part of Sinai. They are deeply convinced that the Israeli settlements constitute a serious obstacle to the peace process in the Middle East. The Nine consider that these settlements, as well as modifications in population and property in the occupied Arab territories, are illegal under international law.

10.   Concerned as they are to put an end to violence, the Nine consider that only the renunciation of force or the threatened use of force by all the parties can create a climate of confidence in the area, and constitute a basic element for a comprehensive settlement of the conflict in the Middle East.

11.   The Nine have decided to make the necessary contacts with all the parties concerned. The objective of these contacts would be to ascertain the position of the various parties with respect to the principles set out in this declaration and in the light of the results of this consultation process to determine the form which such an initiative on their part could take.

11. Chairman Brezhnev Peace Plan, 15 September, 1982 [Excerpts]

As we are profoundly convinced, a just and lasting peace in the Middle East can and must be based on the following principles according both to the general norms of international law and specific decisions of the U.N. Security Council and the General Assembly pertaining to that problem.

In the first place, the principle of inadmissibility of seizure of foreign lands through aggression should be strictly observed. And this means that all territories occupied by Israel since 1967 — the Golan Heights, the West Bank of the Jordan river, the Gaza sector and the Lebanese lands — must be returned to the Arabs. The border between Israel and its Arab neighbours must be declared inviolable.

Second, the inalienable right of the Arab people of Palestine to self-determination, to the creation of their own independent state on the Palestinian lands, which will be freed from the Israeli occupation — on the West Bank of the Jordan River and in the Gaza sector — must be ensured in practice. The Palestinian refugees must be granted the possibility envisaged by the U.N. decisions to return to their homes or get appropriate compensation for the property left by them.

Third, the eastern part of Jerusalem, which was occupied by Israel in 1967 and where one of the main Muslim holy shrines is situated, must be returned to the Arabs and become and inseparable part of the Palestinian state. Free access of believers to the holy shrines of the three religions must be ensured in the whole of Jerusalem.

Fourth, the right of all states of the area must be ensured to safe and independent existence and development, of course, with the observance of full reciprocity, as it is impossible to ensure the security of some people, while flouting the security of others.

Fifth, an end must be put to the state of war, and peace must be established between the Arab States and Israel. And this means that all sides in the conflict, including Israel and the Palestinian State, must commit themselves to mutually respect each other's sovereignty, independence and territorial integrity, and resolve disputes that crop up through peaceful means, through negotiations.

Sixth, international guarantees of settlement must be drawn up and adopted, the role of guarantors could be assumed, let us say, by the permanent members of the U.N. Security Council, or by the U.N. Security Council as a whole.

Such a comprehensive, truly just and really lasting settlement can be drawn up and implemented only through collective efforts with the participation of all sides concerned, including, certainly, PLO — the sole legitimate representative of the Arab people of Palestine.

This is precisely the way of settlement implied in our proposal to convene an international conference on the Middle East, which has gained broad support, also from Democratic Yemen.

I would like to stress that in the present situation the unity of the Arab States in the struggle against the Israeli aggressors is important as never before. The Arabs need this unity like air like water, and the stronger and more reliable this unity is, the sooner, the imperialist intrigues in the Middle East are foiled.

An Arab summit meeting ended the other day. The statement issued on the results of its work has reflected the well-founded alarm and concern about the Israeli aggression in Lebanon and the continuing occupation of Arab lands by it. We positively assess the principles for the settlement of the Palestinian issue and of the Middle East settlement as a whole, which were adopted by the meeting. They are not at variance with what the Soviet Union has been struggling for many years now, and which has been once again expressed by me above in a condensed form."

U.S. Documents

1. President Johnson, Statement on Principles for Peace, 19 June, 1967 [Excerpts]

Our country is committed — and we here reiterate that commitment today to a peace that is based on five principles:
— first, the recognized right of national life;
— second, justice for the refugees;
— third, innocent maritime passage;
— fourth, limits on the wasteful and destructive arms race; and
— fifth, political independence and territorial integrity for all.

This is a time not for malice, but for magnanimity; not for propaganda, but for patience; not for vituperation, but for vision.

We are not here to judge whose fears are right or whose are wrong. Right or wrong, fear is the first obstacle to any peacemaking. Each side must do its share to overcome it. A major step in this direction would be for each party to issue promptly a clear, unqualified public assurance that it is now ready to commit itself to recognize the right of each of its neighbors to national life.

Second, the political independence and territorial integrity of all the states in the area must be assured.

We are not the ones to say where other nations should draw lines between them that will assure each the greatest security. It is clear, however, that a return to the situation of June 4, 1967, will not bring peace. There must be secure, and there must be recognized borders.

Some such lines must be agreed to by the neighbors involved as part of the transition from armistice to peace.

At the same time, it should be equally clear that boundaries cannot and should not reflect the weight of conquest. Each change must have a reason which each side, in honest negotiation, can accept as a part of a just compromise.

Third, it is more certain than ever that Jerusalem is a critical issue of any peace settlement. No one wishes to see the Holy City again divided by barbed wire and by machine guns. I therefore tonight urge an appeal to the parties to stretch their imaginations so that their interests and all the world's interest in Jerusalem, can be taken fully into account in any final settlement.

Fourth, the number of refugees is still increasing. The June war added some 200,000 refugees to those already displaced by the 1948 war. They face a bleak prospect as the winter approaches. We share a very deep concern for these refugees. Their plight is a symbol in the minds of the Arab peoples. In their eyes, it is a symbol of a wrong that must be made right before 20 years of war can end. And that fact must be dealt with in reaching a condition of peace.

All nations who are able, including Israel and her Arab neighbors, should participate directly and wholeheartedly in a massive program to assure these people a better and a more stable future.

Fifth, maritime rights must be respected. Their violation led to war in 1967. Respect for those rights is not only a legal consequence of peace. It is a symbolic recognition that all nations in the Middle East enjoy equal treatment before the law.

And no enduring peace settlement is possible until the Suez Canal and the Straits of Tiran are open to the ships of all nations and their right of passage is effectively guaranteed.

Sixth, the arms race continues. We have exercised restraint while recognizing the legitimate needs of friendly governments. But we have no intention of allowing the balance of forces in the area to ever become an incentive for war.

We continue to hope that our restraint will be matched by the restraint of others, though I must observe that has been lacking since the end of the June war.

We have proposed, and I reiterate again tonight, the urgent need now for an international understanding on arms limitation for this region of the world.

2. The Rogers Plan: Address by Secretary of State Rogers, Washington, D.C., 9 December, 1969

Address before the 1969 GALAXY Conference on Adult Education

I am very happy to be with you this evening and be a part of this impressive conference. The Galaxy Conference represents one of the largest and most significant efforts in the Nation's history to further the goals of all phases of adult and continuing education.

The State Department, as you know, has an active interest in this subject. It is our belief that foreign policy issues should be more broadly understood and considered. As you know, we are making a good many efforts toward providing continuing education in the foreign affairs field. I am happy tonight to join so many staunch allies in those endeavors.

In the hope that I may further that cause I want to talk to you tonight about a foreign policy matter which is of great concern to our nation.

I am going to speak tonight about the situation in the Middle East. I want to refer to the policy of the United States as it relates to that situation in the hope that there may be a better understanding of that policy and the reasons for it.

Following the third Arab-Israeli war in 20 years, there was an upsurge of hope that a lasting peace could be achieved. That hope has unfortunately not been realized. There is no area of the world today that is more important, because it could easily again be the source of another serious conflagration.

When this administration took office, one of our first actions in foreign affairs was to examine carefully the entire situation in the Middle East. It was obvious that a continuation of the unresolved conflict there would be extremely dangerous, that the parties to the conflict alone would not be able to overcome their legacy of suspicion to achieve a political settlement, and that international efforts to help needed support.

The United States decided it had a responsibility to play a direct role in seeking a solution.

Thus, we accepted a suggestion put forward both by the French Government and the Secretary General of the United Nations. We agreed that the major powers — the United States, the Soviet Union, the United Kingdom, and France — should cooperate to assist the Secretary General's representative, Ambassador Jarring, in working out a settlement in accordance with the resolution of the Security Council of the United Nations of November 1967. We also decided to consult directly with the Soviet Union, hoping to achieve as wide an area of agreement as possible between us.

These decisions were made in full recognition of the following important factors:

First, we knew that nations not directly involved could not make a durable peace for the peoples and governments involved. Peace rests with the parties to the conflict. The efforts of major powers can help, they can provide a catalyst, they can stimulate the parties to talk, they can encourage, they can help define a realistic framework for agreement; but an agreement among other powers cannot be a substitute for agreement among the parties themselves.

Second, we knew that a durable peace must meet the legitimate concerns of both sides.

Third, we were clear that the only framework for a negotiated settlement was one in accordance with the entire text of the U.N. Security Council resolution. That resolution was agreed upon after long and arduous negotiations: it is carefully balanced; it provides the basis for a just and lasting peace — a final settlement — not merely an interlude between wars.

Fourth, we believe that a protracted period of no war, no peace, recurrent violence, and spreading chaos would serve the interests of no nation, in or out of the Middle East.

U.S.—Soviet Discussions

For 8 months we have pursued these consultations in four-power talks at the United Nations and in bilateral discussions with the Soviet Union.

In our talks with the Soviets we have proceeded in the belief that the stakes are so high that we have a responsibility to determine whether we can achieve parallel views which would encourage the parties to work out a stable and equitable solution. We are under no illusions; we are fully conscious of past difficulties and present realities. Our talks with the Soviets have brought a measure of understanding, but very substantial differences remain. We regret that the Soviets have delayed in responding to new formulations submitted to them on October 28. However, we will continue to discuss these problems with the Soviet Union as long as there is any realistic hope that such discussions might further the cause of peace.

The substance of the talks that we have had with the Soviet Union has been conveyed to the interested parties through diplomatic channels. This process has served to highlight the main roadblocks to the initiation of useful negotiations among the parties.

On the one hand, the Arab leaders fear that Israel is not in fact prepared to withdraw from Arab territory occupied in the 1967 war.

On the other hand, Israeli leaders fear that the Arab States are not in fact prepared to live in peace with Israel.

Each side can cite from its viewpoint considerable evidence to support its fears. Each side has permitted its attention to be focused solidly and to some extent solely on these fears.

What can the United States do to help to overcome these roadblocks?

Our policy is and will continue to be a *balanced* one.

We have friendly ties with both Arabs and Israelis. To call for Israeli withdrawal as envisaged in the U.N. resolution without achieving agreement on peace would be partisan toward the Arabs. To call on the Arabs to accept peace without Israeli withdrawal would be partisan toward Israel. Therefore, our policy is to encourage the Arabs to accept a permanent peace based on a binding agreement and to urge the Israelis to withdraw from occupied territory when their territorial integrity is assured as envisaged by the Security Council resolution.

Basic Elements of the U.N. Resolution

In an effort to broaden the scope of discussion we have recently resumed four-power negotiations at the United Nations.

Let me outline our policy on various elements of the Security Council resolution. The basic and related issues might be described as peace, security, withdrawal, and territory.

Peace Between the Parties

The resolution of the Security Council makes clear that the goal is the establishment of a state of peace between the parties instead of the state of belligerency which has characterized relations for over 20 years. We believe the conditions and obligations of peace must be defined in specific terms. For example, navigation rights in the Suez Canal and in the Straits of Tiran should be spelled out. Respect for sovereignty and obligations of the parties to each other must be made specific.

But peace, of course, involves much more than this. It is also a matter of the attitudes and intentions of the parties. Are they ready to coexist with one another? Can a live-and-let-live attitude replace suspicion, mistrust, and hate? A peace agreement between the parties must be based on clear and stated intentions and a willingness to bring about basic changes in the attitudes and conditions which are characteristic of the Middle East today.

Security

A lasting peace must be sustained by a sense of security on both sides. To this end, as envisaged in the Security Council resolution, there should be demilitarized zones and related security arrangements more reliable than those which existed in the area in the past. The parties themselves, with Ambassador Jarring's help, are in the best position to work out the nature and the details of such security arrangements. It is, after all, their interests which are at stake and their territory which is involved. They must live with the results.

Withdrawal and Territory

The Security Council resolution endorses the principle of the nonacquisition of territory by war and calls for withdrawal of Israeli armed forces from territories occupied in the 1967 war. We support this part of the resolution, including withdrawal, just as we do its other elements.

The boundaries from which the 1967 war began were established in the 1949 armistice agreements and have defined the areas of national jurisdiction in the Middle East for 20 years. Those boundaries were armistice lines, not final political borders. The rights, claims, and positions of the parties in an ultimate peaceful settlement were reserved by the armistice agreements.

The Security Council resolution neither endorses nor precludes these armistice lines as the definitive political boundaries. However, it calls for withdrawal from occupied territories, the nonacquisition of territory by war, and the establishment of secure and recognized boundaries.

We believe that while recognized political boundaries must be established, and agreed upon by the parties, any changes in the preexisting lines should not reflect the weight of conquest and should be confined to insubstantial alterations required for mutual security. We do not support expansionism. We believe troops must be withdrawn as the resolution provides. We support Israel's security and the security of the Arab States as well. We are for a lasting peace that requires security for both.

Issues of Refugees and Jerusalem

By emphasizing the key issues of peace, security, withdrawal, and territory, I do not want to leave the impression that other issues are not equally important. Two in particular deserve special mention: the question of refugees and of Jerusalem.

There can be no lasting peace without a just settlement of the problem of those Palestinians whom the wars of 1948 and 1967 have made homeless. This human dimension of the Arab-Israeli conflict has been of special concern to the United States for over 20 years. During this period the United States has contributed about $500 million for the support and education of the Palestine refugees. We are prepared to contribute generously along with others to solve this problem. We believe its just settlement must take into account the desires and aspirations of the refugees and the legitimate concerns of the governments in the area.

The problem posed by the refugees will become increasingly serious if their future is not resolved. There is a new consciousness among the young Palestinians who have grown up since 1948 which needs to be channeled away from bitterness and frustration toward hope and justice.

The question of the future status of Jerusalem, because it touches deep emotional, historical, and religious wellsprings, is particularly complicated. We have made clear repeatedly in the past 2½ years that we cannot accept unilateral actions by any party to decide the final status of the city. We believe its status can be determined only through the agreement of the parties concerned, which in practical terms means primarily the Governments of Israel and Jordan, taking into account the interests of other countries in the area and the international community. We do, however, support certain principles which we believe would provide an equitable framework for a Jerusalem settlement.

Specifically, we believe Jerusalem should be a unified city within which there would no longer be restrictions on the movement of persons and goods. There should be open access to the unified city for persons of all faiths and nationalities. Arrangements for the administration of the unified city should take into account the interests of all its inhabitants and of the Jewish, Islamic, and Christian communities. And there should be roles for both Israel and

Jordan in the civic, economic, and religious life of the city.

It is our hope that agreement on the key issues of peace, security, withdrawal, and territory will create a climate in which these questions of refugees and of Jerusalem, as well as other aspects of the conflict, can be resolved as part of the overall settlement.

3. Memorandum of Agreement Between the Governments of Israel and the United States, September 1975

The Geneva Peace Conference

1. The Geneva Peace Conference will be reconvened at a time coordinated between the United States and Israel.

2. The United States will continue to adhere to its present policy with respect to the Palestine Liberation Organization, whereby it will not recognize or negotiate with the Palestine Liberation Organization so long as the Palestine Liberation Organization does not recognize Israel's right to exist and does not accept Security Council Resolutions 242 and 338. The United States Government will consult fully and seek to concert its position and strategy at the Geneva Peace Conference on this issue with the Government of Israel. Similarly, the United States will consult fully and seek to concert its position and strategy with Israel with regard to the participation of any other additional states. It is understood that the participation at a subsequent phase of the Conference of any possible additional state, group or organization will require the agreement of all the initial participants.

3. The United States will make every effort to ensure at the Conference that all the substantive negotiations will be on a bilateral basis.

4. The United States will oppose and, if necessary, vote against any initiative in the Security Council to alter adversely the terms of reference of the Geneva Peace Conference or to change Resolutions 242 and 338 in ways which are incompatible with their original purpose.

5. The United States will seek to ensure that the role of the co-sponsors will be consistent with what was agreed in the Memorandum of Understanding between the United States Government and the Government of Israel of December 20, 1973.

6. The United States and Israel will concert action to assure that the Conference will be conducted in a manner consonant with the objectives of this document and with the declared purpose of the Conference, namely the

advancement of a negotiated peace between Israel and each one of its neighbors.

Henry A. Kissinger	Yigal Allon
Secretary of State	Deputy Prime Minister &
for the Government of	Minister of Foreign Affairs
the United States	For the Government of Israel

4. Deputy Assistant Secretary of State for Near Eastern and South Asian Affairs, Harold H. Saunders, Statement on the Palestinians. 12 November, 1975

Before House Foreign Affairs Subcommittee on the Middle East.

Mr. Chairman, a just and durable peace in the Middle-East is a central objective of the United States. Both President Ford and Secretary Kissinger have stated firmly on numerous occasions that the United States is determined to make every feasible effort to maintain the momentum of practical progress toward a peaceful settlement of the Arab-Israeli conflict.

We have also repeatedly stated that the legitimate interests of the Palestinian Arabs must be taken into account in the negotiation of an Arab-Israeli peace. In many ways, the Palestinian dimension of the Arab-Israeli conflict is the heart of that conflict. Final resolution of the problems arising from the partition of Palestine, the establishment of the State of Israel, and Arab opposition to those events will not be possible until agreement is reached defining a just and permanent status for the Arab peoples who consider themselves Palestinians.

The total number of Palestinian Arabs is estimated at a little more than three million. Of these, about 450,000 live in the area of Israel's pre-1967 borders; about one million are in the Israeli-occupied West Bank, East Jerusalem and Gaza; something less than a million, about 900,000, are in Jordan; half a million are in Syria and Lebanon; and somewhat more than 20-0,000 or so are elsewhere, primarily in the Gulf States. Those in Israel are Israeli nationals. The great majority of those in the West Bank, East Jerusalem and Jordan are Jordanian nationals. Palestinian refugees, who live outside of pre-1967 Israel and number 1.6 million, are eligible for food and/or services from the United Nations Relief and Works Agency (UNRWA); more than 650,000 of these live in camps.

The problem of the Palestinians was initially dealt with essentially as one involving displaced persons. The United States and other nations responded to the immediate humanitarian task of caring for a large number of refugees and trying to provide them with some hope in life. In later years there has been considerable attention given to the programs of UNRWA that help not only to sustain those people's lives but to lift the young people out of the refugee camps and to train them and give them an opportunity to lead productive lives. Many have taken advantage of this opportunity, and an unusually large number of them have completed secondary and university education. One finds Palestinians occupying leading positions throughout the Arab world as professionals and skilled workers in all fields. The U.S. has provided some $620 million in assistance — about sixty-two percent of the total international support ($1 billion) for the Palestinian refugees over the past quarter of a century.

Today, however, we recognize that, in addition to meeting the human needs and responding to legitimate personal claims of the refugees, there is another interest that must be taken into account. It is a fact that many of the three million or so people who call themselves Palestinians today increasingly regard themselves as having their own identity as a people and desire a voice in determining their political status. As with any people in this situation, there are differences among themselves, but the Palestinians collectively are a political factor which must be dealt with if there is to be a peace between Israel and its neighbors.

The statement is often made in the Arab world that there will not be peace until the "rights of the Palestinians" are fulfilled, but there is no agreed definition of what is meant and a variety of viewpoints have been expressed on what the legitimate objectives of the Palestinians are:

Some Palestinian elements hold to the objective of a bi-national secular state in the area of the former mandate of Palestine. Realization of this objective would mean the end of the present state of Israel, a member of the United Nations, and its submergence in some larger entity. Some would be willing to accept merely as a first step toward this goal the establishment of a Palestinian State comprising the West Bank of the Jordan River and Gaza.

Other elements of Palestinian opinion appear willing to accept an independent Palestinian state comprising the West Bank and Gaza, based on acceptance of Israel's right to exist as an independent state within roughly its pre-1967 borders.

Some Palestinians and other Arabs envisage as a possible solution a unification of the West Bank and Gaza with Jordan. A variation of this which has been suggested would be the reconstitution of the country as a federated state, with the West Bank becoming an autonomous Palestinian province.

Still others, including many Israelis, feel that with the West Bank returned to Jordan, and with the resulting existence of two communities — Palestinian and Jordanian — within Jordan, opportunities would be created thereby for the Palestinians to find self-expression.

In the case of a solution which would rejoin the West Bank to Jordan or a solution involving a West Bank/Gaza State, there would still arise the property claims of those Palestinians who before 1948 resided in areas that became the State of Israel. These claims have been acknowledged as a serious problem by the international community ever since the adoption by the United Nations of Resolution 194 on this subject in 1948, a resolution which the United Nations has repeatedly reaffirmed and which the United States has supported. A solution will be further complicated by the property claims against Arab States of the many Jews from those states who moved to Israel in its early years after achieving statehood.

In addition to property claims, some believe they should have the option of returning to their original homes under any settlement.

Other Arab leaders, while pressing the importance of Palestinian involvement in a settlement, have taken the position that the definition of Palestinian interests is something for the Palestinian people themselves to sort out, and the view has been expressed by responsible Arab leaders that realization of Palestinian rights need not be inconsistent with the existence of Israel.

No one, therefore, seems in a position today to say exactly what Palestinian objectives are. Even the Palestine Liberation Organization (PLO), which is recognized by the Arab League and the United Nations General Assembly as the representative of the Palestinian people, has been ambivalent. Officially and publicly, its objective is described as a binational secular state, but there are some indications that coexistence between separate Palestinian and Israeli states might be considered.

When there is greater precision about those objectives, there can be clearer understanding about how to relate them to negotiations. There is the aspect of the future of the West Bank and Gaza — how those areas are to be defined and how they are to be governed. There is the aspect of the relationship between Palestinians in the West Bank and Gaza to those Palestinians who are not living in those areas, in the context of a settlement.

What is needed as a first step is a diplomatic process which will help bring forth a reasonable definition of Palestinian interests — a position from which negotiations on a solution of the Palestinian aspects of the problem might begin. The issue is not whether Palestinian interests should be expressed in a final settlement, but how. There will be no peace unless an answer is found.

Another requirement is the development of a framework for negotiations — a statement of the objectives and the terms of reference. The framework for the negotiations that have taken place thus far and the agreements they have produced involving Israel, Syria, and Egypt, has been provided by the United Nations Security Council Resolutions 242 and 338. In accepting that framework, all of the parties to the negotiation have accepted that the objective of the negotiations is peace between them based on mutual recognition, territorial integrity, political independence, the right to live in peace within secure and recognized borders, and the resolution of the specific issues which comprise the Arab-Israeli conflict.

The major problem that must be resolved in establishing a framework for bringing issues of concern to the Palestinians into negotiation, therefore, is to find a common basis for the negotiation that Palestinians and Israelis can both accept. This could be achieved by common acceptance of the above-mentioned Security Council resolutions, although they do not deal with the political aspect of the Palestinian problem.

A particularly difficult aspect of the problem is the question of who negotiates for the Palestinians. It has been our belief that Jordan would be a logical negotiator for the Palestinian related issues. The Rabat Summit, however, recognized the Palestinian Liberation Organization as the "sole legitimate representative of the Palestinian people".

The PLO was formed in 1964, when 400 delegates from Palestinian communities throughout the Arab world met in Jerusalem to create an organization to represent and speak for the Palestinian people. Its leadership was originally middle class and relatively conservative, but by 1969 control had passed into the hands of the Palestinian fedayeen, or commando, movement, that had existed since the mid 1950's but had come into prominence only after the 1967 war. The organization became an umbrella organization for six separate fedayeen groups: Fatah; the Syrian-backed Saiqa; the Popular Democratic Front for the Liberation of Palestine; Popular Front for the Liberation of Palestine; the General Command — a subgroup of the PFLP; and the Iraqi-backed Arab Liberation Front. Affiliated with the PLO are a number of "popular organizations" — labour and professional unions, student groups, women's groups and so on. Fatah, the largest fedayeen group, also has a welfare apparatus to care for widows and orphans of deceased Fatah members.

However, the PLO does not accept the United Nations Security Council resolutions, does not recognize the existence of Israel, and has not stated its readiness to negotiate peace with Israel; Israel does not recognize the PLO or the idea of a separate Palestinian entity. Thus we do not at this point have the framework for a negotiation involving the PLO. We cannot envision or urge a negotiation between two parties as long as one professed to hold the objective of eliminating the other — rather than the objective of negotiating peace with it.

There is one other aspect to this problem. Elements of the PLO have used terrorism to gain attention for their cause. Some Americans as well as many Israelis and others have been killed by Palestinian terrorists. The international community cannot condone such practices, and it seems to us that there must be some assurance if Palestinians are drawn into the negotiating process that these practices will be curbed.

This is the problem which we now face. If the progress toward peace which has now begun is to continue, a solution to this question must be found. We have not devised an American solution, nor would it be appropriate for us to do so. This is the responsibility of the parties and the purpose of the negotiating process. But we have not closed our minds to any reasonable solution which can contribute to progress toward our overriding objective in the Middle East — an Arab-Israeli peace. The step-by-step approach to negotiations which we have pursued has been based partly on the understanding that issues in the Arab-Israeli conflict take time to mature. It is obvious that thinking on the Palestinian aspects of the problem must evolve on all sides. As it does, what is not possible today may become possible.

Our consultations on how to move the peace negotiations forward will recognize the need to deal with this subject. As Secretary Kissinger has said, "We are prepared to work with all the parties toward a solution of all the issues yet remaining — including the issue of the future of the Palestinians." We will do so because the issues of concern to the Palestinians are important in themselves and because the Arab governments participating in the negotiations have made clear that progress in the overall negotiations will depend in part on progress on issues of concern to the Palestinians. We are prepared to consider any reasonable proposal from any quarter, and we will expect other parties to the negotiation to be equally open minded.

5. Brookings Institution, Toward Peace in the Middle East, December 1975, [Summary]

The Brookings Report, endorsed by Presidential candidate Jimmy Carter among others, was drafted by a distinguished panel of diplomats and academicians, several of whom later became associated with the Carter administration.

Summary

The study group reached five main conclusions.

1. *U.S. interests.* The United States has a strong moral, political, and economic interest in a stable peace in the Middle East. It is concerned for the security, independence, and well-being of Israel and the Arab states of the area and for the friendship of both. Renewed hostilities would have far-reaching and perilous consequences which would threaten those interests.

2. *Urgency.* Whatever the merits of the interim agreement on Sinai, it still leaves the basic elements of the Arab-Israeli dispute substantially untouched. Unless these elements are soon addressed, rising tensions in the area will generate increased risk of violence. We believe that the best way to address these issues is by the pursuit of a comprehensive settlement.

3. *Process.* We believe that the time has come to begin the process of negotiating such a settlement among the parties, either at a general conference or at more informal multilateral meetings. While no useful interim step toward settlement should be overlooked or ignored, none seems promising at the present time and most have inherent disadvantages.

4. *Settlement.* A fair and enduring settlement should contain at least these elements as an integrated package:

(a) *Security.* All parties to the settlement commit themselves to respect the sovereignty and territorial integrity of the others and to refrain from the threat or use of force against them.

(b) *Stages.* Withdrawal to agreed boundaries and the establishment of peaceful relations carried out in stages over a period of years, each stage being undertaken only when the agreed provisions of the previous stage have been faithfully implemented.

(c) *Peaceful relations.* The Arab parties undertake not only to end such hostile actions against Israel as armed incursions, blockades, boycotts, and propaganda attacks, but also to give evidence of progress toward the development of normal international and regional political and economic relations.

(d) *Boundaries.* Israel undertakes to withdraw by agreed stages to the June 5, 1967, lines with only such modifications as are mutually accepted. Boundaries will probably need to be safeguarded by demilitarized zones supervised by UN forces.

(e) *Palestine.* There should be provision for Palestinian self-determination, subject to Palestinian acceptance of the sovereignty and integrity of Israel within agreed boundaries. This might take the form either of an independent Palestine state accepting the obligations and commitments of the peace agreements or of a Palestine entity voluntarily federated with Jordan but exercising extensive political autonomy.

(f) *Jerusalem.* The report suggests no specific solution for the particularly difficult problem of Jerusalem but recommends that, whatever the solution may be, it meet as a minimum the following criteria:

— there should be unimpeded access to all of the holy places and each should be under the custodianship of its own faith;

— there should be no barrier dividing the city which would prevent free circulation throughout it; and

— each national group within the city should, if it so desires, have substantial political autonomy within the area where it predominates.

(g) *Guarantees.* It would be desirable that the UN Security Council endorse the peace agreements and take whatever other actions to support them the agreements provide. In addition, there may well be need for unilateral or multilateral guarantees to some or all of the parties, substantial economic aid, and military assistance pending the adoption of agreed arms control measures.

5. *U.S. role.* The governments directly concerned bear the responsibility of negotiation and agreement, but they are unlikely to be able to reach agreement alone. Initiative, impetus, and inducement may well have to come from outside. The United States, because it enjoys a measure of confidence of parties on both sides and has the means to assist them economically and militarily, remains the great power best fitted to work actively with them in bringing about a settlement. Over and above helping to provide a framework for negotiation and submitting concrete proposals from time to time, the United States must be prepared to take other constructive steps, such as offering aid and providing guarantees where desired and needed. In all of this, the United States should work with the USSR to the degree that Soviet willingness to play a constructive role will permit.

6. Ambassador William W. Scranton, Statements on Occupied Territories, 23 March, 1976, [Excerpts]

Address before the U.N. Security Council

The occupation of territories in the 1967 war has always been seen by the world community to be an abnormal state of affairs that would be brought to an end as part of a peace settlement. Resolution 242, adopted by the Council shortly after the end of the 1967 war that led to the occupation, established the basic bargain that would constitute a settlement. This bargain was withdrawal of Israeli forces in return for termination of all claims or states of belligerency and respect for and acknowledgment of the sovereignty, territorial integrity, and political independence of every state in the area and their right to live in peace within secure and recognized boundaries free from threats or acts of force.

My government has committed itself to do all it can to bring about this settlement and, in the words of Resolution 338, to implement Council Resolution 242 in all of its parts and to further negotiations between the parties concerned under appropriate auspices aimed at establishing a just and durable peace in the Middle East, which is what we are here for. We are engaged at this moment in an effort to regain momentum, as all of you know, in the negotiating process that has brought some unusual progress — and it must bring more.

The second focus of our consideration must be the conduct of the occupation itself. In asking for this meeting, the letter of complaint circulated by the Permanent Representatives of the Libyan Arab Republic and of Pakistan identifes three issues:

— The administration of the holy sites;

— The situation in Jerusalem; and

— Israeli actions in regard to the civilian population of the occupied territories and the Israeli settlements in the occupied territories.

The position of the United States on these issues is clear and of long standing. I propose to review the U.S. position today once more to point out that there are proper principles and there are procedures under international law and practice which, when applied and maintained, will contribute to civil order and will, over the longer run, facilitate a just and a lasting peace.

First, there is a matter of the holy sites and practice of religion in the occupied areas. The deep religious attachment of Moslems and Jews and Christians to the holy places of Jerusalem has added a uniquely volatile element to the tensions that inhere in an occupation situation. The area known to Moslems as the Haram as-Sharif and to Jews as the Temple Mount is of particular sensitivity. Israel's punctilious administration of the holy places in Jerusalem has, in our judgment, greatly minimized the tensions. To my government, the standard to be followed in administering the holy sites is contained in article 27 of the Fourth Geneva Convention Relative to the Protection of Civilian Persons in Time of War. All parties to the Arab-Israeli conflict are signatories of the convention. Article 27 of the convention prescribes, inter alia, that:

"Protected persons are entitled, in all circumstances, to respect for their persons, their honour, their family rights, their religious convictions and practices, and their manners and customs."

With regard to the immediate problem before us — a ruling by a lower Israeli court which would have the effect of altering the status of the Haram — it is our view that Israel's responsibilities under article 27 to preserve religious practices as they were at the time the occupation began cannot be changed by the ruling of an Israeli court. We are gratified, deeply gratified, that the Supreme Court of Israel has upheld the Israeli Government's position.

The status of the holy places is, of course, only one facet, however important, very important, of the problem of the status of Jerusalem itself. The U.S. position on the status of Jerusalem has been stated here on numerous occasions since the Arab portion of that city was occupied by Israel in 1967.

Ambassador Yost said in 1969:

"... the part of Jerusalem that came under the control of Israel in the June war, like other areas occupied by Israel, is occupied territory and hence subject to the provisions of international law governing the rights and obligations of an occupying power."

Ambassador Goldberg said in 1968, to this Council:

"The United States does not accept or recognize unilateral actions by any states in the area as altering the status of Jerusalem."

I emphasize, as did Ambassador Goldberg, that as far as the United States is concerned such unilateral measures, including expropriation of land or other administrative action taken by the Government of Israel, cannot be considered other than interim and provisional and cannot affect the present international status nor prejudge the final and permanent status of Jerusalem. The U.S. position could not be clearer. Since 1967 we have restated here, in other forums, and to the Government of Israel that the future of Jerusalem will be determined only through the instruments and processes of negotiation, agreement, and accommodation. Unilateral attempts to predetermine that future have no standing.

Next I turn to the question of Israeli settlements in the occupied territories. Again, my government believes that international law sets the appropriate standards. An occupier must maintain the occupied area as intact and unaltered as possible, without interfering with the customary life of the area, and any changes must be necessitated by the immediate needs of the occupation and be consistent with international law. The Fourth Geneva Convention speaks directly to the issue of population transfer in article 49:

"The Occupying Power shall not deport or transfer parts of its own civilian population into the territory it occupies."

Clearly, then, substantial resettlement of the Israeli civilian population in occupied territories, including East Jerusalem, is illegal under the convention and cannot be considered to have prejudged the outcome of future negotiations between the parties on the location of the borders of states of the Middle East. Indeed, the presence of these settlements is seen by my government as an obstacle to the success of the negotiations for a just and final peace between Israel and its neighbors.

7. President Jimmy Carter, on Middle East Peace, Town Meeting, Clinton, Mass., 16 March, 1977

I think all of you know that there has been either war or potential war in the Middle East for the last 29 years, ever since Israel became a nation. I think one of the finest acts of the world nations that's ever occurred was to establish the State of Israel.

So, the first prerequisite of a lasting peace is the recognition of Israel by her neighbors, Israel's right to exist, Israel's right to exist permanently, Israel's right to exist in peace. That means that over a period of months or years that the borders between Israel and Syria, Israel and Lebanon, Israel and Jordan, Israel and Egypt must be opened up to travel, to tourism, to cultural exchange, to trade, so that no matter who the leaders might be in those countries, the people themselves will have formed a mutual understanding and comprehension and a sense of a common purpose to avoid the repetitious wars and death that have afflicted that region so long. That's the first prerequisite of peace.

The second one is very important and very, very difficult; and that is, the establishment of permanent borders for Israel. The Arab countries say that Israel must withdraw to the pre-1967 borderlines, Israel says that they must adjust those lines to some degree to insure their own security. That is a matter to be negotiated between the Arab countries on the one side and Israel on the other.

But borders are still a matter of great trouble and a matter of great difficulty, and there are strong differences of opinion now.

And the third ultimate requirement for peace is to deal with the Palestinian problem. The Palestinians claim up to this day this moment that Israel has no right to be there, that the land belongs to the Palestinians, and they've never yet given up their publicly professed commitment to destroy Israel. That has to be overcome.

There has to be a homeland provided for the Palestinian refugees who have suffered for many, many years. And the exact way to solve the Palestinian problem is one that first of all addresses itself right now to the Arab countries and then, secondly, to the Arab countries negotiating with Israel.

Those three major elements have got to be solved before a Middle Eastern solution can be prescribed.

I want to emphasize one more time, we offer our good offices. I think it's accurate to say that of all the nations in the world, we are the one that's most trusted, not completely, but most trusted by the Arab countries and also Israel. I guess both sides have some doubt about us. But we'll have to act as kind of a catalyst to being about their ability to negotiate successfully with one another.

We hope that later on this year, in the latter part of this year, that we might get all of these parties to agree to come together at Geneva, to start talking to one another. They haven't done that yet. And I believe if we can get them to sit down and start talking and negotiating that we have an excellent chance to achieve peace. I can't guarantee that. It's a hope.

I hope that we will all pray that that will come to pass, because what happens in the Middle East in the future might very well cause a major war there which would quickly spread to all the other nations of the world; very possibly it could do that.

Many countries depend completely on oil from the Middle East for their life. We don't. If all oil was cut off to us from the Middle East, we could survive; but Japan imports more than 98 percent of all its energy, and other countries, like in Europe — Germany, Italy, France are also heavily dependent on oil from the Middle East.

So, this is such a crucial area of the world that I will be devoting a major part of my own time on foreign policy between now and next fall trying to provide for a forum within which they can discuss their problems and, hopefully, let them seek out among themselves some permanent solution.

8. President Carter, Statement on Recognition of Palestinians, Aswan, Egypt, 4 January, 1978

It is an honor and a pleasure for us to be in this great country, led by such a strong and courageous man.

Mr. President, your bold initiative in seeking peace has aroused the admiration of the entire world. One of my most valued possessions is the warm, personal relationship which binds me and President Sadat together and which exemplifies the friendship and the common purpose of the people of Egypt and the people of the United States of America.

The Egyptian-Israeli peace initiative must succeed, while still guarding the sacred and historic principles held by the nations who have suffered so much in this region. There is no good reason why accommodation cannot be reached.

In my own private discussions with both Arab and Israeli leaders, I have been deeply impressed by the unanimous desire for peace. My presence here today is a direct result of the courageous initiative which President Sadat undertook in his recent trip to Jerusalem.

The negotiating process will continue in the near future. We fully support this effort, and we intend to play an active role in the work of the Political Committee of Cairo, which will soon reconvene in Jerusalem.

We believe that there are certain principles, fundamentally, which must be observed before a just and a comprehensive peace can be achieved.

*   First, true peace must be based on normal relations among the parties to the peace. Peace means more than just an end to belligerency.

*   Second, there must be withdrawal by Israel from territories occupied in 1967 and agreement on secure and recognized borders for all parties in the context of normal and peaceful relations in accordance with U.N. Resolutions 242 and 338.

*   Third, there must be a resolution of the Palestinian problem in all its aspects. The problem must recognize the legitimate rights of the Palestinian people and enable the Palestinians to participate in the determination of their own future.

Some flexibility is always needed to insure successful negotiations and the resolution of conflicting views. We know that the mark of greatness among leaders is to consider carefully the views of others and the greater benefits that can result among the people of all nations which can come from a successful search for peace.

Mr. President, our consultations this morning have reconfirmed our common commitment to the fundamentals which will, with God's help, make 1978 the year for permanent peace in the Middle East.

9. The Reagan Peace Plan — U.S. Involvement in Mideast Peace Effort, 'A Moral Imperative'. President Ronald Reagan, 1 September, 1982

Following is the full text of the President's address:

Today has been a day that should make all of us proud. It marked the end of the successful evacuation of the PLO from Beirut, Lebanon. This peaceful step could never have been taken without the good offices of the United States and, especially, the truly heroic work of a great American diplomat, Philip Habib. Thanks to his efforts, I am happy to announce that the U.S. Marine contingent helping to supervise the evacuation has accomplished its mission.

Our young men should be out of Lebanon within two weeks. They, too, have served the cause of peace with distinction and we can all be very proud of them.

But the situation in Lebanon is only part of the overall problem of the conflict in the Middle East. So, over the past weeks, while events in Beirut dominated the front page, America was engaged in a quiet behind-the-scenes effort to lay the groundwork for a broader peace in the region. For once, there were no premature leaks as U.S. diplomatic missions travelled to mid-East capitals and I met here at home with a wide range of experts to map out an American peace initiative for the long-suffering peoples of the Middle East, Arab and Israeli alike.

It seemed to me that, with the agreement in Lebanon, we had an opportunity for a more far-reaching peace effort in the region — and I was determined to seize that moment. In the words of the Scripture, the time had come to "follow after the things which make for peace."

Tonight, I want to report to you on the steps we have taken, and the prospects they can open up for a just and lasting peace in the Middle East.

America has long been committed to bringing peace to this troubled region. For more than a generation, successive U.S. Administrations have endeavored to develop a fair and workable process that could lead to a true and lasting Arab-Israeli peace. Our involvement in the search for mid-East peace is not a matter of preference, it is a moral imperative. The strategic importance of the region to the U.S. is well known.

But our policy is motivated by more than strategic interests. We also have an irreversible commitment to the survival and territorial integrity of friendly states. Nor can we ignore the fact that the well-being of much of the world's economy is tied to stability in the strife-torn Middle East. Finally, our traditional humanitarian concerns dictate a continuing effort to peacefully resolve conflicts.

When our Administration assumed office in January 1981, I decided that the general framework for our Middle East policy should follow the broad guidelines laid down by my predecessors.

There were two basic issues we had to address. First, there was the strategic threat to the region posed by the Soviet Union and its surrogates, best demonstrated by the brutal war in Afghanistan; and, second, the peace process between Israel and its Arab neighbors. With regard to the Soviet threat, we have strengthened our efforts to develop with our friends and allies a joint policy to deter the Soviets and their surrogates from further expansion in the region, and, if necessary, to defend against it. With respect to the Arab-Israeli conflict, we have embraced the Camp David framework as the only way to proceed. We have also recognized, however, that solving the Arab-Israeli conflict, in and of itself, cannot assure peace throughout a region as vast and troubled as the Middle East.

Our first objective under the Camp David process was to ensure the successful fulfillment of the Egyptian-Israeli peace treaty. This was achieved with the peaceful return of the Sinai to Egypt in April 1982. To accomplish this, we worked hard with our Egyptian and Israeli friends, and eventually with other friendly countries, to create the multinational force which now operates in the Sinai.

Throughout this period of difficult and time-consuming negotiations, we never lost sight of the next step of Camp David: autonomy talks to pave the way for permitting the Palestinian people to exercise their legitimate rights. However, owing to the tragic assassination of President Sadat and other crises in the area, it was not until January 1982 that we were able to make a major effort to renew these talks. Secretary of State Haig and Ambassador Fairbanks made three visits to Israel and Egypt this year to pursue the autonomy talks. Considerable progress was made in developing the basic outline of an American approach which was to be presented to Egypt and Israel after April.

The successful completion of Israel's withdrawal from Sinai and the courage shown on this occasion by Prime Minister Begin and President Mubarak in living up to their agreements convinced me the time had come for a new American policy to try to bridge the remaining differences between Egypt and Israel on the autonomy process. So, in May, I called for specific measures and a timetable for consultations with the governments of Egypt and Israel on the next steps in the peace process. However, before this effort could be launched, the conflict in Lebanon preempted our efforts. The autonomy talks were basically put on hold while we sought to untangle the parties in Lebanon and still the guns of war.

The Lebanon war, tragic as it was, has left us with a new opportunity for

Middle East peace. We must seize it now and bring peace to this troubled area so vital to world stability while there is still time. It was with this strong conviction that over a month ago, before the present negotiations in Beirut had been completed, I directed Secretary of State Shultz to again review our policy and to consult a wide range of outstanding Americans on the best ways to strengthen chances for peace in the Middle East. We have consulted with many of the officials who were historically involved in the process, with members of the Congress, and with individuals from the private sector, and I have held extensive consultations with my own advisors on the principles I will outline to you tonight.

The evacuation of the PLO from Beirut is now complete. And we can now help the Lebanese to rebuild their war-torn country. We owe it to ourselves, and to posterity, to move quickly to build upon this achievement. A stable and revived Lebanon is essential to all our hopes for peace in the region. The people of Lebanon deserve the best efforts of the international community to turn the nightmares of the past several years into a new dawn of hope.

But the opportunities for peace in the Middle East do not begin and end in Lebanon. As we help Lebanon rebuild, we must also move to resolve the root causes of conflict between Arabs and Israelis.

The war in Lebanon has demonstrated many things, but two consequences are key to the peace process:

First, the military losses of the PLO have not diminished the yearning of the Palestinian people for a just solution of their claims; and second, while Israel's military successes in Lebanon have demonstrated that its armed forces are second to none in the region, they alone cannot bring just and lasting peace to Israel and her neighbors.

The question now is how to reconcile Israel's legitimate security concerns with the legitimate rights of the Palestinians. And that answer can only come at the negotiating table. Each party must recognize that the outcome must be acceptable to all and that true peace will require compromises by all.

So, tonight, I am calling for a fresh start. This is the moment for all those directly concerned to get involved — or lend their support — to a workable basis for peace. The Camp David Agreement remains the foundation of our policy. Its language provides all parties with the leeway they need for successful negotiations.

I call on Israel to make clear that the security for which she yearns can only be achieved through genuine peace, a peace requiring magnanimity, vision and courage.

I call on the Palestinian people to recognize that their own political aspirations are inextricably bound to recognition of Israel's right to a secure future.

And I call on the Arab States to accept the reality of Israel — and the reality that peace and justice can be gained only through hard, fair, direct negotiations.

In making these calls upon others, I recognize that the United States has a special responsibility. No other nation is in a position to deal with the key parties to the conflict on the basis of trust and reliability.

The time has come for a new realism on the part of all the peoples of the Middle East. The state of Israel is an accomplished fact; it deserves unchallenged legitimacy within the community of nations. But Israel's legitimacy has thus far been recognized by too few countries, and has been denied by every Arab State except Egypt. Israel exists; it has a right to exist in peace behind secure and defensible borders, and it has a right to demand of its neighbors that they recognize those facts.

I have personally followed and supported Israel's heroic struggle for survival ever since the founding of the state of Israel 34 years ago. In the pre-1967 borders, Israel was barely 10 miles wide at its narrowest point. The bulk of Israel's population lived within artillery range of hostile Arab armies. I am not about to ask Israel to live that way again.

The war in Lebanon has demonstrated another reality in the region. The departure of the Palestinians from Beirut dramatizes more than ever the homelessness of the Palestinian people. Palestinians feel strongly that their cause is more than a question of refugees. I agree. The Camp David Agreement recognized that fact when it spoke of the legitimate rights of the Palestinian people and their just requirements. For peace to endure, it must involve all those who have been most deeply affected by the conflict. Only through broader participation in the peace process — most immediately by Jordan and by the Palestinians — will Israel be able to rest confident in the knowledge that its security and integrity will be respected by its neighbors. Only through the process of negotiation can all the nations of the Middle East achieve a secure peace.

These then are our general goals. What are the specific new American positions, and why are we taking them?

In the Camp David talks thus far, both Israel and Egypt have felt free to express openly their views as to what the outcome should be. Understandably, their views have differed on many points.

The United States has thus far sought to play the role of mediator; we have avoided public comment on the key issues. We have always recognized — and continue to recognize — that only the voluntary agreement of those parties most directly involved in the conflict can provide an enduring solution. But it has become evident to me that some clearer sense of America's position on the key issues is necessary to encourage wider support for the peace process.

First, as outlined in the Camp David accords, there must be a period of time during which the Palestinian inhabitants of the West Bank and Gaza will have full autonomy over their own affairs. Due consideration must be given to the principle of self-government by the inhabitants of the territories and to the legitimate security concerns of the parties involved.

The purpose of the five-year period of transition which would begin after free elections for a self-governing Palestinian authority is to prove to the Palestinians that they can run their own affairs, and that such Palestinian autonomy poses no threat to Israel's security.

The United States will not support the use of any additional land for the purpose of settlements during the transition period. Indeed, the immediate adoption of a settlement freeze by Israel, more than any other action, could create the confidence needed for wider participation in these talks. Further settlement activity is in no way necessary for the security of Israel and only diminishes the confidence of the Arabs that a final outcome can be freely and fairly negotiated.

I want to make the American position clearly understood: the purpose of this transition period is the peaceful and orderly transfer of domestic authority from Israel to the Palestinian inhabitants of the West Bank and Gaza. At the same time, such a transfer must not interfere with Israel's security requirements.

Beyond the transition period, as we look to the future of the West Bank and Gaza, it is clear to me that peace cannot be achieved by the formation of an independent Palestinian State in those territories. Nor is it achievable on the basis of Israeli sovereignty or permanent control over the West Bank and Gaza.

So the United States will not support the establishment of an independent Palestinian State in the West Bank and Gaza, and we will not support annexation or permanent control by Israel.

There is, however, another way to peace. The final status of these lands must, of course, be reached through the give-and-take of negotiations. But it is the firm view of the United States that self-government by the Palestinians of the West Bank and Gaza in association with Jordan offers the best chance for a durable, just and lasting peace.

We base our approach squarely on the principle that the Arab-Israeli conflict should be resolved through negotiations involving an exchange of territory for peace. This exchange is enshrined in United Nations Security Council Resolution 242, which is, in turn, incorporated in all its parts in the Camp David Agreements. U.N. Resolution 242 remains wholly valid as the foundation stone of America's Middle East peace effort.

It is the United States' position that — in return for peace — the withdrawal provision of Resolution 242 applies to all fronts, including the West Bank and Gaza.

When the border is negotiated between Jordan and Israel, our view on the extent to which Israel should be asked to give up territory will be heavily affected by the extent of true peace and normalization and the security arrangements offered in return.

Finally, we remain convinced that Jerusalem must remain undivided, but its final status should be decided through negotiations.

In the course of the negotiations to come, the United States will support positions that seem to us fair and reasonable compromises, and likely to promote a sound agreement. We will also put forward our own detailed proposals when we believe they can be helpful. And, make no mistake, the United States will oppose any proposal — from any party and at any point in the negotiating process — that threatens the security of Israel. America's commitment to the security of Israel is iron-clad. And I might add, so is mine.

During the past few days, our ambassadors in Israel, Egypt, Jordan, and Saudi Arabia have presented to their host governments the proposals in full detail that I have outlined here tonight.

I am convinced that these proposals can bring justice, bring security, and bring durability to an Arab-Israeli peace.

The United States will stand by these principles with total dedication. They are fully consistent with Israel's security requirements and the aspirations of the Palestinians. We will work hard to broaden participation at the peace table as envisaged by the Camp David accords. And I fervently hope that the Palestinians and Jordan, with the support of their Arab colleagues, will accept this opportunity.

Tragic turmoil in the Middle East runs back to the dawn of history. In our modern day, conflict after conflict has taken its brutal toll there. In an age of nuclear challenge and economic interdependence, such conflicts are a threat to all the people of the world, not just the Middle East itself. It is time for us all — in the Middle East and around the world — to call a halt to conflict, hatred and prejudice; it is time for us all to launch a common effort for reconstruction, peace and progress.

It has often been said — and regrettably too often been true — that the story of the search for peace and justice in the Middle East is a tragedy of opportunities missed.

In the aftermath of the settlement in Lebanon we now face an opportunity for a broader peace. This time we must not let it slip from our grasp. We must look beyond the difficulties and obstacles of the present and move with fairness and resolve toward a brighter future. We owe it to ourselves — and to posterity — to do no less. For if we miss this chance to make a fresh start, we may look back on this moment from some later vantage point and realize how much that failure cost us all.

These, then, are the principles upon which American policy towards the Arab-Israeli conflict will be based. I have made a personal commitment to see that they endure and, God willing, that they will come to be seen by all reasonable, compassionate people as fair, achievable, and in the interests of all who wish to see peace in the Middle East.

Tonight, on the eve of what can be a dawning of new hope for the people of the troubled Middle East — and for all the world's people who dream of a just and peaceful future — I ask you, my fellow Americans, for your support and your prayers in this great undertaking.

10. Text of 'Talking Points' Sent to Prime Minister Begin by President Reagan. Washington D.C., 8 September, 1982

Following is the text of what U.S. Administration officials called 'talking points' accompanying a letter sent by President Reagan to Prime Minister Menachem Begin of Israel. The same points were presented to Arab governments as a prelude to Mr. Reagan's peace proposals.

General Principles

A.   We will maintain our commitment to Camp David.

B.   We will maintain our commitment to the conditions we require for recognition of and negotiation with the P.L.O.

C.   We can offer guarantees on the position we will adopt in negotiations. We will not be able, however, to guarantee in advance the results of these negotiations.

Transitional Measures

A.   Our position is that the objective of the transitional period is the peaceful and orderly transfer of authority from Israel to the Palestinian inhabitants.

B.   We will support:

*   The decision of full autonomy as giving the Palestinian inhabitants real authority over themselves, the land and its resources, subject to fair safeguards on water.

*   Economic, commercial, social and cultural ties between the West Bank, Gaza and Jordan.

*   Participation by the Palestinian inhabitants of East Jerusalem in the election of the West Bank—Gaza authority.

*   Real settlement freeze.

*   Progressive Palestinian responsibility for internal security based on capability and performance.

C.   We will oppose:

*   Dismantlement of the existing settlements.

*   Provisions which represent a legitimate threat to Israel's security,

reasonably defined.

    *   Isolation of the West Bank and Gaza from Israel.

    *   Measures which accord either the Palestinians or the Israelis generally recognized sovereign rights with the exception of external security, which must remain in Israel's hands during the transitional period.

Final Status Issues

    A.   U.N.S.C. Resolution 242.

It is our position that Resolution 242 applies to the West Bank and Gaza and requires Israeli withdrawal in return for peace. Negotiations must determine the borders. The U.S. position in these negotiations on the extent of the withdrawal will be significantly influenced by the extent and nature of the peace and security arrangements offered in return.

    B.   Israeli Sovereignty.

It is our belief that the Palestinian problem cannot be resolved (through) Israeli sovereignty or control over the West Bank and Gaza. Accordingly, we will not support such a solution.

    C.   Palestinian State.

The preference we will pursue in the final status negotiation is association of the West Bank and Gaza with Jordan. We will not support the formation of a Palestinian State in those negotiations. There is no foundation of political support in Israel or the United States for such a solution. The outcome, however, must be determined by negotiations.

    D.   Self-Determination.

In the Middle East context the term self-determination has been identified exclusively with the formation of a Palestinian State. We will not support this definition of self-determination. We believe that the Palestinians must take the leading role in determining their own future and fully support the provision in Camp David providing for the elected representatives of the inhabitants of the West Bank and Gaza to decide how they shall govern themselves consistent with the provision of their agreement in the final status negotiations.

    E.   Jerusalem.

We will fully support the position that the status of Jerusalem must be determined through negotiations.

    F.   Settlements.

The status of Israeli settlements must be determined in the course of the final status negotiations. We will not support their continuation as extraterritorial outposts.

Additional Talking Points

    1.   Approach to Hussein.

The President has approached Hussein to determine the extent to which he may be interested in participating.

    * King Hussein has received the same U.S. positions as you.

    * Hussein considers our proposals serious and gives them serious attention.

    * Hussein understands that Camp David is the only base that we will accept for negotiations.

    * We are also discussing these proposals with the Saudis.

    2.   Public Commitment.

Whatever the support from these or other Arab States, this is what the President has concluded must be done.

The President is convinced his positions are fair and balanced and fully protective of Israel's security. Beyond that they offer the practical opportunity of eventually achieving the peace treaties Israel must have with its neighbors.

He will be making a speech announcing these positions, probably within a week.

    3.   Next Procedural Steps

Should the response to the President's proposal be positive, the U.S. would take immediate steps to relaunch the autonomy negotiations with the broadest possible participation as envisaged under the Camp David agreements.

We also contemplate an early visit by Secretary Shultz in the area.

Should there not be a positive response, the President, as he has said in his letter to you, will nonetheless stand by his position with proper dedication.

Sadat's Visit and the Autonomy Negotiations

1. Statement to the Israeli Knesset by President Sadat, 20 November 1977

In the name of God, the Gracious and Merciful.

Mr. Speaker, Ladies and Gentlemen:

Peace and the mercy of God Almighty be upon you and may peace be for us all, God willing. Peace for us all on the Arab land, and in Israel as well, as in every part of this big world, which is so complexed by its sanguinary conflicts, disturbed by its sharp contradictions, menaced now and then by destructive wars launched by man to annihilate his fellow man. Finally, amidst the ruins of what man has built and the remains of the victims of Mankind, there emerges neither victor nor vanquished. The only vanquished remains man, God's most sublime creation, man whom God has created — as Ghandi the apostle of peace puts it: to forge ahead to mould the way of life and worship God Almighty.

I come to you today on solid ground, to shape a new life, to establish peace. We all, on this land, the land of God; we all, Muslims, Christians and Jews, worship God and no one but God. God's teachings and commandments are love, sincerity, purity and peace.

I do not blame all those who received my decision — when I announced it to the entire world before the Egyptian People's Assembly — with surprise and amazement. Some, gripped by the violent surprise, believed that my decision was no more than verbal juggling to cater for world public opinion. Others, still, interpreted it as political tactics to camouflage my intention of launching a new war. I would go as far as to tell you that one of my aides at the Presidential Office contacted me at a late hour following my return home from the People's Assembly and sounded worried as he asked me: "Mr. President, what would be our reaction if Israel should actually extend an invitation to you?" I replied calmly, I will accept it immediately. I have declared that I will go to the end of the world; I will go to Israel, for I want to put before the People of Israel all the facts.

I can see the point of all those who were astounded by my decision or those who had any doubts as to the sincerity of the intentions behind the declaration of my decision. No one would have ever conceived that the President of the biggest Arab State, which bears the heaviest burden and the top responsibility pertaining to the cause of war and peace in the Middle East, could declare his readiness to go to the land of the adversary while we were still in a state of war. Rather, we all are still bearing the consequences of four fierce wars waged within thirty years. The families of the 1973 October War are still moaning under the cruel pains of widowhood and bereavement of sons, fathers and brothers.

As I have already declared, I have not consulted, as far as this decision is concerned, with any of my colleagues and brothers, the Arab Heads of State or the confrontation States. Those of them who contacted me, following the declaration of this decision, expressed their objection, because the feeling of utter suspicion and absolute lack of confidence between the Arab States and the Palestinian People on the one hand, and Israel on the other, still surges in us all. It is sufficient to say that many months in which peace could have been brought about had been wasted over differences and fruitless discussions on the procedure for the convocation of the Geneva Conference, all showing utter suspicion and absolute lack of confidence.

But, to be absolutely frank with you, I took this decision after long thinking, knowing that is constitutes a grave risk for, if God Almighty has made it my fate to assume the responsibility on behalf of the Egyptian People and to share in the fate-determining responsibility of the Arab Nation and the Palestinian People, the main duty dictated by this responsibility is to exhaust all and every means in a bid to save my Egyptian Arab People and the entire Arab Nation the horrors of new, shocking and destructive wars, the dimensions of which are foreseen by no other than God himself.

After long thinking, I was convinced that the obligation of responsibility before God, and before the people, make it incumbent on me that I should go to the farthest corner of the world, even to Jerusalem, to address Members of the Knesset, the representatives of the People of Israel, and acquaint them with all the facts surging in me. Then, I would leave you to decide for yourselves. Following this, may God Almighty determine our fate.

Ladies and Gentlemen, there are moments in the lives of nations and peoples when it is incumbent on those known for their wisdom and clarity of vision to overlook the past, with all its complexities and weighing memories, in a bold drive towards new horizons. Those who, like us, are shouldering the same responsibility entrusted to us, are the first who should have the courage to take fate-determining decisions which are in consonance with the circumstances. We must all rise above all forms of fanaticism, self-deception and obsolete theories of superiority. The most important thing is never to forget that infallibility is the prerogative of God alone.

If I said that I wanted to save all the Arab People the horrors of shocking and destructive wars, I most sincerely declare before you that I have the same feelings and bear the same responsibility towards all and every man on earth, and certainly towards the Israeli People.

Any life lost in war is a human life, irrespecitve of its being that of an Israeli or an Arab. A wife who becomes a widow is a human being entitled to a happy family life, whether she be an Arab or an Israeli. Innocent children who are deprived of the care and compassion of their parents are ours, be they living on Arab or Israeli land. They command our top responsibility to afford them a comfortable life today and tomorrow.

For the sake of them all, for the safeguard of the lives of all our sons and brothers, for affording our communities the opportunity to work for the progress and happiness of man and his right to a dignified life, for our responsibilities before the generations to come, for a smile on the face of every child born on our land — for all that, I have taken my decision to come to you, despite all hazards, to deliver my address.

I have shouldered the prerequisites of the historical responsibility and, therefore, I declared — on 4 February 1971, to be precise — that I was willing to sign a peace agreement with Israel. This was the first declaration made by a responsible Arab official since the outbreak of the Arab-Israel conflict.

Motivated by all these factors dictated by the responsibilities of leadership, I called, on 16 October 1973, before the Egyptian People's Assembly, for an international conference to establish permanent peace based on justice. I was not in the position of he who was pleading for peace or asking for a ceasefire.

Motivated by all these factors dictated by duties of history and leadership, we signed the first disengagement agreement, followed by the second disengagement agreement in Sinai. Then we proceeded trying both open and closed doors in a bid to find a certain path leading to a durable and just peace. We opened our hearts to the peoples of the entire world to make them understand our motivations and objectives, and to leave them actually convinced of the fact that we are advocates of justice and peace-makers.

Motivated by all these factors, I decided to come to you with an open mind and an open heart, and with a conscious determination, so that we might establish permanent peace based on justice.

It is so fated that my trip to you, the trip of peace, should coincide with the Islamic feast, the holy Feast of Courban Bairam, the Feast of Sacrifice when

Abraham — peace be upon him — great-grandfather of the Arabs and Jews, submitted to God; I say when God Almighty ordered him, and to Him Abraham went, with dedicated sentiments, not out of weakness, but through a giant spiritual force and by a free will, to sacrifice his very own son, prompted by a firm and unshakable belief in ideals that lend life a profound significance.

This coincidence may carry a new meaning to us all, which may become a genuine aspiration heralding security and peace.

Ladies and Gentlement, let us be frank with each other, using straightforward words and a clear conception, with no ambiguity. Let us be frank with each other today while the entire world, both East and West, follows these unparalleled moments which could prove to be a radical turning point in the history of this part of the world, if not in the history of the world as a whole. Let us be frank with each other as we answer this important question: how can we achieve permanent peace based on justice?

I have come to you carrying my clear and frank answer to this big question, so that the people in Israel as well as the whole world might hear it, and so that all those whose devoted prayers ring in my ears, pleading to God Almighty that this historic meeting may eventually lead to the results aspired to by millions, might also hear it.

Before I proclaim my answer, I wish to assure you that, in my clear and frank answer, I am basing myself on a number of facts which no one can deny.

The first fact: no one can build his happiness at the expense of the misery of others.

The second fact: never have I spoken or will ever speak in two languages. Never have I adopted or will adopt two policies. I never deal with anyone except in one language, one policy, and with one face.

The third fact: direct confrontation and a straight line are the nearest and most successful methods to reach a clear objective.

The fourth fact: the call for a permanent and just peace, based on respect for the United Nations resolutions, has now become the call of the whole world. It has become a clear expression of the will of the international community, whether in official capitals, where policies are made and decisions taken, or at the level of world public opinion which influences policy-making and decision-taking.

The fifth fact: and this is probably the clearest and most prominent, is that the Arab Nation, in its drive for permanent peace based on justice, does not proceed from a position of weakness or hesitation, but it has the potential of power and stability which tells of a sincere will for peace. The Arab-declared intention stems from an awareness prompted by a heritage of civilization that, to avoid an inevitable disaster that will befall us, you and the entire world, there is no alternative to the establishment of permanent peace based on justice — peace that is not shaken by storms, swayed by suspicion, or jeopardized by ill intentions.

In the light of these facts which I meant to place before you the way I see them, I would also wish to warn you in all sincerity; I warn you against some thoughts that could cross your minds; frankness makes it incumbent upon me to tell you the following:

First: I have not come here for a separate agreement between Egypt and Israel. This is not part of the policy of Egypt. The problem is not that of Egypt and Israel. Any separate peace between Egypt and Israel, or between any Arab confrontation State and Israel, will not bring permanent peace based on justice in the entire region. Rather, even if peace between all the confrontation States and Israel were achieved, in the absence of a just solution to the Palestinian problem, never will there be that durable and just peace upon which the entire world insists today.

Second: I have not come to you to seek a partial peace, namely to terminate the state of belligerency at this stage, and put off the entire problem to a subsequent stage. This is not the radical solution that would steer us to permanent peace.

Equally, I have not come to you for a third disengagement agreement in Sinai, or in the Golan and the West Bank. For this would mean that we are merely delaying the ignition of the fuse; it would mean that we are lacking the courage to confront peace, that we are too weak to shoulder the burdens and responsibilities of a durable peace based on justice.

I have come to you so that together we might build a durable peace based on justice, to avoid the shedding of one single drop of blood from an Arab or an Israeli. It is for this reason that I have proclaimed my readiness to go to the farthest corner of the world.

Here, I would go back to the answer to the big question: how can we achieve a durable peace based on justice?

In my opinion, and I declare it to the whole world from this forum, the answer is neither difficult nor impossible, despite long years of feud, blood vengeance, spite and hatred, and breeding generations on concepts of total rift and deep-rooted animosity. The answer is not difficult, nor is it impossible, if we sincerely and faithfully follow a straight line.

You want to live with us in this part of the world. In all sincerity, I tell you, we welcome you among us, with full security and safety. This, in itself, is a tremendous turning point; one of the landmarks of a decisive historical change.

We used to reject you. We had our reasons and our claims, yes. We used to brand you as "so-called" Israel, yes. We were together in international conferences and organizations and our representatives did not, and still do not, exchange greetings, yes. This has happened and is still happening.

It is also true that we used to set, as a precondition for any negotiations with you, a mediator who would meet separately with each party. Through this procedure, the talks of the first and second disengagement agreements took place.

Our delegates met in the first Geneva Conference without exchanging a direct word. Yes, this has happened.

Yet, today I tell you, and declare it to the whole world, that we accept to live with you in permanent peace based on justice. We do not want to encircle you or be encircled ourselves by destructive missiles ready for launching, nor by the shells of grudges and hatred. I have announced on more than one occasion that Israel has become a *fait accompli,* recognized by the world, and that the two superpowers have undertaken the responsibility of its security and the defence of its existence.

As we really and truly seek peace, we really and truly welcome you to live among us in peace and security.

There was a huge wall between us which you tried to build up over a quarter of a century, but it was destroyed in 1973. It was a wall of a continuously inflammable and escalating psychological warfare. It was a wall of fear of the force that could sweep the entire Arab Nation. It was a wall of propaganda, that we were a Nation reduced to a motionless corpse. Rather, some of you had gone as far as to say that, even after 50 years, the Arabs would not regain any strength. It was a wall that threatened always with the long arm that could reach and strike anywhere. It was a wall that warned us against extermination and annihilation if we tried to use our legitimate right to liberate the occupied territories. Together we have to admit that that wall fell and collapsed in 1973.

Yet, there remained another wall. This wall constitutes a psychological barrier between us. A barrier of suspicion. A barrier of rejection. A barrier of fear of deception. A barrier of hallucinations around any action, deed or decision. A barrier of cautious and erroneous interpretations of all and every event or statement. It is this psychological barrier which I described in official statements as representing 70 percent of the whole problem.

Today through my visit to you, I ask you: why don't we stretch out our hands with faith and sincerity so that, together, we might destroy this barrier? Why shouldn't our and your will meet meet with faith and sincerity, so that together we might remove all suspicion of fear, betrayal and ill intentions? Why don't we stand together with the bravery of men and the boldness of heroes who dedicate themselves to a sublime objective? Why don't we stand together with the same courage and boldness to erect a huge edifice of peace that builds and does not destroy? An edifice that is a beacon for generations to come — the human message for construction, development and the dignity of man? Why should we bequeath to the coming generations the plight of bloodshed, death, orphans, widowhood, family disintegration, and the wailing of victims?

Why don't we believe in the wisdom of God conveyed to us by the Proverbs of Solomon:

"Deceit is in the heart of them that imagine evil; but to the counsellors of peace is joy. Better is a dry morsel, and quietness therewith, than a house full of sacrifices with strife."

Why don't we repeat together from the Psalms of David:

"Hear the voice of my supplications, when I cry unto thee, when I lift up my hands towards the holy oracle. Draw me not away with the wicked, and with the workers of iniquity, which speak peace to their neighbours, but mischief is in their hearts. Give them according to their deeds, and according to the wickedness of their endeavours."

To tell you the truth, peace cannot be worth its name unless it is based on justice, and not on the occupation of the land of others. It would not be appropriate for you to demand for yourselves what you deny others. With all frankness, and with the spirit that has prompted me to come to you today, I tell you: you have to give up, once and for all, the dreams of conquest, and give up the belief that force is the best method for dealing with the Arabs. You should clearly understand and assimilate the lesson of confrontation between you and us.

Expansion does not pay. To speak frankly, our land does not yield itself to bargaining. It is not even open to argument. To us, the national soil is equal to the holy valley where God Almighty spoke to Moses — peace be upon him. None of us can, or accept to, cede one inch of it, or accept the principle of debating or bargaining over it.

I sincerely tell you that before us today lies the appropriate chance for peace, if we are really serious in our endeavours for peace. It is a chance that time cannot afford once again. It is a chance that, if lost or wasted, the plotter against it will bear the curse of humanity and the curse of history.

What is peace for Israel? It means that Israel lives in the region with her Arab neighbours, in security and safety. To such logic, I say yes. It means that Israel lives within her borders, secure against any aggression. To such logic, I say yes. It means that Israel obtains all kinds of guarantees that ensure those two factors. To this demand, I say yes. More than that: we declare that we accept all the international guarantees you envisage and accept. We declare that we accept all the guarantees you want from the two superpowers or from either of them, or from the Big Five, or some of them.

Once again, I declare clearly and unequivocally that we agree to any guarantees you accept because, in return, we shall obtain the same guarantees.

In short, then, when we ask: what is peace for Israel, the answer would be: it is that Israel live within her borders with her Arab neighbours, in safety and security within the framework of all the guarantees she accepts and which are offered to the other party. But how can this be achieved? How can we reach this conclusion which would lead us to permanent peace based on justice?

There are facts that should be faced with all courage and clarity. There are Arab territories which Israel has occupied by armed force. We insist on complete withdrawal from these territories, including Arab Jerusalem.

I have come to Jerusalem, as the City of Peace, which will always remain as a living embodiment of coexistence among believers of the three religions. It is inadmissable that anyone should conceive the special status of the City of Jerusalem within the framework of annexation or expansionism, but it should be a free and open city for all believers.

Above all, the city should not be severed from those who have made it their abode for centuries. Instead of awakening the prejudices of the Crusaders, we should revive the spirit of Omar ibn el-Khattab and Saladdin, namely the spirit of tolerance and respect for rights. The holy shrines of Islam and Christianity are not only places of worship, but a living testimony of our uninterrupted presence here politically, spiritually and intellectually. Let us make no mistake about the importance and reverence we Christians and Muslims attach to Jerusalem.

Let me tell you, without the slightest hesitation, that I did not come to you under this dome to make a request that your troops evacuate the occupied territories. Complete withdrawal from the Arab territories occupied in 1967 is a logical and undisputed fact. Nobody should plead for that. Any talk about permanent peace based on justice, and any move to ensure our coexistence in peace and security in this part of the world, would become meaningless, while you occupy Arab territories by force of arms. For there is no peace that could be in consonance with, or be built on, the occupation of the land of others. Otherwise, it would not be a serious peace.

Yes, this is a foregone conclusion which is not open to discussion or debate — if intentions are sincere and if endeavours to establish a just and durable peace for ours and the generations to come are genuine.

As for the Palestinians' cause, nobody could deny that it is the crux of the entire problem. Nobody in the world could accept, today, slogans propagated here in Israel, ignoring the existence of the Palestinian People, and questioning their whereabouts. The cause of the Palestinian People and their legitimate rights are no longer ignored or denied today by anybody. Rather, nobody who has the ability of judgement can deny or ignore it.

It is an acknowledged fact received by the world community, both in the East and in the West, with support and recognition in international documents and official statements. It is of no use to anybody to turn deaf ears to its resounding voice which is being heard day and night, or to overlook its historical reality. Even the United States, your first ally which is absolutely committed to safeguard Israel's security and existence, and which offered and still offers Israel every moral, material and military support — I say — even the United States has opted to face up to reality and facts, and admit that the

Palestinian People are entitled to legitimate rights and that the Palestinian problem is the core and essence of the conflict and that, so long as it continues to be unresolved, the conflict will continue to aggravate, reaching new dimensions. In all sincerity, I tell you that there can be no peace without the Palestinians. It is a grave error of unpredictable consequences to overlook or brush aside this cause.

I shall not indulge in past events since the Balfour Declaration sixty years ago. You are well acquainted with the relevant facts. If you have found the legal and moral justification to set up a national home on a land that did not all belong to you, it is incumbent upon you to show understanding of the insistence of the People of Palestine on establishing, once again *(sic)* a state on their land. When some extremists ask the Palestinians to give up this sublime objective, this, in fact, means asking them to renounce their identity and every hope for the future.

I hail the Israeli voices that called for the recognition of the Palestinian People's rights to achieve and safeguard peace. Here I tell you, ladies and gentlemen, that it is no use to refrain from recognizing the Palestinian People and their rights to statehood and rights of return.

We, the Arabs, have faced this experience before, with you and with the reality of Israeli existence. The struggle took us from war to war, from victims to more victims, until you and we have today reached the edge of a horrifying abyss and a terrifying disaster, unless together we seize the opportunity today of a durable peace based on justice.

You have to face reality bravely as I have done. There can never be any solution to a problem by evading it or turning a deaf ear to it. Peace cannot last if attempts are made to impose fantasy concepts on which the world has turned its back and announced its unanimous call for the respect of rights and facts. There is no need to enter a vicious circle as to Palestinian rights. It is useless to create obstacles. Otherwise the march of peace will be impeded or peace will be blown up.

As I have told you, there is no happiness to the detriment of others. Direct confrontation and straight-forwardness are the short-cut and the most successful way to reach a clear objective. Direct confrontation concerning the Palestinian problem, and tackling it in one single language with a view to achieving a durable and just peace, lie in the establishment of their state. With all the guarantees you demand, there should be no fear of a newlyborn state that needs the assistance of all countries of the world. When the bells of peace ring, there will be no hands to beat the drums of war. Even if they existed, they would be soundless.

Conceive with me a peace agreement in Geneva that we would herald to a world thirsty for peace, a peace agreement based on the following points:

First: ending the Israeli occupation of the Arab territories occupied in 1967.

Second: achievement of the fundamental rights of the Palestinian People and their right to self-determination, including their right to establish their own state.

Third: the right of all states in the area to live in peace within their boundaries, which will be secure and guaranteed through procedures to be agreed upon, which provide appropriate security to international boundaries, in addition to appropriate international guarantees.

Fourth: commitment of all states in the region to administer the relations among them in accordance with the objectives and principles of the United Nations Charter, particularly the principles concerning the non-resort to force and the solution of differences among them by peaceful means.

Fifth: ending the state of belligerency in the region.

Ladies and Gentlemen, peace is not the mere endorsement of written lines; rather, it is a rewriting of history. Peace is not a game of calling for peace to defend certain whims or hide certain ambitions. Peace is a giant struggle against all and every ambition and whim. Perhaps the examples taken from ancient and modern history teach us all that missiles, warships and nuclear weapons cannot establish security. Rather, they destroy what peace and security build. For the sake of our peoples, and for the sake of the civilizations made by man, we have to defend man everywhere against the rule of the force of arms, so that we may endow the rule of humanity with all the power of the values and principles that promote the sublime position of Mankind.

Allow me to address my call from this rostrum to the People of Israel. I address myself with true and sincere words to every man, woman and child in Israel.

From the Egyptian People who bless this sacred mission of peace, I convey to you the message of peace, the message of the Egyptian People who do not know fanaticism, and whose sons, Muslims, Christians, and Jews, live together in a spirit of cordiality, love and tolerance. This is Egypt whose people have entrusted me with that sacred message, the message of security, safety and peace. To every man, woman and child in Israel, I say: encourage your leadership to struggle for peace. Let all endeavours be channelled towards building a huge edifice for peace, instead of strongholds and hideouts defended by destructive rockets. Introduce to the entire world the image of the new man in this area, so that he might set an example to the man of our age, the man of peace everywhere.

Be the heralds to your sons. Tell them that past wars were the last of wars and the end of sorrows. Tell them that we are in for a new beginning to a new life — the life of love, prosperity, freedom and peace.

You, bewailing mother; you, widowed wife; you, the son who lost a brother or a father; you, all victims of wars — fill the earth and space with recitals of peace. Fill bosoms and hearts with the aspirations of peace. Turn the song into a reality that blossoms and lives. Make hope a code of conduct and endeavour. The will of peoples is part of the will of God.

Ladies and Gentlemen, before I came to this place, with every beat of my heart and with every sentiment, I prayed to God Almighty, while performing the Curban Bairam prayers, and while visiting the Holy Sepulchre, to give me strength and to confirm my belief that this visit may achieve the objectives I look forward to, for a happy present and a happier future.

I have chosen to set aside all precedents and traditions known by warring countries, in spite of the fact that occupation of the Arab territories is still there. Rather, the declaration of my readiness to proceed to Israel came as a great surprise that stirred many feelings and astounded many minds. Some opinions even doubted its intent. Despite that, the decision was inspired by all the clarity and purity of belief, and with all the true expression of my People's will and intentions.

And I have chosen this difficult road which is considered, in the opinion of many, the most difficult road. I have chosen to come to you with an open heart and an open mind. I have chosen to give this great impetus to all international efforts exerted for peace. I have chosen to present to you, and in your own home, the realities devoid of any schemes or whims, not to manoeuvre or to win a round, but for us to win together, the most dangerous of rounds and battles in modern history — the battle of permanent peace based on justice.

It is not my battle alone, nor is it the battle of the leadership in Israel alone. It is the battle of all and every citizen in all our territories whose right it is to live in peace. It is the commitment of conscience and responsibility in the hearts of millions.

When I put forward this initiative, many asked what is it that I conceived as possible to achieve during this visit, and what my expectations were. And, as I answered the questioners, I announce before you that I have not thought of carrying out this initiative from the concept of what could be achieved during this visit, but I have come here to deliver a message. I have delivered the message, and may God be my witness.

I repeat with Zechariah, *"Love right and justice."*

I quote the following verses from the holy Koran:

"We believe in God and in what has been revealed to us and what was revealed to Abraham, Ismail, Isaac, Jacob, and the tribes and in the books given to Moses, Jesus, and the prophets from their Lord. We make no distinction between one and another among them and to God we submit."

2. Prime Minister Begin Knesset Speech, 20 November, 1977

Mr. Speaker, Mr. President of the State of Israel, Mr. President of the Arab Republic of Egypt, ladies and gentlemen, members of the Knesset: We send our greetings to the president, to all the people of the Islamic religion in our country, and wherever they may be, on this occasion of the feast of the festival of the sacrifice 'Id al-Adha. This feast reminds us of the binding of Isaac. This was the way in which the Creator of the World tested our forefather, Abraham, our common forefather, to test his faith, and Abraham passed this test. However, from the moral aspect and the advancement of humanity, it was forbidden to sacrifice human beings. Our two peoples in their ancient traditions know and taught what the Lord, blessed be He, taught while peoples around us still sacrified human beings to their gods. Thus, we contributed, the people of Israel and the Arab people, to the progress of mankind, and thus we are continuing to contribute to human culture to this day.

I greet and welcome the president of Egypt for coming to our country and on his participating in the Knesset session. The flight time between Cairo and Jerusalem is short, but the distance between Cairo and Jerusalem was until last night almost endless. President el-Sadat crossed this distance courageously. We, the Jews, know how to appreciate such courage, and we know how to appreciate it in our guest, because it is with courage that we are here, and this is how we continue to exist, and we shall continue to exist.

Mr. Speaker, this small nation, the remaining refuge of the Jewish people who returned to their historic homeland, has always wanted peace, and since the dawn of our independence, on 14 May 1948, 5 Iyar Tashah, in the declaration of independence in the founding scroll of our national freedom, David Ben-Gurion said: "We extend a hand of peace and neighborliness to all the neighboring countries and their peoples. We call upon them to cooperate, to help each other, with the Hebrew people independent in their own country. One year earlier, even from the underground, when we were in the midst of the fateful struggle for the liberation of the country and the redemption of the people, we called in our neighbors in these terms: In this country we will live together and we will advance together and we will live lives of freedom and happiness. Our Arab neighbors, do not reject the hand stretched out to you in peace."

But it is my bounden duty, Mr. Speaker, and not only my right, not to pass over the truth that our hand outstretched for peace was not grasped and one day after we had renewed our independence, as was our right, our eternal right, which cannot be disputed, we were attacked on three fronts, and we stood almost without arms, the few against many, the weak against the strong, while an attempt was made, one day after the declaration of independence, to strangle it at birth, to put an end to the last hope of the Jewish people, the yearning renewed after the years of destruction and holocaust. No, we did not believe in might and we have never based our attitude towards the Arab people on might. Quite the contrary, force was used against us. Over all the years of this generation we have never stopped being attacked by might, of the strong arm stretched out to exterminate our people, to destroy our independence, to deny our rights. We defended ourselves, it is true. We defended our rights, our existence, our honor, our women and our children, against these repeated and recurring attempts to crush us through the force of arms, and not only on one front. That, too, is true. With the help of God Almighty, we overcame the forces of aggression, and we have guaranteed existence for our nation. Not only for this generation, but for the coming generations, too. We do not believe in might. We believe in right, only in right. And therefore our aspiration, from the bottom of our hearts, has always been, to this very day, for peace.

Mr. President, Mr. President of Egypt, the commanders of all the underground Hebrew fighting organizations are sitting in this democratic house. They had to conduct a campaign of the few against the many, against a huge, a world power. Sitting here are the veteran commanders and captains who had to go forth into battle because it was forced upon them and forward to victory, which was unavoidable because they were defending their rights. They belong to different parties. They have different views, but I am sure, Mr. President, that I am expressing the views of everyone, with no exceptions, that we have one aspiration in our hearts, one desire in our souls, and all of us are united in all these aspirations and desires — to bring peace, peace for our nation, which has not known peace for even one day since we started returning to Zion, and peace for our neighbors, whom we wish all the best, and we believe that if we make peace, real peace, we will be able to help our neighbors, in all walks of life, and a new era will open in the Middle East, an era of blossoming and growth, development and expansion of the economy, its growth as it was in the past.

Therefore, permit me today to set forth the peace program as we understand it. We want full, real peace with complete reconciliation between the Jewish and the Arab peoples. I do not wish to dwell on the memories of the past, but there have been wars; there has been blood spilt; wonderful young people have been killed on both sides. We will live all our life with the memories of our heroes who gave their lives so this day would arrive, this day, too, would come, and we respect the bravery of a rival and we honor all the members of the younger generation among the Arab people who also fell.

I do not wish to dwell on memories of the past, although they be bitter memories. We will bury them; we will worry about the future, about our people, our children, our joint and common future. For it is true indeed that we will have to live in this area, all of us together will live here, for generations upon generations: The great Arab people in their various states and countries, and the Jewish people in their country, Eretz Yisrael. Therefore, we must determine what peace means.

Let us conduct negotiations, Mr. President, as free negotiating partners for a peace treaty, and, with the aid of the Lord, we fully believe the day will come when we can sign it with mutual respect, and we will then know that the era of wars is over, that hands have been extended between friends, that each has shaken the hand of his brother and the future will be shining for all the peoples of this area. The beginning of wisdom in a peace treaty is the abolition of the state of war. I agree, Mr. President, that you did not come here, we did not invite you to our country in order, as has been said in recent days, to divide the Arab peoples. Somebody quoted an ancient Roman, saying: Divide and rule. Israel does not want to rule and therefore does not need to divide. We want peace with all our neighbors: with Egypt, with Jordan, with Syria and with Lebanon. We would like to negotiate peace treaties.

And there is no need to distinguish between a peace treaty and an abolition of the state of war. Quite the contrary, we are not proposing this nor are we asking for it. The first clause of a peace treaty is cessation of the state of war, forever. We want to establish normal relations between us, as they exist between all nations, even after wars. We have learned from history, Mr. President, that war is avoidable, peace is unavoidable. Many nations have waged war among themselves, and sometimes they used the tragic term perennial enemy. There are no perennial enemies. And after all the wars the inevitable comes — peace. And so we want to establish, in a peace treaty, diplomatic relations as is the custom among civilized nations.

Today two flags are flying over Jerusalem: the Egyptian flag and the Israeli flag. And we saw together, Mr. President, little children waving both the flags. Let us sign a peace treaty and let us establish this situation forever, both in Jerusalem and in Cairo, and I hope the day will come when the Egyptian children wave the Israeli flag and the Egyptian flag, just as the children of Israel waved both these flags in Jerusalem.

And you, Mr. President, will have a loyal ambassador in Jerusalem, and we will have an ambassador in Cairo. And even if differences of opinion arise between us, we will clarify them like civilized peoples through our authorized envoys.

We are proposing economic cooperation for the development of our countries. These are wonderful countries in the Middle East. The Lord created it thus: oases in the desert, but there are deserts as well and we can make them flourish. Let us cooperate in this field. Let us develop our countries. Let us eliminate poverty, hunger, the lack of shelter. Let us raise our peoples to the level of developed countries and let them not call us "developing countries".

And with all due respect, I am willing to confirm the words of his majesty the king of Morocco, who said — in public too — that if peace arises in the Middle East, the combination of Arab genius and Jewish genius together can turn this area into a paradise on earth.

Let us open our countries to free traffic. You come to our country and we will visit yours. I am ready to announce, Mr. Speaker, this day that our country is open to the citizens of Egypt and I make no conditions on our part. I think it is only proper and just that there should be a joint announcement on this matter. But, just as there are Egyptian flags in our streets, and there is also an honored delegation from Egypt in our capital and in our country, let the number of visitors increase: our border will be open to you, and also all the other borders.

And as I pointed out, we want this in the south and in the north and in the east. And so I am renewing my invitation to the president of Syria to follow in your footsteps, Mr. President, and come to us to open negotiations for achieving peace between Israel and Syria and to sign a peace treaty between us. I am sorry to say that there is no justification for the mourning they have declared beyond our northern border. Quite the contrary, such visits, such links, such clarifications can and must be days of joy, days of lifting spirits for all the peoples. I invite King Hussein to come to us to discuss all the problems which need to be discussed between us. Also genuine representatives of the Arabs of Eretz Yisrael, I invite them to come and hold talks with us to clarify our common future, to guarantee the freedom of man, social justice, peace, mutual respect. And if they invite us to go to their capitals, we will accept their invitations. If they invite us to open negotiations in Damascus, in Amman or in Beirut, we will go to those capitals in order to hold negotiations with them there. We do not want to divide. We want real peace with all our neighbors, to be expressed in peace treaties whose contents I have already made clear. [interruptions indistinct from the audience].

Mr. Speaker, it is my duty today to tell our guest and the peoples watching us and listening to our words about the link between our people and this country. The president recalled the Balfour Declaration. No, sir, we did not take over any strange land; we returned to our homeland. The link between our people and this country is eternal. It arose in the earliest days of the history of humanity and has never been disrupted. In this country we developed our civilization, we had our prophets here, and their sacred words stand to this day. Here the kings of Judah and Israel knelt before their God. This is where we became a people; here we established our kingdom. And when we were expelled from our land because of force which was used against us, the farther we went from our land, we never forgot this country for even a single day. We prayed for it, we longed for it, we believed in our return to it from the day the words were spoken: When the Lord restores the fortunes of Zion, we will be like dreamers. Our mouths will be filled with laughter, and our tongues will speak with shouts of joy. These verses apply to all our exiles and all our sufferings, giving the consolation that the return to Zion would come.

This, our right, was recognized. The Balfour Declaration was included in the mandate laid down by the nations of the world, including the United States, and the preface to this recognized international document says: [speaks in English] "Whereas recognition has the Bible given to the historical connection of the Jewish people with Palestine and to the grounds for reconstituting their national home in that country", [ends English] — the historic connection between the Jewish people and Palestine [in English] — or, in Hebrew, Eretz Yisrael, was given reconfirmation — reconfirmation — as the national homeland in that country, that is, in Eretz Yisrael.

In 1919 we also won recognition of this right by the spokesman of the Arab people and the agreement of 3 January 1919, which was signed by Emir Faysal and Chaim Weizmann. It reads: [speaks in English] Mindful of the racial kinship and ancient bonds existing between the Arabs and the Jewish people and realizing that the surest means of working out the consummation of the national aspirations in the closest possible collaboration in the development of the Arab State and of Palestine. [ends English]. And afterward come all the clauses about cooperation between the Arab State and Eretz Yisrael. This is our right. The existence — truthful existence.

What happened to us when our homeland was taken from us? I accompanied you this morning, Mr. President, to Yad Vashem. With your own eyes you saw the fate of our people when this homeland was taken from it. It cannot be told. Both of us agreed, Mr. President, that anyone who has not seen with his own eyes everything there is in Yad Vashem cannot understand what happened to this people when it was without a homeland, when its own homeland was taken from it. And both of us read a document dated 30 January 1939, where the word "Vernichtung" — annihilation — appears. If war breaks out, the Jewish race in Europe will be exterminated. Then, too, we were told that we should not pay attention to the racists. The whole world heard. Nobody came to save us. Not during the nine fateful, decisive months after the announcement was made, the like of which had not been seen since the Lord created man and man created the Devil.

And during those six years, too, when millions of our people, among them one and a half million of the little children of Israel who were burned on all the strange beds [as heard], nobody came to save them, not from the East nor from the West. And because of this, we took a solemn oath, this entire generation, the generation of extermination and revival, that we would never again put our people in danger, that we would never again put our women and our children, whom it is our duty to defend — if there is a need for this, even at the cost of our lives — in the hell of the exterminating fire of an enemy. Since then, it has been our duty for generations to come to remember that certain things said about our people must be taken with complete seriousness. And we must not, heaven forbid, for the sake of the future of our people, take any advice whatsoever against taking these things seriously.

President el-Sadat knows, and he knew from us before he came to Jerusalem, that we have a different position from his with regard to the permanent borders between us and our neighbors. However, I say to the president of Egypt and to all our neighbors: Do not say, there is not negotiation, there will not be negotiations about any particular issue. I propose, with the agreement of the decisive majority of this parliament, that everything be open to negotiation. Anyone who says, with reference to relations between the Arab people, or the Arab peoples around us, and the State of Israel, that there are things which should be omitted from negotiations is taking upon himself a grave responsibility. Everything can be negotiated.

No side will say the contrary. No side will present prior conditions. We will conduct the negotiations honorably. If there are difference of opinion between us, this is not unusual. Anyone who has studied the histories of wars and the signing of peace treaties knows that all negotiations over a peace treaty began with differences of opinion between the sides. And in the course of the negotiations they reached an agreement which permitted the signing of peace treaties and agreements. And this is the road which we propose to take.

And we will conduct the negotiations as equals. There are no vanquished and there are no victors. All the peoples of the area are equal and all of them should treat each other with due respect. In this spirit of openness, of willingness to listen to each other, to hear the facts and the reasoning and the explanations, accepting all the experience of human persuasion, let us conduct the negotiations as I have asked and am proposing, open them and carry them out, carry them on constantly until we reach the longed-for hour of the signing of a peace treaty between us.

We are not only ready to sit with the representatives of Egypt, and also with the representatives of Jordan and Syria and Lebanon, if they are ready, we are prepared to sit together at a peace conference in Geneva. We propose that the Geneva conference be renewed, on the basis of the two Security Council resolutions: 242 and 338. If there are problems between us by convening the Geneva conference, we will be able to clarify them. And if the president of Egypt wants to continue clarifying them in Cairo, I am for it. If in a neutral place, there is no objection. Let us clarify anywhere, even before the Geneva conference convenes, the problems which should be clarified before it is convened. And our eyes will be open and our ears will listen to all proposals.

Permit me to say a word about Jerusalem. Mr. President, you prayed today in the house of prayer sacred to the Islamic religion, and from there you went to the Church of the Holy Sepulchre. You realized, as those coming from all over the world have realized, that ever since this city was unified, there has been completely free access, without interference and without any obstacle, for the members of every religion to the places sacred to them. This positive phenomenon did not exist for 19 years. It has existed for about 11 years, and we can promise the Moslem world and the Christian world, all the peoples, that there will always be free access to the sacred places of every religion. We will defend this right to free access, for we believe in it. We believe in equal rights for all men and citizens and respect for every faith.

Mr. Speaker, this is a special day for our legislative chamber, and certainly this day will be remembered for many years in the history of our nation, and perhaps also in the history of the Egyptian nation, maybe in the history of all nations. And this day, with your agreement, ladies and gentlemen, members of the Knesset, let us pray that the God of our fathers, our common fathers, will give us the wisdom needed to overcome difficulties and obstacles, calumnies and slander, incitement and attacks. And with the help of God, may we arrive at the longed-for day for which all our people pray — peace. For it is indeed true that the sweet singer of Israel [King David] said: "Righteousness and peace will kiss each other", and the Prophet Zachariah said: Love, truth and peace."

3. Prime Minister Begin's Autonomy Plan, 28 December, 1977

As announced in the Knesset

1. The administration of the Military Government in Judea, Samaria and the Gaza district will be abolished.

2. In Judea, Samaria and the Gaza district, administrative autonomy of the residents, by and for them, will be established.

3. The residents of Judea, Samaria and the Gaza district will elect an Administrative Council composed of 11 members. The Administrative Council will operate in accordance with the principles laid down in this paper.

4. Any resident, 18 years old and above, without distinction of citizenship, or if stateless, will be entitled to vote in the elections to the Administrative Council.

5. Any resident whose name is included in the list of candidates for the Administrative Council and who, on the day the list is submitted, is 25 years old or above, will be entitled to be elected to the Council.

6. The Administrative Council will be elected by general, direct, personal, equal and secret ballot.

7.   The period of office of the Administrative Council will be four years from the day of its election.

8.   The Administrative Council will sit in Bethlehem.

9.   All the administrative affairs relating to the Arab residents of the areas of Judea, Samaria and the Gaza district will be under the direction and within the competence of the Administrative Council.

10.   The Administrative Council will operate the following Departments: education; religious affairs; finance; transportation; construction and housing; industry, commerce and tourism; agriculture; health, labour and social welfare; rehabilitation of refugees; and the administration of justice and supervision of local police forces; and promulgate regulations relating to the operation of these Departments.

11.   Security and public order in the areas of Judea, Samaria and the Gaza district will be the responsibility of the Israeli authorities.

12.   The Administrative Council will elect its own chairman.

13.   The first session of the Administrative Council will be convened 30 days after the publication of the election results.

14.   Residents of Judea, Samaria and the Gaza district, without distinction of citizenship, or if stateless, will be granted free choice (option) of either Israeli or Jordanian citizenship.

15.   A resident of the areas of Judea, Samaria and the Gaza district who requests Israeli citizenship will be granted such citizenship in accordance with the citizenship law of the state.

16.   Residents of Judea, Samaria and the Gaza district who, in accordance with the right of free option, choose Israeli citizenship, will be entitled to vote for, and be elected to, the Knesset in accordance with the election law.

17.   Residents of Judea, Samaria and the Gaza district who are citizens of Jordan or who, in accordance with the right of free option will become citizens of Jordan, will elect and be eligible for election to the Parliament of the Hashemite Kingdom of Jordan in accordance with the election law of that country.

18.   Questions arising from the vote to the Jordanian Parliament by residents of Judea, Samaria and the Gaza district will be clarified in negotiations between Israel and Jordan.

19.   A committee will be established of representatives of Israel, Jordan and the Administrative Council to examine existing legislation in Judea, Samaria and the Gaza district, and to determine which legislation will continue in force which will be abolished, and what will be the competence of the Administrative Council to promulgate regulations. The rulings of the committee will be adopted by unanimous decision.

20.   Residents of Israel will be entitled to acquire land and settle in the areas of Judea, Samaria and the Gaza district. Arabs, residents of Judea,

Samaria and the Gaza district who, in accordance with the free option granted them, will become Israeli citizens, will be entitled to acquire land and settle in Israel.

21. A committee will be established of representatives of Israel, Jordan and the Administrative Council to determine norms of immigration to the areas of Judea, Samaria and the Gaza district. The committee will determine the norms whereby Arab refugees residing outside Judea, Samaria and the Gaza district will be permitted to immigrate to these areas in reasonable numbers. The rulings of the committee will be adopted by unanimous decision.

22. Residents of Israel and residents of Judea, Samaria and the Gaza district will be assured freedom of movement and freedom of economic activity in Israel Judea, Samaria and the Gaza district.

23. The Administrative Council will appoint one of its members to represent the Council before the Government of Israel for deliberation on matters of common interest, and one of its members to represent the Council before the Government of Jordan for deliberation on matters of common interest.

24. Israel stands by its right and its claim of sovereignty to Judea, Samaria and the Gaza district. In the knowledge that other claims exist, it proposes, for the sake of the agreement and the peace, that the question of sovereignty in the areas be left open.

25. With regard to the administration of the holy places of the three religions in Jerusalem, a special proposal will be drawn up and submitted that will include the guarantee of freedom of access to members of all the faiths to the shrines holy to them.

26. These principles will be subject to review after a five-year period.

4. A Framework for Peace in the Middle East Agreed at Camp David, 17 September, 1978

Following is the text of the Agreement reached at the Camp David Summit and signed September 17 at the White House.

Mohammed Anwar el-Sadat, President of the Arab Republic of Egypt, and Menachem Begin, Prime Minister of Israel, met with Jimmy Carter, President of the United States of America, at Camp David from September 5 to September 17, 1978, and have agreed on the following framework for peace in the Middle East. They invite other parties to the Arab-Israel conflict to adhere to it.

The search for peace in the Middle East must be guided by the following:

— The agreed basis for a peaceful settlement of the conflict between Israel and its neighbors in United Nations Security Council Resolution 242, in all its parts.

— After four wars during thirty years, despite intensive human efforts, the Middle East, which is the cradle of civilization and the birthplace of three great religions, does not yet enjoy the blessing of peace. The people of the Middle East yearn for peace so that the vast human and natural resources of the region can be turned to the pursuits of peace and so that this area can become a model for coexistence and cooperation among nations.

— The historic initiative of President Sadat in visiting Jerusalem and the reception accorded to him by the Parliament, Government and People of Israel, and the reciprocal visit of Prime Minister Begin to Ismailia, the peace proposals made by both leaders, as well as the warm reception of these missions by the peoples of both countries, have created an unprecedented opportunity for peace which must not be lost if this generation and future generations are to be spared the tragedies of war.

— The provisions of the Charter of the United Nations and the other accepted norms of international law and legitimacy now provide accepted standards for the conduct of relations among all states.

— To achieve a relationship of peace, in the spirit of Article 2 of the United Nations Charter, future negotiations between Israel and any neighbor prepared to negotiate peace and security with it, are necessary for the purpose of carrying out all the provisions and principles of Resolutions 242 and 338.

— Peace requires respect for the sovereignty, territorial integrity and political independence of every state in the area and their right to live in peace within secure and recognized boundaries free from threats or acts of force. Progress toward that goal can accelerate movement toward a new era of reconciliation in the Middle East marked by cooperation in promoting economic development, in maintaining stability, and in assuring security.

— Security is enhanced by a relationship of peace and by cooperation between nations which enjoy normal relations. In addition, under the terms of peace treaties, the parties can, on the basis of reciprocity, agree to special security arrangements such as demilitarized zones, limited armaments areas, early warning stations, the presence of international forces, liaison, agreed measures for monitoring, and other arrangements that they agree are useful.

Framework

Taking these factors into account, the parties are determined to reach a just, comprehensive, and durable settlement of the Middle East conflict through the conclusion of peace treaties based on Security Council Resolutions 242 and 338, in all their parts. Their purpose is to achieve peace and good neighborly relations. They recognize that, for peace to endure, it must involve all those who have been most deeply affected by the conflict. They therefore agree that this framework as appropriate is intended by them to constitute a basis for peace not only between Egypt and Israel, but also between Israel and each of its other neighbors which is prepared to negotiate peace with Israel on this basis. With that objective in mind, they have agreed to proceed as follows:

A.   West Bank and Gaza.

1.   Egypt, Israel, Jordan and the representatives of the Palestinian people should participate in negotiations on the resolution of the Palestinian problem in all its aspects. To achieve that objective, negotiations relating to the West Bank and Gaza should proceed in three stages:

(a)   Egypt and Israel agree that, in order to ensure a peaceful and orderly transfer of authority, and taking into account the security concerns of all the parties, there should be transitional arrangements for the West Bank and Gaza for a period not exceeding five years. In order to provide full autonomy to the inhabitants, under these arrangements the Israeli military government and its civilian administration will be withdrawn as soon as a self-governing authority has been freely elected by the inhabitants of these areas to replace the existing military government. To negotiate the details of a transitional arrangement, the Government of Jordan will be invited to join the negotiations on the basis of this framework. These new arrangements should give due consideration both to the principle of self-government by the inhabitants of these territories and to the legitimate security concerns of the parties involved.

(b)   Egypt, Israel, and Jordan will agree on the modalities for establishing the elected self-governing authority in the West Bank and Gaza. The delegations of Egypt and Jordan may include Palestinians from the West Bank and Gaza or other Palestinians as mutually agreed. The parties will negotiate an agreement which will define the powers and responsibilities of the self-governing authority to be exercised in the West Bank and Gaza. A withdrawal of Israeli Armed Forces will take place and there will be a redeployment of the remaining Israeli forces into specified security locations. The agreement will also include arrangements for assuring internal and external security and public order. A strong local police force will be established, which may include Jordanian citizens. In addition, Israeli and Jordanian forces will participate in joint patrols and in the manning of control posts to assure the security of the borders.

(c)   When the self-governing authority (administrative council) in the West Bank and Gaza is established and inaugurated, the transitional period of five years will begin. As soon as possible, but not later than the third year after the beginning of the transitional period, negotiations will take place to determine the final status of the West Bank and Gaza and its relationship with its neighbors, and to conclude a peace treaty between Israel and Jordan by the end of the transitional period. These negotiations will be conducted between

Egypt, Israel, Jordan, and the elected representatives of the inhabitants of the West Bank and Gaza. Two separate but related committees will be convened, one committee, consisting of representatives of the four parties which will negotiate and agree on the final status of the West Bank and Gaza, and its relationship with its neighbors, and the second committee, consisting of representatives of Israel and representatives of Jordan to be joined by the elected representatives of the inhabitants of the West Bank and Gaza, to negotiate the peace treaty between Israel and Jordan, taking into account the agreement reached on the final status of the West Bank and Gaza. The negotiations shall be based on all the provisions and principles of U.N. Security Council Resolution 242. The negotiations will resolve, among other matters, the location of the boundaries and the nature of the security arrangements. The resolution from the negotiations must also recognize the legitimate rights of the Palestine people and their just requirements. In this way, the Palestinians will participate in the determination of their own future through:

1) The negotiations between Egypt, Israel, Jordan and the representatives of the inhabitants of the West Bank and Gaza to agree on the final status of the West Bank and Gaza and other outstanding issues by the end of the transitional period.

2) Submitting their agreement to a vote by the elected representatives of the inhabitants of the West Bank and Gaza.

3) Providing for the elected representatives of the inhabitants of the West Bank and Gaza to decide how they shall govern themselves consistent with the provisions of their agreement.

4) Participating as stated above in the work of the committee negotiating the peace treaty between Israel and Jordan.

2. All necessary measures will be taken and provisions made to assure the security of Israel and its neighbors during the transitional period and beyond. To assist in providing such security, a strong local police force will be constituted by the self-governing authority. It will be composed of inhabitants of the West Bank and Gaza. The police will maintain continuing liaison on internal security matters with the designated Israeli, Jordanian, and Egyptian officers.

3. During the transitional period, representatives of Egypt, Israel, Jordan, and the self-governing authority will constitute a continuing committee to decide by agreement on the modalities of admission of persons displaced from the West Bank and Gaza in 1967, together with necessary measures to prevent disruption and disorder. Other matters of common concern may also be dealt with by this committee.

4. Egypt and Israel will work with each other and with other interested parties to establish agreed procedures for a prompt, just and permanent implementation of the resolution of the refugee problem.

B. Egypt-Israel

1. Egypt and Israel undertake not to resort to the threats or the use of force to settle disputes. Any disputes shall be settled by peaceful means in accordance with the provisions of Article 33 of the Charter of the United Nations.

2. In order to achieve peace between them, the parties agree to negotiate in good faith with a goal of concluding within three months from the signing of this framework a peace treaty between them, while inviting the other parties to the conflict to proceed simultaneously to negotiate and conclude similar peace treaties with a view to achieving a comprehensive peace in the area. The framework for the conclusion of a peace treaty between Egypt and Israel will govern the peace negotiations between them. The parties will agree on the modalities and the timetable for the implementation of their obligations under the treaty.

C. Associated Principles

1. Egypt and Israel state that the principles and provisions described below should apply to peace treaties between Israel and each of its neighbors — Egypt, Jordan, Syria and Lebanon.

2. Signatories shall establish among themselves relationships normal to states at peace with one another. To this end, they should undertake to abide by all the provisions of the Charter of the United Nations. Steps to be taken in this respect include:

(a) Full recognition;

(b) Abolishing economic boycotts;

(c) Guaranteeing that under their jurisdiction the citizens of the other parties shall enjoy the protection of the due process of law.

3. Signatories should explore possibilities for economic development in the context of final peace treaties, with the objective of contributing to the atmosphere of peace, cooperation and friendship which is their common goal.

4. Claims Commissions may be established for the mutual settlement of all financial claims.

5. The United States shall be invited to participate in the talks on matters related to the modalities of the implementation of the Agreements and working out the timetable for the carrying out of the obligations of the parties.

6. The United Nations Security Council shall be requested to endorse the peace treaties and ensure that their provisions shall not be violated. The permanent members of the Security Council shall be requested to underwrite the peace treaties and ensure respect for their provisions. They shall also be requested to conform their policies and actions with the undertakings contained in this framework.

5. Government of Egypt Proposed Model of Full Autonomy for the West Bank and Gaza Strip, 28 January, 1980

I — Introduction

(a)   The Camp David Framework stipulates the withdrawal of the military government and its civilian administration, and the transfer of its authority to the self-governing authority which will replace it.

(b)   In reviewing the powers and responsibilities of the military government and its civilian administration, the working group was seeking to envisage, through a practical approach, the powers and responsibilities to be exercised by the SGA in the context of its replacement of the military government and its civilian administration as stated in the Camp David Framework. That was the purpose of the survey of the current situation, it was a way out of the deadlock caused by the conceptual discussions of the comprehensive approach, and a step to provide the parties with basic information for discussing the transfer of authority. Indeed, the presentations of the powers and responsibilities of the military government and its civilian administration were meant to lead the working group, in the light of these presentations, and in the context of the transfer of authority, to prepare a model for the powers and responsibilities to be exercised by the SGA.

This method was endorsed by the decision taken at the London meeting of the heads of delegation on October 26, 1979:

"... Presentations on the current situation will provide the parties with basic information for discussing transfer of authority as stated in the Camp David Framework."

This led subsequently to the call of the plenary on December 19, 1979 to the working group:

"To proceed to prepare for the plenary's future consideration a proposed model for the powers and responsibilities to be exercised by the SGA".

(c)   When the method is thus set in perspective, it becomes clear that when a model of the powers and responsibilities of the SGA is to be prepared, the guiding frame should be the powers and responsibilities of the military government and its civilian administration and that the focal points in discussing such a model should be:

1 — Withdrawal of the Israeli military government and its civilian administration.

2 — The transfer of authority.

3 — Organs of the SGA which will take over from, and replace, the military government and its civilian administration.

II — The Military Government and its Civilian Administration

(a)   On June 7, 1967, the Israeli military command published proclamation

No. 2 entitled "Laws and administration proclamation". A section of which is concerned with the assumption of government by the Israeli defence forces, and under the title "Assumption of powers" it reads:

"Any power of government, legislation, appointment, or administration with respect to the region or its inhabitants shall henceforth vest in me alone and shall be exercised only by me or a person appointed by me to that end or acting on my behalf."

(b) The Israel military government currently existing in the West Bank and Gaza Strip has full comprehensive authority. It assumes the power of formulating all policies and coordinating all activities. Its decision making emanates from different and interconnected channels of Israeli cabinet and interministerial levels as well as a chain of military command leading to the area or regional commander (one for the West Bank and one for Gaza) who was vested with full legislative and executive authority in the area as shown in the aforementioned proclamation. Mandatory orders issued by the military commander presented legislative enactments and revisions. Policy is determined according to considerations adopted by the office of the coordinator of activities, the Israeli ministry concerned and the regional command.

(c) Administrative authority is delegated to regional and district commanders. Routine administrative duties and conduct of ordinary activities are left to the relevant institutions that were already operating in the West Bank and Gaza or to newly organized units of administrative service.

The civil administration of the military government is carried out by branches, each branch supervising a number of units. The units carry out the conduct of every day life. Heads of units who operate in the areas are directly subordinated through the chief of branch to the military commander while they come, at the same time, under the corresponding ministries in Israel on professional matters. From the ministry they get instructions on professional matters, how to act, how to deal with the problems arising out of the daily life. From the commander, through the chief of branch, they get the policy, the command.

(d) The military government and its civilian administration is therefore composed of different levels manifesting different layers of authority. One layer legislates and formulates policies while another layer executes and carries out the policies.

The Camp David Framework stipulates the transfer of both. It is not a matter of transferring the administrative set-up which implements the orders but first and foremost transferring the strata of authority which holds the power to issue the orders.

(e) It may be recalled that the civil administration of the military government is mainly composed, even now, of local inhabitants. According to the figures of December 1978 there were in the West Bank 11,165 local employees in the civil administration (and only 980 Israelis) while in Gaza there are local director-generals heading 14 of the main units.

So, it may be said, that even now the Palestinian people in the West Bank and Gaza Strip are bearing most of the responsibility for running the affairs of their daily life but only carrying out decisions which were made for them and implementing policies which were formulated over their heads.

When the Camp David Framework promises them full autonomy, it can only mean that under the SGA they will be able to take their own decisions and formulate their own policies.

The full autonomy which the Camp David Framework provides for cannot amount to a reorganization of what the Palestinians in the West Bank and Gaza Strip already have, but rather the transformation of that set-up in an authority which is self-governing. Hence, the withdrawal of the military government and the transfer of its manifold authority to the inhabitants.

III — Withdrawal of the Military Government and the Transfer of Authority

(a)   The first step in establishing the SGA should be the withdrawal of the military government, the Camp David Framework for peace states clearly that: "The Israeli military government and its civilian administration will be withdrawn as soon as a self-governing authority has been freely elected by the inhabitants of these areas to replace the existing military government."

The joint letter of March 26, 1979 states that: "The Military Government and its civilian administration will be withdrawn, to be replaced by the SGA."

(b)   Distinction is made in both the Camp David Framework and the joint letter between two kinds of withdrawals:

1 — The withdrawal of the military government and its civilian administration which is total and absolute. It is an unqualified withdrawal; and

2 — A withdrawal of Israeli armed forces which is going to be partial and there will be a redeployment of the remaining forces into specified security locations.

(c)   The withdrawal of the military government and its civilian administration, which occurs as soon as the SGA is elected, is the first step towards the assumption by the SGA of its powers and responsibilities. The transfer of authority takes place by handing over the powers and responsibilities of the military government and its civilian administration to the newly elected SGA. The SGA replaces the outgoing regime.

(d)   In this respect, the following elements should be stressed:

(1)   The transfer of authority implies the handing over of all powers and responsibilities presently exercised by the military government and its civilian administration.

(2)   The transfer of authority should be carried out in a peaceful and orderly manner.

(3)   Whenever Palestinian Institutions already exist in the West Bank and Gaza Strip, as part of the prevailing system of civil service, they will, in the course of such transfer of authority, take over the functions of, and replace, the military government and its civilian administration. It is only when new functions, or new powers, are transferred to the SGA which were not exercised before under the military regime by the Palestinian people that new organs should be sought.

(e)   Stress should be focused more on the powers and functions that are not exercised by the Palestinian people under the military regime so that the necessary relevant organs would be suggested. The Palestinian people already played the major role in the civil service which obeyed the commands and implemented the policies of the military regime. Under the autonomy there will be need for an organ to fulfill their newly acquired power to make their own decisions and formulate their own policies. The elected body of the SGA is obviously that organ.

IV — Powers and Responsibilities to be Exercised by the Self-Governing Authority

For a model of powers and responsibilities to be exercised by the SGA, some keywords and guidelines from the Camp David Framework for peace should be stressed at the outset.

(a)   It is a self-governing authority, which means that it governs itself by itself. It is a self-generating authority. No outside source vests it with its authority.

(b)   It provides full autonomy, and not an impaired or partial autonomy.

(c)   This self-governing authority with full autonomy comes through free elections. It is a democratic structure of government by the people and for the people. As an elected body it has a representative character and its membership fulfill the functions and exercise the powers that an elected representative body usually does.

1 — Nature of the SGA

The SGA is an interim arrangement for a period not exceeding 5 years. This transitional process, at the outset of which the Israeli military government and its civilian administration will be withdrawn and the SGA established, can demonstrate that the practical problems arising from a transition to peace can be satisfactorily resolved. The transitional period is aimed at bringing about the changes in attitudes that can assure a final settlement which realizes the legitimate rights of the Palestinian people while assuring the security of all the parties. The purpose of this transitional arrangement is:

(a)   To ensure a peaceful and orderly transfer of authority to the Palestinian people in the West Bank and Gaza Strip.

(b)   To help the Palestinian people to develop their own political, economic and social institutions in the West Bank and Gaza Strip so as to give expression to the principle of full autonomy which the SGA provides.

(c)   To provide the proper conditions for the Palestinian people to participate in negotiations leading to the solution of the Palestinian problem in all its aspects and the realization of their legitimate rights including their right to self-determination.

2 — Scope of the SGA:

(a)   The jurisdiction of the SGA will encompass all of the Palestinian territories occupied after 5 June 1967 and which are delineated in the relevant armistice agreements of 1949 (Egyptian Israeli armistice agreement of 2 April, 1949 regarding the Gaza Strip and Jordanian Israeli armistice agreement of 24 February, 1949 regarding the West Bank including Arab Jerusalem).

(b)   Authority of the SGA extends to the inhabitants as well as the land in the West Bank and the Gaza Strip.

(c)   All powers and responsibilities of the SGA apply to the West Bank and Gaza Strip which shall be regarded under the autonomy as one territory and integral whole.

(d)   All changes in the geographic character, the demographic composition and the legal status of the West Bank and Gaza Strip or any part thereof are null and void and must be rescinded as they jeopardize the attainment of the legitimate rights of the Palestinian people as provided for in the Camp David Framework.

This applies in particular to:

1 — East Jerusalem, the annexation of which by Israel is null and void and must be rescinded. Relevant Security Council Resolutions, particularly Resolutions 242 and 267 must be applied to Jerusalem which is an integral part of the West Bank. Legal and historical Arab rights in the City must be respected and restored.

2 — Israeli settlements in the West Bank and Gaza Strip are illegal and, in the course of a final settlement should be withdrawn.

During the transitional period there should be a ban on the establishment of new settlements or enlarging the existing ones. After the inauguration of the SGA all settlers in the West Bank and Gaza will come under the authority of the SGA.

3 — General Powers and Responsibilities of the SGA
1 — Promulgation of laws and regulations
2 — Policy formulation and supervision
3 — Budgetary provisions
4 — Taxation
5 — Employment of staff

6 — Issuance of identity and travel documents
7 — Control of in and out movement of persons and goods
8 — Power to assume obligations and own property
9 — Power to hold title to public land
10 — Power to sue and to be sued
11 — Power to enter into contracts
12 — Power to participate in negotiations on the final status of the West Bank and Gaza Strip and to ascertain in the views of the Palestinians
13 — Assuming responsibility for:
(a) Public administration;
(b) Public services;
(c) Public order and internal security and police;
(d) Public domain and natural resources;
(e) Economic and financial fields;
(f) Social and cultural fields;
(g) Human rights and fundamental freedoms;
14 — Administration of Justice.

4 — Structure of the SGA

(a) The SGA will be composed of 80—100 members freely elected from the Palestinian people in the West Bank and Gaza Strip.

(b) The structure of the SGA contains two main organs:
— An assembly composed of all freely elected representatives from the West Bank and Gaza.
— A council composed of 10—15 members to be elected from among the membership of the assembly.

(c) The Assembly:
(1) It will take over, and replace, the authority of the military government in enacting laws and regulations, formulating and supervising policies, adopting the budget, levying taxes, etc...
(2) Its internal organization of a chairman with one or more vice-chairmen, its rules of procedure and the number and composition of its committees will be determined by the Assembly itself.

(d) The Council:
(1) It assumes the actual administration of the West Bank and Gaza and implements the policies formulated by the assembly in the different domains.
(2) It covers the whole range of activities and has full power in organizing, operating, employing staff and supervising the following executive branches; Education — Information and Culture — Transportation and Communications — Health — Social Welfare — Labour — Tourism — Internal Security — Housing — Religious Affairs — Agriculture — Economy and Finance — Commerce — Industry — Administration of Justice.

(3)   The Council will constitute its divisions as it deems necessary for the proper conduct of its functions and will determine the number of divisions, the internal organization of divisions and the machinery for coordination as befits the best and the most effective conduct of its activities. It may get in this respect, and if requested, expert help from the parties.

(e)   The Judicial authority will be manifested in a system of courts of law, courts of appeal and supreme court enjoying full guarantees for independence and efficiency in their administration of justice.

(f)   The SGA will have a representative, alongside with the representatives of Israel, Egypt (and Jordan), on the continuing committee in accordance with Article 3 of the Camp David Framework. Matters of common concern to Israel and the SGA which need mutual arrangements could be dealt with through the committee.

5 — Seat of the SGA
The seat of the SGA will be East Jerusalem.

6 — Additional Arrangements
(a)   As soon as the SGA is established and inaugurated in the West Bank and Gaza Strip, a withdrawal of Israeli armed forces will take place and there will be a redeployment of the remaining Israeli forces into specified security locations. Permission will be required for any movement of military troops into or through the territory.

(b)   The Camp David Framework requires the parties to negotiate an agreement which includes, inter alia, arrangements for assuring internal security and public order. Responsibility for security and public order will be decided jointly by the parties including the Palestinians, the Israelis, the Egyptians (and the Jordanians).

(c)   A strong police force will be established in the West Bank and Gaza Strip. It will be constituted by the SGA and composed of the people of the West Bank and Gaza Strip.

6. Israel, Autonomy Proposal, January 1982

In the Camp David Agreement signed on 17 September 1978 between Egypt and Israel, with the United States signing as a witness, agreement was reached on a plan for the solution of the problem of the Palestinian Arabs, that includes a proposal for full autonomy for the Palestinian Arabs living in Judea, Samaria and Gaza. The manner of establishing this autonomy, as well as its powers, were to be determined in negotiations between the signatories (Jordan was invited to participate, but did not respond). It was Israel that first raised the idea of autonomy that was later to serve as the basis of the Camp David agreement. For the first time in the history of the Palestinian Arab inhabitants of Judea-Samaria and the Gaza district, they were offered an opportunity of this kind to conduct their own affairs by themselves. Since 1979, talks have been held for the implementation of this agreement; there were intermissions in the negotiations, but talks were resumed intensively in the summer of 1981, leading to a thorough-going clarification of the positions of the parties. At these talks Israel put forward its proposals with regard to the self-governing authority (administrative council), its powers, responsibilities and structure as well as other related issues. The main points of Israel's proposals, as submitted in the course of the negotiations were as follows:

Scope, Jurisdiction and Structure of the Self-Governing Authority (Administrative Council):

1. The Camp David accords set forth the establishment of a self-governing authority (administrative council) that will comprise one body representing the Arab inhabitants of Judea, Samaria and the Gaza district, who will choose this body in free elections, and it will assume those functional powers that will be transferred to it. Thus the Palestinian Arabs will for the first time have an elected and representative body, in accordance with their own wishes and free choice, that will be able to carry out the functions assigned to it as an administrative council.

2. The members of the administrative council will be able, as a group, to discuss all subjects within the council's competence, apportioning among themselves the spheres of responsibility for the various functions. Within the domain of its assigned powers and responsibilities, the council will be responsible for planning and carrying out its activities.

Powers of the Self-Governing Authority (Administrative Council):

1.a. Under the terms of the Camp David agreement, the parties have to reach an agreement on the powers and responsibilities of the authority. Israel's detailed proposals include a list of powers that will be given to the authority and that, by any reasonable and objective criterion, represent a wide and comprehensive range of fields of operation. Without any doubt, the transferring of these powers constitutes the bestowal of full autonomy — in the full meaning of that term.

b. The powers to be granted the authority, under these proposals, are in the following domains:

1. *Administration of Justice:* Supervision of the administrative system of the courts in the areas; dealing with matters connected with the prosecution system and with the registration of companies, partnerships, patents, trademarks, etc.

2.   *Agriculture:* All branches of agriculture and fisheries, nature reserves and parks.

3.   *Finance:* Budget of the administrative council and allocations among its various divisions; taxation.

4.   *Civil Service:* Appointment and working conditions of the Council's employees. (Today, the civil service of the inhabitants of Judea-Samaria and Gaza, within the framework of the Military Government's Civilian Administration, numbers about 12,000 persons.)

5.   *Education and Culture:* Operation of the network of schools in the areas, from kindergarten to higher education; supervision of cultural, artistic and sporting activities.

6.   *Health:* Supervision of hospitals and clinics; operation of sanitary and other services related to public health.

7.   *Housing and Public Works:* Construction, housing for the inhabitants and public works projects.

8.   *Transportation and Communications:* Maintenance and coordination of transport, road traffic, meteorology; local postal and communications services.

9.   *Labour and Social Welfare:* Welfare, labour and employment services, including the operation of labour exchanges.

10.   *Municipal Affairs:* Matters concerning municipalities and their effective operation.

11.   *Local Police:* Operation of a strong local police force, as provided for in the Camp David agreement, and maintenance of prisons for criminal offenders sentenced by the courts in the areas.

12.   *Religious Affairs:* Provision and maintenance of religious facilities for all religious communities among the Arab inhabitants of Judea-Samaria and the Gaza district.

13.   *Industry, Commerce and Tourism:* Development of industry, commerce, workshops and tourist services.

2.   The council will have full powers in its spheres of competence to determine its budget, to enter into contractual obligations, to sue and be sued and to engage manpower. It will, moreover, have wide powers to promulgate regulations, as required by a body of this kind. In the nature of things, in view of the free movement that will prevail between Judea-Samaria and the Gaza district and Israel and for the general welfare of the inhabitants, arrangements will be agreed upon in the negotiations, in a number of domains, for cooperation and coordination with Israel. The administrative council will, hence, have full scope to exercise its wide-ranging powers under the terms of the autonomy agreement. These powers embrace all walks of life, and will enable the inhabitants of the areas concerned to enjoy full autonomy.

3.   Size: The size of the administrative council must reflect its functions and its essential purpose: it is an administrative council, whose representative character finds expression in its establishment through free elections, by the Arab inhabitants of Judea, Samaria and Gaza. Clearly, the criterion for determining the number of its members must be the functions that the council is empowered to perform. We propose, therefore, that the number of members will conform with the functions listed above.

4.   Free Elections: Elections to the administrative council, under Israel's proposals, will be absolutely free, as stipulated in the Camp David agreement. Under the terms of the agreement, the parties will agree upon the modalities of the elections; as a matter of fact, in past negotiations a long list of principles and guidelines has already been prepared in this matter. In these free elections, all the rights pertaining to a peaceful assembly, freedom of expression and secret balloting will be preserved and assured, and all necessary steps will be taken to prevent any interference with the election process. The holding of an absolutely free and unhampered election process will thus be assured in full, under the law, and in keeping with the tradition of free elections practiced in democratic societies. These elections will, in many respects, constitute a new departure in the region around us which in most of its parts is not too close to the ways of democracy, and in which free elections are a rare phenomenon. It is of some interest, therefore, to note that Judea-Samaria and Gaza, under Israel's Military Government since 1967, have exemplified the practical possibility of totally free elections in these areas. In 1972, and again in 1976, Israel organized free elections in these areas based on the tradition and model of its own democratic and liberal tradition and custom; voters and elected officials alike concede that these were free elections in the fullest sense. The elections in the administrative council will be organized and supervised by a central elections committee whose composition has been agreed upon by the parties.

5.   Time of elections and establishment of the self-governing authority (administrative council): The elections will be held as expeditiously as possible after agreement will have been reached on the autonomy. This was set forth in the joint letter of the late President Sadat and of Prime Minster Begin to President Carter, dated 26 March 1979, setting for the manner in which the self-governing authority (administrative council) is to be established, under the terms of the Camp David agreement.

6.   Within one month following the elections, the self-governing authority (administrative council) is to be established and inaugurated, and at that time the transitional period of five years will begin — again, in conformity with the Camp David agreement and the joint letter.

7.   Hence, every effort will be made to hold elections without delay, once an agreement is reached, to be followed by the establishment of the self-governing authority (administrative council).

8. Following the elections and the establishment of the self-governing authority (administrative council) the military government and its civilian administration will be withdrawn, a withdrawal of Israeli armed forces will take place, and there will be a redeployment of the remaining Israeli forces into specified security locations, in full conformity with the Camp David agreement. Israel will present to the other parties in the negotiations the map of the specified security locations of the redeployment. It goes without saying that all this will be done for the purpose of safeguarding the security of Israel as well as of the Arab inhabitants of Judea-Samaria and Gaza and of the Israeli citizens residing in these areas.

9. All of the above indicates Israel's readiness to observe the Camp David agreement fully and in every detail, in letter and spirit, while safeguarding the interests of all concerned.

Israeli Documents

1. Principles Guiding Israel's Policy in the Aftermath of the June 1967 War as Outlined by Prime Minister Eshkol. Jerusalem, 9 August, 1967 [Excerpts]

(a)   The Government of Israel will endeavour to achieve peace with the neighbouring Arab countries. We shall never permit a return to a situation of constant threat to Israel's security, of blockade and of aggression.

(b)   The Government of Israel is prepared for direct negotiations with all the Arab States together, or with any Arab State separately.

(c)   The State of Israel strives for economic cooperation and regional planning with all States in the Middle East.

(d)   Israel will cooperate fully in the solution of the refugees problem . . . within the framework of an international and regional plan.

(e)   The Government endeavours to maintain fair and equitable relations with the population in the new areas, while maintaining order and security.

After our military victory, we confront a fateful dilemma; immigration or stagnation . . . By the end of the century, we must have five million Jews in Israel. We must work hard so that Israel may be able to maintain decent human, cultural, technical and economic standards. This is the test of Israel's existence as a Jewish State in the Middle East.

2. The Nine-Point Peace Plan, Israel's Foreign Minister Abba Eban, 8 October, 1968

Statement to the U.N. General Assembly

Mr. President, my Government has decided to give the members of the United Nations a detailed account of its views on the establishment of a just and lasting peace in the Middle East. Amidst the tumult of a rancorous public debate, the deeper motives of our policy have not always been clearly perceived. A structure of peace cannot, of course, be built by speeches at this rostrum. It may, however, be useful for the parties to clarify their intentions and to draw a picture of their policies beyond the routine vocabulary in which this discussion has been held down for sixteen months.

In the interest of peace, I shall refrain from detailed comment on the polemical observations made here by Foreign Ministers of Arab States. The total and unblemished self-satisfaction with which these Ministers have spoken, the complete absence in their worlds of any self-criticism or innovation, the lack of detailed and organized comment on concrete issues — all these illustrate the inhibition which still prevents Arab Governments from thinking lucid and constructive thoughts about their relations with Israel. Indeed, the Foreign Minister of Sudan actually recommended that Israel be dismantled and its people dispersed. Here we have the oldest and most tenacious link in all human history between a people and a land. And an Arab leader speaks of Israel as though it were a temporary international exhibition to be folded up and taken away! Such intellectual frivolity and self-delusion are not heard on any other international issue.

Israel cannot easily forget the immense loss and burden which it has borne through the implacable hostility directed against it for twenty years, culminating in the unforgettable summer of 1967. For there has not been a Six-Day War. There has been a twenty-year war conducted by the Arab States in varying degrees of intensity with the candid hope of Israel's ruin and destruction. The issue is whether this war is now going to be ended by a final peace or merely interrupted in order to be resumed in conditions more propitious for Arab success.

Our danger in 1967 was the climax and not the whole story of our predicament. No other people has had to live all its days with a mark of interrogation hanging over its collective and individual survival. And behind Israel's quest for secure life, there is a particular and hideous legacy of wholesale death in the European slaughter-house. In May 1967, we found ourselves beset by deadly peril which we faced in utter solitude of action and responsibility. Maritime blockade, murderous incursions, military encirclement, declarations of overt war, a frenzied torrent of violent threats and a formal announcement by President Nasser that the battle was joined for Israel's extinction, all came together in cumulative assault on Israel's life and security.

All the acts which fall under the widely supported definitions of aggression were simultaneously concerted against us. The universal conscience was deeply stirred. Millions across the world trembled for Israel's fate. The memory of those dark days broods over Israel's life. Our nation still lives intimately with the dangers which then confronted us. We still recall how the imminent extinction of Israel's statehood and the massacre of its population were seriously discussed across the world: in wild intoxication of spirit in Arab capitals, and with deep, but impotent, sorrow in other lands. To prevent the renewal of those dangers is the first law of our policy. The gravest danger is lest through a lassitude of spirit, or imprecision of diplomatic craftsmanship, or collapse of patience, we again revert to fragile, false and ambiguous solutions which carry within them the seed of future wars. Those of us who bear responsibility for our nation's survival and our children's lives cannot have anything to do with vague solutions which fall short of authentic and lasting peace. June 1967 must be the last of the Middle Eastern wars.

This resolve has moved our policy at every stage of the political discussion from the outbreak of hostilities to this very day.

In June and July 1967, the General Assembly rejected all proposals which sought to condemn Israel's resistance or to reconstruct the conditions which had led to the outbreak of war. A new milestone was reached when the Security Council adopted its unanimous Resolution on 22 November 1967. That Resolution was presented to us for our acquiescence, not as a substitute for specific agreement, but as a list of principles on which the parties could base their agreement. It was drafted, as Ambassador George Ball said on 11 September, as 'a skeleton of principles on which peace could be erected'. It was not meant to be self-executing. As Lord Caradon said on 22 November, it was not 'a call for a temporary truce or a superficial accommodation'; it reflected, as he said, a refusal 'to be associated with any so-called settlement which was only a continuation of a false truce'. Its author stated that any 'action to be taken must be within the framework of a permanent peace, and withdrawal must be to secure boundaries'. The term 'secure and recognized boundaries' had first appeared in a United States draft, the author of which pointed out that this meant something different from the old armistice demarcation lines. Secure and recognized boundaries, he said, had never existed in the Middle East. They must, therefore, be fixed by the parties in the course of the peacemaking process.

Now these were the understandings on which Israel's cooperation with Ambassador Jarring's mission was sought and obtained. Whatever our views might be on these formulations by other Governments, it has been evident at every stage that the two central issues are the establishment of a permanent peace and an agreement for the first time on the delineation of secure and recognized boundaries. These are the conditions prerequisite for any movement. It is here that the peacemaking process must begin. If these problems are solved, all the other issues mentioned in the Resolution fall into place. To seek a change in the cease-fire dispositions, without the framework of a just and lasting peace and the determination of agreed boundaries, is an irrational course for which there is no international authority or precedent. This would be a short and certain route to renewed war in conditions hostile to Israel's security and existence.

Our contacts with the Special Representative of the Secretary-General began in December 1967. At the end of that month, on 27 December, I conveyed a document to the Egyptian Foreign Minister, through Ambassador Jarring, proposing an agenda for a discussion on the establishment of a just and lasting peace. In this letter, I expressed a willingness to hear the UAR's views, and suggested that representatives of our two Governments be brought together informally in order to explore each other's intentions and to derive assurance and confidence for future contacts. In our letter we made it clear that the establishment of the boundary was fully open for negotiation and agreement.

The UAR made no reply, offered no comment, presented no counter-proposals. Indeed, from that day to this, the UAR has not sent us a single document referring to or commenting on any Israeli letters.

On 7 January, I conveyed to the Jordan Government, through Ambassador Jarring, a letter in which I sought to open a constructive dialogue. This letter reads in part:

"History and geography create an objective affinity of interest between the two countries. More than any other relationship between Middle Eastern States, this one involves human interests in a close degree of interdependence. A close and confident association would seem to be as necessary for Jordanian as for Israeli welfare.

"The major problems at issue between Jordan and Israel are closely interconnected. Territorial security, economic and humanitarian problems impinge directly on each other. Moreover, the political and juridical basis of this relationship is of overriding importance. If there is a prior agreement to establish relations of permanent peace, the specific problems at issue between the two countries can be effectively and honourably solved."

I went on to list the five major subjects on which we shall seek agreement. These included the establishment of the boundary and security arrangements. No reply was made to this approach.

On 12 February, I requested Ambassador Jarring to convey the following to the Governments of Egypt and Jordan:

"Israel has cooperated and will cooperate with you in your mission. We accept the Security Council's call, in its Resolution of 22 November 1967, for the promotion of agreement on the establishment of peace with secure and recognized boundaries.

"Once agreement is reached on a peace settlement, it will be faithfully implemented by Israel.

"As I indicated to you on 1 February 1968, Israel is prepared to negotiate on all matters included in the Security Council Resolution which either side wishes to raise. Our views on the problems of peace and our interpretation of the Resolution were stated by me in the Security Council on 2 November 1967.

"The next step should be to bring the parties together. I refer to the agreement which I expressed to you on 1 February for the Special Representative of the Secretary-General to convene the two Governments."

This message elicited no response. On February 19, I communicated another message to Ambassador Jarring for transmission to Cairo. This message assured the Secretary-General's Representative of Israel's full cooperation in his efforts to promote agreement and to achieve an accepted settlement for the establishment of a just and lasting peace in accordance with his mandate under the Security Council Resolution of 22 November 1967.

It further pointed out that the UAR is aware of Israel's willingness to negotiate on all matters included in the Security Council Resolution. It drew attention to the fact that the Resolution is a framework for agreement, and that it cannot be fulfilled without a direct exchange of views and proposals leading to bilateral contractual commitments. It accepted the sponsor's view that the principles recommended for inclusion in the peace settlement are integrally linked and interdependent, and it proposed to move forward to a more substantive stage and to embark on a meaningful negotiation for achieving a just and lasting peace called for by the Security Council.

Early in March 1968, Ambassador Jarring sought our reaction on a proposal to convene Israel, the UAR and Jordan in conferences under his auspices to seek an agreed settlement in fulfilment of his mandate under the Security Council's Resolution. We were later informed that the UAR had rejected and that Jordan had not accepted this course. On 1 May, Ambassador Tekoah was empowered to indicate, in the Security Council, Israel's acceptance of the November Resolution for the promotion of agreement on the establishment of a just and lasting peace. The Israeli Representative was authorized to reaffirm that we were willing to seek agreement with each Arab State on all the matters included in the Resolution, and that we accepted the proposal of Dr. Jarring of bringing about meetings between Israel and its neighbours under his auspices in fulfilment of his mandate for the purpose of peaceful and accepted settlement.

On 29 May, after a discussion in our Cabinet, I made a statement in the

Knesset proposing a method of implementing the Security Council Resolution through negotiation, agreement and the signature and application of treaty engagements to be worked out between the parties. In this, as in previous documents, it was made clear that we regarded the establishment of the boundary as a matter for negotiation and agreement.

On 14 June, I was informed that this proposal had been conveyed to the UAR's Permanent Representative, who had noted it without any reaction. At the end of August, I submitted to the UAR Foreign Minister, through Ambassador Jarring, a series of ideas and viewpoints on the implications of the term "a just and final peace". This was developed in further communications early in September. To all these detailed proposals, the UAR replied declining any specific comment, and limiting itself to a general reference to the text of the Security Council's Resolution. The UAR would recite the Resolution in a declaration of acceptance without any specification of how it proposed to reach concrete agreement. During this time, Egyptian policy was authoritatively defined by President Nasser in a formal utterance on 23 June. In that statement, the UAR President expressed willingness to attempt, as in March 1957, "a political solution" on condition that certain principles of Egyptian policy be recognized. He said:

"The following principles of Egyptian policy are immutable:

1) No negotiation with Israel
2) No peace with Israel
3) No recognition of Israel
4) No transactions will be made at the expense of Palestinian territories or the Palestinian people."

How one can build peace out of such negative and immutable principles defeats the imagination.

Mr. President, I have taken the General assembly into the knowledge of our initiatives and proposals. I leave it to my fellow delegates to judge whether their complete rejection was justified or compatible with a sincere attempt to explore the conditions of a permanent peace and to reach agreement.

In discussing the reasons for the lack of substantive progress, we cannot fail to perceive that the discussion on peace has revolved too much around semantic expressions, too little around the solution of contentious issues. There is no instance in history in which a stubborn and complex conflict has been brought to an end by the mere recitation of texts without precise agreement on the issues of which the conflict is composed. Israel has accepted the Security Council's Resolution for the establishment of a just and lasting peace and declared its readiness to negotiate agreements on all the principles mentioned therein. We hold that the Resolution should be implemented through negotiation, agreement and the joint signature and application of appropriate treaty engagements.

When the parties accept a basis for settlement — their least duty is to clarify what they mean by their acceptance.

To make identical and laconic statements with diametrically opposed motives and interpretations would come dangerously close to international deceit. All parties must say what they mean, and mean what they say. And the heart of the problem is not what we say, but what we do. The construction of a peaceful edifice requires sustained action in order to bring the vital interests of the parties into an acceptable harmony. There is no such thing as peace by incantation. Peace cannot be advanced by recitations accompanied by refusal to negotiate viable agreements. The Security Council's Resolution has not been used as an instrument for peace. It has been invoked as an obstacle and alibi to prevent the attainment of peace.

In these conditions, my Government has given intensive consideration to the steps that we should now take. Our conclusion is this. Past disappointment should not lead to present despair. The stakes are too high. While the cease-fire agreements offer important security against large-scale hostilities, they do not represent a final state of peace. They must, of course, be maintained and respected until there is peace. They must be safeguarded against erosion by military assault and murderous incursion. But at the same time, the exploration of a lasting peace should be constant. Unremitting, resilient and, above all, sincere, my Government deems the circumstances and atmosphere afforded by our presence here as congenial for a new attempt. We suggest that a new effort be made in the coming weeks to cooperate with Ambassador Jarring in his task of promoting agreements on the establishment of peace.

It is important to break out of the declaratory phase in which the differences of formulation are secondary and in any case legitimate, in order to give tangible effect to the principles whereby peace can be achieved in conformity with the central purposes of the United Nations Charter or the Security Council Resolution and with the norms of international law. Instead of a war of words, we need acts of peace.

I come to enumerate the nine principles by which peace can be achieved:

1) The establishment of peace

The situation to follow the cease-fire must be a just and lasting peace, duly negotiated and contractually expressed.

Peace is not a mere absence of fighting. It is a positive and clearly defined relationship with far-reaching political, practical and juridical consequences. We propose that the peace settlement be embodied in treaty form. It would lay down the precise conditions of our co-existence, including a map of the secure and agreed boundary. The essence of peace is that it commits both parties to the proposition that their twenty-year-old conflict is at a permanent end. Peace is much more than what is called "non-belligerency". The elimination of belligerency is one of several conditions which compose the establishment of a just and lasting peace. If there had previously been peace between the States of our area and temporary hostilities had erupted, it might have been sufficient to terminate belligerency and to return to the previously existing peace. But the Arab-Israel area has had no peace. There is nothing normal or legitimate or established to which to return. The peace structure must be built from its foundations. The parties must define affirmatively what their relations shall be, not only what they will have ceased to be. The Security Council, too, called for the establishment of peace and not for any intermediate or ambiguous or fragmentary arrangement such as that which had exploded in 1967.

2) Secure and Recognized Boundaries

Within the framework of peace, the cease-fire lines will be replaced by permanent, secure and recognized boundaries between Israel and each of the neighbouring Arab States, and the disposition of forces will be carried out in full accordance with the boundaries under the final peace. We are willing to seek agreement with each Arab State on secure and recognized boundaries within the framework of a permanent peace.

It is possible to work out a boundary settlement compatible with the security of Israel and with the honour of Arab States. After twenty years, it is time that Middle Eastern States ceased to live in temporary "demarcation lines" without the precision and permanence which can come only from the definite agreement of the States concerned. The majority of the United Nations have recognized that the only durable and reasonable solutions are agreed solutions serving the common interests of our peoples. The new peace structure in the Middle East, including the secure and recognized boundaries, must be built by Arab and Israeli hands.

3) Security Agreements

In addition to the establishment of agreed territorial boundaries, we should discuss other agreed security arrangements designed to avoid the kind of vulnerable situation which caused a breakdown of the peace in the summer of 1967. The instrument establishing peace should contain a pledge of mutual non-aggression.

4) The Open Frontier

When agreement is reached on the establishment of peace with permanent boundaries, the freedom of movement now existing in the area, especially in the Israel-Jordan sector, should be maintained and developed. It would be incongruous if our peoples were to intermingle in peaceful contact and commerce only when there is a state of war and cease-fire — and to be separated into ghettos when there is peace. We should emulate the open frontier now developing within communities of States, as in parts of Western Europe.

Within this concept, we include free port facilities for Jordan on Israel's Mediterranean coast and mutual access to places of religious and historic associations.

5) Navigation

Interference with navigation in the international waterways in the area has been the symbol of the state of war and, more than once, an immediate cause of hostilities. The arrangements for guaranteeing freedom of navigation should be unreserved, precise, concrete and founded on absolute equality of rights and obligations between Israel and other littoral States.

6) Refugees

The problem of displaced populations was caused by war and can be solved by peace. On this problem I propose:

One: A conference of Middle Eastern States should be convened, together with the Governments contributing to refugee relief and the specialized agencies of the United Nations, in order to chart a five-year plan for the solution of the refugee problem in the framework of a lasting peace and the integration of refugees into productive life. This conference can be called in advance of peace negotiations.

Two: Under the peace settlement, joint refugee integration and rehabilitation commissions should be established by the signatories in order to approve agreed projects for refugee integration in the Middle East, with regional and international aid.

Three: As an interim measure, my Government has decided, in view of the forthcoming winter, to intensify and accelerate action to widen the uniting of families scheme, and to process "hardship cases" among refugees who had crossed to the East Bank during the June 1967 fighting. Moreover, permits for return which had been granted and not used can be transferred to other refugees who meet the same requirements and criteria as the original recipients.

7) Jerusalem

Israel does not seek to exercise unilateral jurisdiction in the Holy Places of Christianity and Islam. We are willing in each case to work out a status to give effect to their universal character. We would like to discuss appropriate agreements with those traditionally concerned. Our policy is that the Christian and Moslem Holy Places should come under the responsibility of those who hold them in reverence.

8) Acknowledgement and Recognition of Sovereignty, Integrity and Right to National Life

This principle, inherent in the Charter and expressed in the Security Council Resolution of November 1967, is of basic importance. It should be fulfilled through specific contractual engagements to be made by the Governments of Israel and of the Arab States to each other — by name. It follows logically that Arab Governments will withdraw all the reservations which they have expressed on adhering to international conventions, about the non-applicability of their signatures to their relations with Israel.

9) Regional Cooperation

The peace discussion should examine a common approach to some of the resources and means of communication in the region in an effort to lay foundations of a Middle Eastern community of sovereign States.

Mr. President,

The process of exploring peace terms should follow normal precedents. There is no case in history in which conflicts have been liquidated or a transition effected from a state of war to a state of peace on the basis of a stubborn refusal by one State to meet another for negotiation. There would be nothing new in the experience and relationship of Israel and the Arab States for them to meet officially to effect a transition in their relationships. What is new and unprecedented is President Nasser's principle of "no negotiation".

In the meantime, we continue to be ready to exchange ideas and clarifications on certain matters of substance through Ambassador Jarring with any Arab Government willing to establish a just and lasting peace with Israel.

Mr. President,

I have expounded our views on peace in more detail than is usual in General Assembly debates. On each of these nine points we have elaborated detailed views and ideas which we would discuss with neighbouring States in a genuine exchange of views, in which we should, of course, consider comments and proposals from the other side. No Arab spokesman has yet addressed himself to us in similar detail on the specific and concrete issues involved in peacemaking. Behind our proposals lie much thought and planning which can bear fruit when our minds and hearts interact with those of neighbouring States.

We ask friendly Governments outside the region to appraise the spirit as well as the content of the ideas which I have here outlined. We urge the Arab Governments to ponder them in a deliberate mood, and to explore their detailed implications with us in the normal and appropriate frameworks.

The solutions which I have outlined cover all the matters mentioned in the Security Council's Resolution and would constitute the effective fulfilment of its purposes.

We base ourselves on the integral and interdependent character of the points at issue. Nothing is less fruitful than an attempt to give separate identity or precedence to any single principle of international policy, thus destroying its delicate balance.

Moreover, the obligations of Israel and the Arab States to each other are not exhausted by any single text. They are also governed by the Charter, by the traditional precepts of international law, by constructive realism and by the weight of human needs and potentialities.

Lest Arab Governments be tempted out of sheer routine to rush into impulsive rejection, let me suggest that tragedy is not what men suffer but what they miss. Time and again Arab Governments have rejected proposals today — and longed for them tomorrow. The fatal pattern is drawn across the whole period since 1947 — and before. There is nothing unrealistic about a negotiated peace inspired by a sense of innovation and constructed by prudent and flexible statecraft. Indeed, all other courses are unrealistic. The idea of a solution imposed on the parties by a concert of Powers is perhaps the most unrealistic of all. The positions of the Powers have not moved any closer in the last fifteen months than have the positions of the parties themselves. Moreover, the Middle East is not an international protectorate. It is an area of sovereign States which alone have the duty and responsibility of determining the conditions of their co-existence. When the parties have reached agreement, it would be natural for their agreement to receive international support. To the Arab States, we say: "For you and us alone, the Middle East is not a distant concern, or a strategic interest, or a problem of conflict, but the cherished home in which our cultures were born, in which our nationhood was fashioned and in which we and you and all our posterity must henceforth live together in mutuality of interest and respect."

It may seem ambitious to talk of a peaceful Middle Eastern design at this moment of tension and rancour. But there is such a thing in physics as fusion at high temperatures. In political experience, too, the consciousness of peril often brings a thaw in frozen situations. In the long run, nations can prosper only by recognizing what their common interest demands. The hour is ripe for the creative adventure of peace.

3. Israel's Foreign Minister Abba Eban Knesset Statement on Occupied Territories. Jerusalem, 13 May, 1969 [Excerpts]

Three demands which Israel will not waive are a permanent presence at Sharm el-Sheikh, a unified Jerusalem despite concessions to Jordan over the Holy Places, and a Golan Heights for ever out of Syrian hands.

4. Statement by the Israeli Government Embodying a Reaction to the U.S. Secretary of State Rogers' Address on United States Foreign Policy in the Middle East Tel Aviv, 11 December, 1969

The Israel Government discussed in special session the political situation in the region and the latest speech of the U.S. Secretary of State on the Middle East.

The Government states that the tension in the Middle East referred to by Mr. Rogers derives from the aggressive policy of the Arab governments: The absolute refusal to make peace with Israel and the unqualified support of the Soviet Union for the Arab aggressive stand.

Israel is of the opinion that the only way to terminate the tension and the state of war in the region is by perpetual striving for a durable peace among the nations of the region, based on a peace treaty reached through direct negotiations which will take place without any prior conditions by any party. The agreed, secure and recognized boundaries will be fixed in the peace treaty. This is the permanent and stated peace policy of Israel and is in accordance with accepted international rules and procedures.

The Six Day War, or the situation created in its wake, cannot be spoken of in terms of expansion or conquest. Israel cried out against aggression which threatened its very existence, and used its natural right of national self-defence.

In his speech, Mr. Rogers said that states outside the region cannot fix peace terms; only states in the region are authorized to establish peace by agreement among themselves. The Government states regretfully that this principle does not tally with the detailed reference in the speech to peace terms, including territorial and other basic questions, among them Jerusalem. Jerusalem was divided following the conquest of part of the city by the Jordanian Army in 1948. Only now, after the unification of the city under Israel administration, does there exist freedom of access for members of all faiths to their holy places in the city.

The position of Israel is: The negotiations for peace must be free from prior conditions and external influences and pressures. The prospects for peace will be seriously marred if states outside the region continue to raise territorial proposals and suggestions on other subjects that cannot further peace and security.

When the Four Power talks began, the Government of Israel expressed its view on the harmful consequences involved in this move in its statement of March 27, 1969. The fears expressed then were confirmed.

Peace was not promoted, Arab governments were encouraged by the illusion that an arrangement could be reached by the exertion of external influences and pressures with no negotiations between the parties. In this period Egyptian policy reached the most extreme expressions, especially in President Nasser's speech in which he spoke of rivers flowing with blood and skies lit by fire. In this period, the region has not become tranquil. In an incessant violation of the cease-fire arrangement, fixed by the Security Council and accepted by all sides unconditionally and with no time limit, the Egyptians have intensified their attempts to disturb the cease-fire lines. Conveniently, Arab aggression in other sectors continued and terrorist acts, explicitly encouraged by Arab governments, were intensified. Even the Jarring mission to promote an agreement between the parties was paralyzed.

The focus of the problem as stated by Mr. Rogers lies in the basic intentions and positions of the governments of the region to the principle of peaceful coexistence. The lack of intention of the Arab governments to move towards peace with Israel is expressed daily in proclamations and deeds. The positions and intentions of the parties towards peace cannot be tested unless they agree to conduct negotiations as among states desiring peace. Only when there is a basic change in the Arab position, which denies the principle of negotiations for the signing of peace, will it be possible to replace the state of war by durable peace. This remains the central aim of the policy of Israel.

In his forthcoming talks with the Secretary of State, the Foreign Minister will explain in detail the position of the Government of Israel concerning the situation in the region.

5. Resolution Adopted by the Israel Knesset Rejecting King Hussein's United Arab Kingdom Plan. Jerusalem, 16 March, 1972

The Knesset has duly noted the Prime Minister's statement of March 16, 1972, regarding the speech made by the King of Jordan on March 11, 1972.

The Knesset has determined that the historic right of the Jewish people to the Land of Israel is beyond challenge.

The Knesset authorizes the Government of Israel to continue its policy in accordance with the basic principles, as approved by the Knesset on December 15, 1969, according to which:

The government will steadfastly strive to achieve a durable peace with Israel's neighbours founded in peace treaties achieved by direct negotiations between the parties. Agreed, secure and recognized borders will be laid down in the peace treaties.

The peace treaties will assure cooperation and mutual aid, the solution of any problem that might be a stumbling-block in the path to peace, and the avoidance of any aggression, direct or indirect.

Israel will continue to be willing to negotiate — without prior conditions from either side — with any of the neighbouring states for the conclusion of a peace treaty. Without a peace treaty, Israel will continue to maintain in full the situation as established by the cease-fire and will consolidate its position in accordance with the vital requirements of its security and development.

The Knesset supports the Government in its endeavours to further peace by negotiating with the Arab states according to the resolutions of the Knesset.

6. The "Galili Plan" — Statement by Government Ministers of the Israeli Labour Party on Proposed Policy in the Occupied Territories. August, 1973

Preamble: These points of agreement are not decisions endorsed by the Party and the Labour Alignment, but recommendations by the Labour Party ministers. The Prime Minister has submitted these points of agreement to the authorized organizations (the Party, the Labour Alignment and the Government) for their approval. These points will be set out as guide-lines in the electoral programme of the Labour Alignment and included in the government's general plan of action. Once the basic lines of the plans of action have been approved the projects will be worked out in practical detail, and the budgets for their implementation will be included in the government's annual budgets. The plan of action in the occupied areas for the next four years will not be conditional on any change in the political status of these areas or the civil status of the inhabitants and the refugees.

A. *Principles:* The next government will continue to operate in the occupied areas on the basis of the policy pursued by the present government — development, provision of employment and services, economic links, open bridges, encouragement of initiative and the renewal of municipal representation, orders from the military government, village and town settlement, improvement of the refugee camps, specific and controlled work in Israel for

Arab workers from the occupied areas.

B. *Rehabilitation of Refugees and Economic Development in the Gaza Strip:* A four-year plan of action will be drawn up, and the necessary funds allocated for its execution, with a view to ensuring the rehabilitation of the refugees, and economic development. The main points of this plan of action will be: Changing the housing situation (establishing places of residence for the refugees near the camps, improving the camps and making the municipalities of neighbouring towns responsible for them); vocational training; improving health and livelihood in trades and industry; encouraging the population to take the initiative in improving their standard of living.

C. *Development in Judea and Samaria:* A four-year plan of action will be drawn up and the necessary financing for its execution ensured, with the object of ensuring the development of the economic infrastructure and improving the essential services (health, electrical, etc.); developing the water services to meet the requirements of the population; developing vocational and higher education; developing electrical communications and transport services; improving streets and roads; developing trade and industry as sources of employment for the inhabitants; improving the refugees' housing situation; and help to the municipal authorities.

D. *Financing for Judea and Samaria:* Once it is endorsed by the government, the agreement reached between the Ministries of Finance and Defence will constitute the basis of decisions as to how the plans of action in the Gaza Strip and the West Bank should be financed.

E. *International Financing:* Efforts will be made to obtain from external sources the means to finance projects for the rehabilitation of the refugees and development in the occupied areas.

F. *Encouraging Israeli Business in the Territories:* Facilities and incentives will be provided to encourage Israelis to establish industrial projects in the occupied areas (in accordance with the proposal submitted by the Minister of Trade and Industry to the Governmental Committee for Economic Affairs on August 1).

G. *Encouraging Local Residents' Initiative in Judea and Samaria:* Aid will be given for self-initiative of the inhabitants in the fields of education, religion and services, and in the field of developing democratic forms in social and municipal life. As far as possible local persons will be appointed to high civilian posts in the [Military] Government.

H. *The Policy of Open Bridges:* The policy of open bridges will continue.

I. *Work for the Inhabitants of the Territories in Israel:* Work for the inhabitants of the occupied territories in Israel and in Jewish economic areas in the occupied territories will be subject to control as regards both numbers and the areas in which workers are allowed to work. Necessary measures will be taken to ensure working conditions and wages similar to those in Israel.

J. *Paramilitary and Civilian Settlements:* New settlements will be established and the network of settlements will be reinforced. Efforts will be made to increase their population by developing trade, industry and tourism. When the government's annual budget is drawn up from year to year it will be decided what means are necessary for the new settlements, in accordance with the recommendations of the Settlement Department, and after the approval of the Ministerial Committee on Settlement to establish new settlements in the next four years in the Rafah Approaches, the Jordan Valley and the Golan Heights. They will include a civilian-industrial settlement in the Golan Heights, a regional centre in the Jordan Valley, development of the north-east shore of the Sea of Galilee and the north-west shore of the Dead Sea and executing the planned water projects. Non-governmental organizations, both public and private will be included within the framework of the plans approved by the government for the development of sites for settlement.

K. *The Regional Centre in the Rafah Approaches:* The continued development of the Regional Centre in the Rafah Approaches will be ensured so that it may comprise 800 housing units by the year 1977—1978. Industrial development for settlers prepared to settle at their own expense will be encouraged.

L. *The Unification and Purchase of Land in the Territories:* 1. More intensive action to unify lands for the requirements of existing and planned settlement (purchase, state lands, absentees' lands, exchanges of lands, arrangements with the inhabitants) will be expanded. 2. The Israel Lands Authority will be recommended to expand purchases of land and real estate in the occupied areas for the purposes of settlement, development and land exchange. 3. The Lands Authority will lease to companies and individuals for the execution of approved projects. 4. The Lands Authority will also try to buy lands by all effective means, in particular through companies and individuals who buy lands, in coordination with the Lands Authority on its behalf. 5. Purchases of lands and real estate by companies and individuals will be approved only in cases where it is ascertained that the Directorate is unable to buy or not interested in buying the lands on its own account. 6. A special Cabinet Committee will be authorized to grant permits, on condition that the lands purchased are intended for constructive projects and not for speculation, and within the framework of the government's policy. 7. The Israel Lands Authority will also make a point of acquiring lands already bought by Jews.

M. *Jerusalem and Environs:* Provision of housing and industrial development in the capital and its environs will be continued with a view to consolidation beyond the original area. To achieve this goal, efforts will be made to buy additional land; the government lands in the area to the east and south of Jerusalem which the government has decided to enclose will be exploited.

N. *Nabi Samuel:* The government's decision taken on September 13, 1970, on the settlement of Nabi Samuel will be implemented.

O. *A Deep Sea Port in Southern Gaza:* In preparation for the rapid development of the Rafah Approaches studies will be carried out in the course of two or three years on the basic facts of the proposal to construct a deep sea port south of Gaza — the geographical situation, the economic viability and the political considerations. When the results have been obtained and a practical project has been submitted, the government will take a decision on the matter.

P. *An Industrial Center in Kfar Saba:* The necessary conditions will be ensured for the establishment of an industrial centre attached to Kfar Saba beyond the Green Line, as also for the development of Israeli industry in the areas of Tulkarm and Qalqilya.

7. Statement Issued by Israel's Cabinet Insisting that Jordan Represent the Palestinians in Negotiations. Jerusalem, 21 July, 1974

Israel will continue to strive for peace agreements with the Arab States within defensible borders to be achieved through negotiation without prior conditions.

The Government will work towards negotiations for a peace agreement with Jordan.

The peace will be founded on the existence of two independent states only — Israel with united Jerusalem as her capital and a Jordanian-Palestinian Arab state east of Israel within borders to be determined in negotiations between Israel and Jordan. This state will provide for expression of identity of the Jordanians and the Palestinians, in peace and good-neighbourliness with Israel.

The Cabinet endorses the Prime Minister's statement of June 3, 1974, in the Knesset, that the Government of Israel will not conduct negotiations with terrorist organizations whose aim is the destruction of the State of Israel.

The Minister for Foreign Affairs reported on the latest events in Cyprus.

8. Israel Knesset Statement, Prime Minister, Yitzhak Rabin, Following the Rabat Conference, 5 November, 1974 [Excerpts]

The meaning of [the Rabat] Resolutions is clear. The Rabat Conference decided to charge the organizations of murderers with the establishment of a Palestinian State, and the Arab countries gave the organizations a free hand to decide on their mode of operations. The Arab countries themselves will refrain, as stated in the Resolution, from intervening in the "internal affairs" of this action.

We are not fully aware of the significance of the fourth Resolution, which refers to "outlining a formula" for the coordination of relations between Jordan, Syria, Egypt and the PLO. It is by no means impossible that it is also intended to bring about closer military relations between them.

The significance of these Resolutions is extremely grave. The aim of the terrorist organizations is well known and clear. The Palestine National Covenant speaks bluntly and openly about the liquidation of the State of Israel by means of armed struggle, and the Arab States committed themselves at Rabat to support this struggle. Any attempt to implement them will be accompanied by at least attempts to carry out terrorist operations on a larger scale with the support of the Arab countries.

The decisions of the Rabat Conference are merely a continuation of the resolutions adopted at Khartoum. Only, further to the "no's" of Khartoum, the roof organization of the terrorists has attained the status conferred upon it by the presidents and kings at Rabat. Throughout this conference not a voice was raised expressing readiness for peace. The recurring theme of this conference was the aspiration to destroy a member-state of the United Nations. The content of this gathering has nothing whatsoever in common with social progress or the advancement of humanity among the Arab nations or in the relations with the peoples in the region and throughout the world.

There is no indication of any deviation from the goal and policy of the terrorist organizations, so let us not delude ourselves on this score. The terrorist organizations had no successes in the administered territories, but the successes they achieved at the U.N. General Assembly and at Rabat are encouraging them to believe that the targets they had so confidently set themselves are now within reach.

The policy laid down in Khartoum and Rabat shall not be executed. We have the power to prevent its implementation. The positions of the government of Israel in the face of these resolutions of the Rabat Conference is unequivocal:

A) The government of Israel categorically rejects the conclusions of the Rabat Conference, which are designed to disrupt any progress towards peace, to encourage the terrorist elements, and to foil any step which might lead to peaceful coexistence with Israel.

B)   In accordance with the Knesset's resolutions, the government of Israel will not negotiate with terrorist organizations whose avowed policy is to strive for Israel's destruction and whose method is terrorist violence.

C)   We warn the Arab leaders against making the mistake of thinking that threats or even the active employment of the weapon of violence or of military force will lead to a political solution. This is a dangerous illusion. The aims of the Palestinian National Charter will not be achieved, either by terrorist acts or by limited or total warfare.

The Rabat Conference Resolutions do not justify the adoption of other resolutions, and merely add force to our determination. To anyone who recommends negotiations with the terrorist organizations, I have to say that there is no basis for negotiations with the terrorist organizations. It does not enter our minds to negotiate with a body that denies our existence as a State and follows a course of violence and terrorism for the destruction of our State.

Negotiations with such a body would lend legitimacy and encouragement to its policy and its criminal acts. The U.N. General Assembly's decision to invite this body to its debates is a serious error from the moral and political stand-points, but it has no substance as incompatible with the very existence of the State of Israel. Israel will grant no recognition to those who conspire against her existence.

Rabat is not a surprising innovation, but our policy will not be determined by its decisions. We shall carefully watch the steps the Arab States will take in the wake of this conference and, in particular, we shall watch the moves of those States with whom we were about to embark on negotiations on stages of progress towards peace. Above all, we shall see whether Egypt is in fact ready for this, or whether she has committed herself to the ban on reaching a separate agreement with Israel. We shall be watching Jordan's moves, too, to see whether she surrenders to Arafat.

In the face of this development, we believe that the strength and stability of the State of Israel, and the Israel defense forces, powerful and prepared for any test, are the guarantee for our safety. As long as we are strong and follow a wise and courageous policy, the chances will increase that our neighbors will be ready to seek ways of coming to terms with us.

9. The Allon Plan — Article by Israel Foreign Minister Yigal Allon Reiterating his Plans for Peace. October, 1976 [Excerpts]

The polarized asymmetry between the size and intentions of the Arab States and those of Israel, and the extreme contrast in the anticipated fate of each side in the event of military defeat, obliges Israel to maintain constantly that measure of strength enabling it to defend itself in every regional conflict and against any regional combination of strength confronting it, without the help of any foreign army. To our deep regret, this is the first imperative facing us, the imperative to survive. And I would venture to say every other state in our place would behave exactly as we do.

There are, of course, many elements constituting the essential strength that Israel must maintain, ranging from its social, scientific and economic standards, as well as its idealistic motivation, to the quality and quantity of its armaments. A discussion of all of these elements is not within the compass of this article; my concern here is with one of them — but one essential to them all and without which Israel might well lack the strength to defend itself. I am referring to the territorial element; to what can be defined as defensible borders that Israel must establish in any settlement, as an essential part of any effective mutual security arrangements and without any desire for territorial expansion per se.

The most cursory glance at a map is sufficient to ascertain how little the armistic lines of 1949 — lines which were never in the first place recognized as final — could be considered defensible borders. And even the most superficial fingering of the pages of history should be enough to demonstrate how attractive these lines have been to the Arab States as an encouragement to try their strength again against us. The truth of the matter is that Resolution 242 of the United Nations Security Council has already recognized, in its original English text, the need to provide Israel with secure and recognized boundaries — in other words, that changes must be introduced in the old lines of the armistice agreements.

It is no coincidence that this resolution does not speak about Israel's withdrawal from *all* the territories that came under its control in the war that was forced upon Israel in June 1967, nor even from *the* territories. In the original text (which was the outcome of long and exhaustive negotiation), Resolution 242 speaks only of withdrawal from territories. That the meaning was clear was demonstrated by the statement of the United States at the time, made by its U.N. Ambassador Arthur Goldberg on November 15, 1967, in the Security Council discussions that preceded the passage of Resolution 242. He stated:

"Historically, there never have been secure or recognized boundaries in the area. Neither the Armistice Lines of 1949, nor the Cease-Fire Lines of 1967, have answered that description."

As is known, Israel expressed more than once its willingness to withdraw from the cease-fire lines of 1967, within the framework of a peace agreement. On the other hand, it is clear — even according to the Security Council decision — that Israel is not obliged to withdraw to the armistice lines of 1949 that preceded the 1967 war, but to revised lines. The question is what borders will provide Israel with that essential minimum of security? And without such security it is difficult to expect to pacify the area and provide a lasting solution to the conflict within it.

If the sole consideration were the purely strategic-military one, then possibly the most convenient security borders would have been those Israel maintained following the Six-Day War, or perhaps those which it maintains today. There is even a basis for the claim that the 1973 Yom Kippur War — begun as a surprise attack in concert by the armies of Egypt and Syria — proves that these lines were ideally the best. Had the Yom Kippur War commenced on the 1949 armistice lines, for example, there can be little doubt that the price Israel would have had to pay in repelling the aggressors would have been unimaginably higher than that paid so painfully in October 1973. But we are not merely talking about purely military-strategic matters, to the extent that they ever exist in isolation. Nor are we discussing the maximum security that borderlines can provide Israel. As stated, our preccupation is only with the essential minimum.

One does not have to be a military expert to easily identify the critical defects of the armistice lines that existed until June 4, 1967. A considerable part of these lines is without any topographical security value; and, of no less importance, the lines fail to provide Israel with the essential minimum of strategic depth. The gravest problem is on the eastern boundary, where the entire width of the coastal plain varies between 10 and 15 miles, where the main centers of Israel's population, including Tel Aviv and its suburbs, are situated, and where the situation of Jerusalem is especially perilous. Within these lines a single successful first strike by the Arab armies would be sufficient to dissect Israel at more than one point, to sever its essential living arteries, and to confront it with dangers that no other state would be prepared to face. The purpose of defensible borders is thus to correct this weakness, to provide Israel with the requisite minimal strategic depth, as well as lines which have topographical strategic significance.

Of course I do not wish to overlook the fact that there are some who would claim that in an era of modern technological development such factors are valueless. In a nutshell, their claim is that the appearance of ground-to-ground missiles, supersonic fighter-bombers, and other sophisticated instruments of modern warfare has canceled out the importance of strategic depth and topographical barriers. Personally, I do not know of a single state which is willing and ready to give up a convenient border line for this reason. At any rate, this argument is certainly invalid regarding Israel, and within the context of the Middle East conflict, where the opposite is true. Precisely because of dramatic developments in conventional weaponry the significance of territorial barriers and strategic depth has increased.

With all the heavy damage that warheads and bombs can inflict, they alone cannot be decisive in war, as long as the other side is resolved to fight back. Recent military history demonstrates this only too clearly. The German air "blitz" did not knock England out of World War II, nor did the heavy allied air bombardments bring Germany to its knees. This happened only when the last bunker in berlin fell. Even massive American air bombardments did not defeat North Vietnam which, in the final analysis, proved to be the victor in the war. At least as far as conventional wars are concerned, the following basic truth remains: without an attack by ground forces that physically overrun the country involved, no war can be decisive. This is all the more so in the Middle East where the Arab side is no less vulnerable to rocket and aerial bombardment than Israel, a factor that can greatly minimize the use of this kind of weaponry, and will leave to the ground forces the role of really deciding the issue.

III

Fortunately, the geostrategic conditions that have existed in the Middle East over the past nine years permit a solution based upon a fair political compromise. This could provide Israel with the minimal defensible borders that are indispensible without impairing, to any meaningful extent, the basic interests of the other side, including those of the Palestinian community. As with every other compromise, so, too, is this one likely to be painful in the short term to both sides. But this compromise will, in the long run, grant advantages that both sides do not currently possess nor, without it, ever would in the future.

According to the compromise formula I personally advocate, Israel — within the context of a peace settlement — would give up the large majority of the areas which fell into its hands in the 1967 war. Israel would do so not because of any lack of historical affinity between the Jewish people and many of these areas. With regard to Judea and Samaria, for example, historical Jewish affinity is as great as that for the coastal plain or Galilee. Nonetheless, in order to attain a no less historically exalted goal, namely that of peace, such a deliberate territorial compromise can be made.

For its part, the Arab side would have to concede its claim to those strategic security zones which, together with a number of effective arrangements to be discussed below, will provide Israel with that vital element so lacking in the pre-1967 war lines: a defense posture which would enable the small standing army units of Israel's defense force to hold back the invading Arab armies until most of the country's reserve citizens army could be mobilized. These security zones would thus guarantee enough time to organize and launch the counter offensive needed to defeat any such aggression.

The armistice lines of 1949 extend along the foothills of the Judean and Samarian mountains and along the Mediterranean coastal plain — that is, flat territory without any topographical barriers. This leaves central Israel with a narrow area that comprises the Achilles heel of the lines prior to June 4, 1967. It serves as a constant temptation to a hostile army in possession of hilly Judea and Samaria to attempt to inflict a fatal blow against Israel by severing it in two in one fell swoop. Moreover, this weakness would permit such an army not only to strike at Israel's densest population and industrial centers, but also in effect to paralyze almost all of Israel's airspace with surface-to-air missiles with which the Arab armies are so abundantly equipped.

According to the 1949 lines, Jerusalem was pierced through its heart — the university and the principal hospital on Mount Scopus were cut off, while access from the coastal plain to Jerusalem was restricted to a narrow corridor, threatened on both sides by a pincer attack.

In the northeastern sector, the 1949 line left Syria on the dominating Golan Heights, controlling the Huleh Valley and the Galilee Basin at their foothills, and including the sources of the Jordan River and the Sea of Galilee from which Israel draws a vital part of its water supply. Moreover, after 1949 Syria not only repeatedly shelled the Israeli villages located at the Golan foothills but also attempted to divert the sources of the Jordan and thereby deprive Israel of a vital source of water. Even more important, the Golan Heights served in past wars as the most convenient base for the Syrian army to make swift and major attacks upon Galilee, ultimately aimed at the conquest of the entire northern part of our country.

According to the 1949 armistice agreements, signed by Israel in the naive belief that they would lead swiftly to peace, Egypt was given control of the Gaza Strip. This was a dangerous and needless anomaly. Bordering the unpopulated Sinai desert and without any affinity to Egypt proper, this zone came to serve as a base for large-scale terrorist raids launched at southern Israel. Should the strip be returned to Egyptian control it might easily resume its destructive function. Even worse, it might serve Egypt as a bridgehead for an offensive northward and eastward toward the very heart of Israel, following the historic invasion route from south to north. Another serious defect in the armistice agreements was that it left Israel's southern port entrance at Eilath on a tiny strip of shoreline only six miles long from its border with Egypt to that of Jordan. Moreover, Israel's maritime route to the Red Sea and Indian Ocean passes through the Straits of Tiran at Sharm-el-Sheikh, and the Egyptian blockade there against Israeli ships and cargoes constituted a *casus belli* in both 1956 and 1967.

A reasonable compromise solution can be found for all these weaknesses in the current geostrategic and demographic situation existing in the Middle East. Without going into details or drawing precise maps, an activity that must await direct negotiations between the parties themselves, in my opinion the solution in principle ought to be along the following general lines.

Both to preserve its Jewish character and to contribute toward a solution of the Palestinian issue, Israel should not annex an additional and significant Arab population. Therefore the strategic depth and topographical barriers in the central sector, so totally absent in the lines preceding the 1967 war, cannot be based on moving these lines eastward in a schematic manner, even though this would be logical from a purely strategic point of view. Rather, apart from some minor tactical border alterations along the western section of "the green line", this same goal can be achieved through absolute Israeli control over the strategic zone to the *east* of the dense Arab population, concentrated as it is on the crest of the hills and westward. I am referring to the arid zone that lies between the Jordan River to the east, and the eastern chain of the Samarian and Judean mountains to the west — from Mt. Gilboa in the north through the Judean desert, until it joins the Negev desert. The area of this desert zone is only about 700 square miles and it is almost devoid of population. Thus this type of solution would leave almost all of the Palestinian Arab population of the West Bank under Arab rule.

Cutting through this zone, which continues from north to south, it would be possible to delineate a corridor from west to east under Arab sovereignty. This would permit uninterrupted communication along the Jericho-Ramallah axis, between the Arab populated areas of the West and East banks of the river. In this manner the only realistic solution becomes possible — one that also helps resolve the problem of Palestinian identity that could then find its expression in a single Jordanian-Palestinian State. (After all, the population of both banks, East and West, are Palestinian Arabs. The fact is that the great majority of Palestinians carry Jordanian passports while almost all of Jordan's inhabitants are Palestinians.)

Jerusalem, Israel's capital, which was never the capital of any Arab or Muslim State, but was always the capital and center of the Jewish people, cannot return to the absurd situation of being partitioned. The Holy City and adjacent areas essential for its protection and communications must remain a single, undivided unit under Israel's sovereignty. Because of its universal status, however, in that it is holy to three great religions, as well as the mixed nature of its inhabitants, a solution for the religious interests connected with it can be found, a *religious* and not a political solution. For example, special status could be granted to the representatives of the various faiths in the place holy to them, just as it might be possible to base the municipal structure of the city upon subdistricts that take ethnic and religious criteria into account.

While the strategic zone in the central sector is crucial to Israel's security, so, too, is a zone on the Golan Heights. As past experience has demonstrated, a border not encompassing the Golan Heights would again invite the easy shelling of the villages below in the Huleh Valley, the Galilee Basin and eastern Galilee. More important than the danger of renewed Syrian shelling are sniping at Israeli villages and fishermen below, which is basically a *tactical* question, is that Israel needs an effective defense line on the Golan Heights for two cardinal *strategic* reasons: first, to preclude any new Syrian attempts to deny Israel its essential water resources and, second, to prevent a massive Syrian attack on the whole of Galilee, either independently or in coordination with other Arab armies on Israel's other frontiers.

In my view the city of Gaza and its environs, which is heavily populated by Palestinian Arabs, could comprise a part of the Jordanian-Palestinian unit which would arise to the east of Israel, and serve as that state's Mediterranean port. In this case, it would be necessary to place at the disposal of traffic between Gaza and the Jordanian-Palestinian State the use of a land route (as distinct from a land corridor) similar to that, for example, connecting the United States with Alaska. But Israel must continue to control fully the strategic desert zone from the southern part of the Gaza strip to the dunes on the eastern approaches of the town of El Arish, which itself would be returned to Egypt. This strategic zone, almost empty of population, would block the historic invasion route along the sea coast which many conquerors have taken over the generations to invade the land of Israel, and further north.

A number of border adjustments will also be essential to ensure security sensitive areas of the 1949 Armistice line between Israel and Egypt. These must be made in such a manner as to permit full Israeli control in a number of sectors of crucial importance to its defense and which lack any value for the security of Egypt. I am referring to such areas as those surrounding Abu Aweigila, Kusseima and Kuntilla, which comprise the principal strategic crossroads on the main routes from the desert to Beersheba, and to the Eilath shore line which is the gateway to Israel's maritime routes to the Indian Ocean and the Far East.

An especially sensitive point is that of the area of Sharm-el-Sheikh at the southern tip of the Sinai Peninsula. Although, from this vantage point, there is no danger of a massive surprise attack on Israel proper, a very concrete threat to Israeli freedom of navigation does exist. It should be repeated that Egypt has twice imposed blockades against Israeli ships and cargoes seeking passage through the Straits of Tiran. And, in both instances, Israel was compelled to break this blockade mounted from Sharm-el-Sheikh by capturing the place. In one way or another, unquestionable Israeli control over this corner of the

Sinai — and over a land route reaching it — is not only critical to Israeli defense, but also serves to neutralize a focal point that is liable to set the area on fire once again. Moreover, because of the threat of blockade to Israeli-bound traffic through the Bab-el-Mandeb Strait, which connects the Red Sea with the Indian Ocean, full Israeli control over Sharm-el-Sheikh might serve as a countervailing deterrent against such blockade attempts.

To sum up, there were numerous bitterly deficient points in the pre-1967 lines, and these proposals encompass minimal corrections to them required for an overall peace settlement. The necessity for these corrections is all the more apparent when it is realized that Israel not only faces the military strength of its contiguous neighbours, but may also have to face the combined strength of many other Arab countries. This has already happened to no small extent in the 1973 war, when contingents from Iraq, Libya, Algeria, Saudi Arabia, Morocco, Jordan and other Arab countries participated in the fighting, together with the armies of Egypt and Syria. Thus, in a very practical sense, solid defense lines are indispensible to Israel in order to withstand the attacks of the entire Arab world. In addition, these may well be supported by contingents of so-called volunteers who can be sent from certain countries from outside the area that are hostile to Israel.

Let me stress again that defensible borders are vital to Israel not out of any desire to annex territories per se, not out of a desire for territorial expansion, and not out of any historical and ideological motivation. Israel can compromise on territory but it cannot afford to do so on security. The entire rationale of defensible borders is strategic. This is also the only rationale for the selective settlement policy that Israel is pursuing, as an integral part of its unique defense system, in those strategic zones so vital to its security.

Of course, when the peace for which we strive is achieved, the borders will not divide the two peoples but be freely open to them. In short, good fences make good neighbors.

IV

As I have pointed out, border adjustments essential for Israel's security, and hence for the long-term stability of the entire area, must also be linked with mutually effective security arrangements designed to prevent surprise attacks by one side on the other, or at least to reduce to a minimum the danger of such attacks. In the geostrategic circumstances of the Middle East, to reduce the possibility of surprise offensives is, in fact, to reduce the danger of all offensives. I am referring to such arrangements as the delineation of both totally and partially demilitarized zones under joint Arab-Israeli control, with or without the participation of a credible international factor; or such arrangements as the delineation of parallel early-warning systems like those functioning in the Sinai according to the terms of the 1975 Interim Agreement between

Israel and Egypt.

I will not enter here into the technical details of such arrangements, their nature, placement and scope. Not that they are unimportant or nonessential; on the contrary, without them, Israel could not permit itself to make the far-reaching territorial compromises which, in my opinion, it should be prepared to make within the context of peace agreements with its neighbors. Let me give one example, albeit, the most important, in order to illustrate this point. According to the principles I have already outlined, if Israel were to forfeit the densely populated heartland of Judea and Samaria, it would not be able to forego — under any circumstances — the effective demilitarization of these areas. Apart from civilian police to guarantee internal order, these areas would have to be devoid of offensive forces and heavy arms. In the same way as any other country, Israel would be unable to abandon areas so close to its heartland if they were liable once again to become staging areas for full-scale, limited or guerilla attacks upon its most vital areas.

In short, Israel cannot permit itself to withdraw from a large part of the West Bank unless the area from which it withdraws is shorn of all aggressive potential. For this purpose, absolute Israeli control, as proposed above, of a strategic security zone along the Jordan Basin will not be adequate. Effective demilitarization of the areas from which the Israel Defense Forces withdraw will also be essential. Here as elsewhere, the two elements are interwoven: without a security zone, Israel cannot be satisfied with demilitarization alone; without effective demilitarization, Israel cannot be satisfied with just the security zone.

It should be clear from what I have said, that Israel does not hold most of the territories that fell into its hands in the war, which was imposed on it in 1967, as an end in itself. Despite the paucity of its territory compared with the vast areas of the Arab countries, and despite the historical, strategic and economic importance of these areas, Israel would be prepared to concede all that is not absolutely essential to its security within the context of an overall peace settlement. It is holding most of these territories now only as a means to achieve its foremost goal — peace with all its neighbors.

10. Statement Issued by the Government of Israel Responding to the US—USSR Joint Declaration on the Middle East. Jerusalem, 1 October, 1977

1. The Soviet Union's demand that Israel withdraw to the pre-June 1967 borders — a demand which contravenes the true meaning of Security Council Resolution 242 — is known to all.

2. Despite the fact that the Governments of the U.S. and Israel agreed on July 7, 1977 that the aim of the negotiations at Geneva should be "an overall peace settlement to be expressed in a peace treaty", the concept of a "peace treaty" is not mentioned at all in the Soviet-American statement.

3. There is no reference at all in this statement to Resolutions 242 and 338, despite the fact that the U.S. Government has repeatedly affirmed heretofore that these resolutions constitute the sole basis for the convening of the Geneva Conference.

4. There can be no doubt that this statement, issued at a time when discussions are proceeding on the reconvening of the Geneva Conference, cannot but still further harden the positions of the Arab States and make the Middle East peace process still more difficult.

5. As the Prime Minister has stated, Israel will continue to aspire to free negotiations with its neighbours with the purpose of signing a peace treaty with them.

11. Law Enacted by Israel's Knesset Proclaiming Jerusalem the Capital of Israel. Jerusalem, 29 July, 1980

1. Jerusalem, whole and united, is the capital of Israel.

2. Jerusalem is the seat of the President of the State, the Knesset, the Government and the Supreme Court.

3. The Holy Places shall be protected from desecration and any other offense and from anything likely to prejudice the freedom of access of the members of the different religions to the places sacred to them or their feelings with regard to those places.

4. (1) The government shall preserve the development, the prosperity of Jerusalem and the welfare of its inhabitants by means of allocating special funds, including a special annual grant for the Municipality of Jerusalem (capitals' grant) [subject to] the approval of the Knesset Committee on Financial Affairs.

(2)   Jerusalem shall be given special priority as regards the activities of the state authorities for its development in the economic and other fields.

(3)   The government shall set up a special body or bodies for the implementation of this provision.

12. Fundamental Policy Guidelines of the Government of Israel as Approved by the Knesset, 5 August, 1981

Articles Relevant to the Israeli-Palestinian Conflict:

1.   Recognition of the common fate and joint struggle for the existence of the Jewish people in the Land of Israel and in the Diaspora.

2.   The right of the Jewish people to the Land of Israel, an eternal right that cannot be called into question, and which is intertwined with the right to security and peace.

3.   The government will continue to place its aspirations for peace at the head of its concerns, and no effort will be spared in order to further peace. The peace treaty between Israel and Egypt is a historic turning point in Israel's status in the Middle East.

4.   The government will continue to use all means to prevent war.

5.   The government will diligently observe the Camp David Agreements.

6.   The government will work for the renewal of negotiations on the implementation of the agreement on full autonomy for the Arab residents of Judea, Samaria, and the Gaza district.

7.   The autonomy agreed upon at Camp David means neither sovereignty nor self-determination. The autonomy agreements set down at Camp David are guarantees that under no conditions will a Palestinian State emerge in the territory of Western *Eretz Yisrael.*

8.   At the end of the transition period set down in the Camp David agreements, Israel will present its claim, and act to realize its right of sovereignty over Judea, Samaria, and the Gaza district.

9.   Settlement in the Land of Israel is a right and an integral part of the nation's security. The government will act to strengthen, expand, and develop settlement. The government will continue to honor the principle that Jewish settlement will not cause the eviction of any person from his land, his village, or his city.

10.   Equality of rights for all residents will continue to exist in the Land of Israel, with no distinction [on the basis] of religion, race, nationality, sex, or ethnic community.

11.   Israel will not descend from the Golan Heights, nor will it remove any settlement established there. It is the government that will decide on the ap-

propriate timing for the application of Israeli law, jurisdiction, and administration to the Golan Heights.

27.   Education will be based on the eternal values of Israel's Torah, on the values of Judaism and Zionism, love of the people of Israel and love of the homeland.

28.   The government will guarantee freedom of conscience and religion to every citizen and resident, will provide for community religious requirements using state means, and will guarantee religious education to all children whose parents so desire.

34.   The government will cultivate an attitude of respect toward the heritage of Israel, implant its values, strengthen the ties between the people in the Land of Israel and the Diaspora, and [strengthen] mutual responsibility and intergenerational ties.

35.   Jerusalem is the eternal capital of Israel, indivisible, entirely under Israeli sovereignty. Free access to their holy places has been and will be guaranteed to followers of all religions.

13. Text of Israel's Communique on the Reagan Plan, Jerusalem, 2 Sept, 1982

Following is the text of the communique issued by the Israeli Cabinet on President Reagan's Middle East proposals.

The Cabinet met in special session today and adopted the following resolution:

The positions conveyed to the Prime Minister of Israel on behalf of the President of the United States consist of partial quotations from the Camp David Agreement or are nowhere mentioned in the agreement or contradict it entirely.

The following are the major positions of the Government of the United States:

1.   Jerusalem

"Participation by the Palestinian inhabitants of East Jerusalem in the election for the West Bank—Gaza Authority."

No mention whatsoever is made in the Camp David agreement of such a voting right. The single meaning of such a vote is the repartition of Jerusalem into two authorities, the one — of the State of Israel, and the other — of the administrative council of the autonomy. Jerusalem is nowhere mentioned in the Camp David agreement. With respect to the capital of Israel letters were forwarded and attached to that agreement. In his letter to the President of the

United States, Mr. Jimmy Carter, the Prime Minister of Israel, Mr. Menachem Begin, stated that "Jerusalem is one city, indivisible, the capital of the State of Israel." Thus shall it remain for all generations to come.

2. Security

"Progressive Palestinian responsibility for internal security based on capability and performance."

In the Camp David agreement it is stated:

"A withdrawal of Israeli armed forces will take place and there will be a redeployment of the remaining Israel forces into specified security locations.

"The agreement will also include arrangements for assuring internal and external security and public order."

It is, therefore, clear that in the Camp David agreement no distinction is made between internal security and external security. There can be no doubt that, were internal security not to be the responsibility of Israel, the terrorist organization called P.L.O. — even after its defeat by the I.D.F. in Lebanon — would act to perpetrate constant bloodshed, shedding the blood of Jews and Arabs alike. For the citizens of Israel this is a question of life and death.

3. A Real Settlement Freeze

In the Camp David agreement no mention whatsoever is made of such a freeze. At Camp David the Prime Minister agreed that new settlements could not be established (though population would be added to existing ones) during the period of the negotiations for the signing of the peace treaty between Egypt and Israel (three months being explicitly stated). This commitment was carried out in full. That three-month period terminated on Dec. 17, 1978. Since then many settlements have been established in Judea, Samaria and the Gaza district without evicting a single person from his land, village or town. Such settlement is a Jewish inalienable right and an integral part of our national security. Therefore there shall be no settlement freeze. We shall continue to establish them in accordance with our natural right. President Reagan announced at the time that the "settlements are not illegal". A double negative makes a positive, meaning that the settlements are legal. We shall act, therefore, in accordance with our natural right and the law, and we shall not deviate from the principle that these vital settlements will not lead to any eviction.

4. The Definition of Full Autonomy

"The definition of full autonomy as giving the Palestinian inhabitants real authority over themselves, the land and its resources, subject to fair safeguards on water."

Such a definition is nowhere mentioned in the Camp David agreement, which states:

"In order to provide full autonomy to the inhabitants (underlined, our emphasis), etc."

In the lengthy discussion at Camp David it was made absolutely clear that the autonomy applies not to the territory (underlined) but to the inhabitants (underlined).

5.   Ties With Jordan

"Economic, commercial and cultural ties between the West Bank, Gaza and Jordan."

In all the clauses of the Camp David agreement there is no reference whatsoever to such ties.

6.   Israeli Sovereignty

There is nothing in the Camp David agreement that precludes the application of Israeli sovereignty over Judea, Samaria and the Gaza district following the transitional period which begins with the establishment and inauguration of the self-governing authority (administrative council). This was also stated by an official spokesman of the Government of the United States.

7.   Palestinian State

The Government of the United States commits itself not to support the establishment of a Palestinian State in Judea, Samaria and the Gaza district.

Regrettably, the visible reality proves this to be an illusion. Were the American plan to be implemented, there would be nothing to prevent King Hussein from inviting his new-found friend, Yasser Arafat, to come to Nablus and hand the rule over to him. Thus would come into being a Palestinian State which would conclude a pact with Soviet Russia and arm itself with every kind of modern weaponry. If the PLO could do this in Lebanon, establishing a state-within-a-state, how much more so will the terrorists do so ruling over Judea, Samaria and the Gaza district. Then a joint front would be established of that "Palestinian State" with Jordan and Iraq behind her, Saudi Arabia to the south and Syria to the north. All these countries, together with other Arab States, would, after a while, launch an onslaught against Israel to destroy her. It is inconceivable that Israel will ever agree to such an "arrangement" whose consequences are inevitable.

Since the positions of the Government of the United States seriously deviate from the Camp David agreement, contradict it and could create a serious danger to Israel, its security and its future, the Government of Israel has resolved that on the basis of these positions it will not enter into any negotiations with any party.

The Government of Israel is ready to renew the autonomy negotiations forthwith with the Governments of the United States and Egypt, signatories to the Camp David agreement, and with other states and elements invited at Camp David to participate in the negotiations, with a view to reaching agreement on the establishment of full autonomy for the Arab inhabitants of Judea, Samaria and the Gaza district, in total conformity with the Camp David accords.

Israeli Party and Extra Parliamentary Platforms

1. The Agudat Israel Party Platform, 1981 [Excerpts]*

We are of the opinion that the myriad declarations and all the talk about the status of the territories and defensible borders do not benefit the state of Israel. On such sensitive matters, discreet action is to be preferred to loud declarations. Our guiding principle is the promise made by God to our forefathers, that we should inherit the land as stated in our holy Bible. According to the eternal precept of our tradition: "the saving of life is above all else". However, we are loyal to the quest for peace as preached by our prophets; we demand the promotion of political initiatives on our side; and that no effort be spared in pursuing peace with our neighbors and establishing friendly relations with all nations and states. Until we attain the prophetic vision of "beat your swords into ploughshares", we have to maintain the military level and moral superiority of the Israel Defense Forces. This will be done in order to fulfil that biblical verse that "God walks in the midst of your camp to save you and to bring down your enemy; let your camp be holy."

2. The HaTehiya Party Platform, 1981 [Excerpts]*

At the core of Hatehiya's political program is our firm conviction that the People of Israel enjoys the inalienable and eternal right to all of the Land of Israel. It is, therefore, our national obligation to translate this right into political reality in all parts of The Land under our control. We cannot, we must not, abandon our Land to foreign rule or desolation.

---

* Agudat Israel is the Orthodox Religious Party.
* HaTehiya is the Zionist Revival Movement.

In light of this faith, we shall strive for the *proclamation of full* Israeli sovereignty over all areas of the Land of Israel under our control and *for a full-scale effort toward massive Jewish settlement of these territories.*

We shall also strive toward *real peace.* Real peace, peace concluded for peace's sake, cannot be established on the basis of Israeli retreats, concessions and demonstrations of weakness. Any agreements concluded along these lines merely encourage the Arab nations to wage war and continue a policy of further weakening Israel as part of a comprehensive plan to destroy her.

The Camp David agreements and the Israeli-Egyptian treaty, though termed "peace agreements", are, in fact, nothing more than retreat agreements, inducements to the Arab states to wage war against a smaller, weaker Israel. The net result of these agreements is:

The loss of Sinai and all its strategically advantageous expanses.

The abandonment of the only energy sources in Israel's possession.

The consequent diminution of our national sovereignty through increased dependence upon the United States.

The setting of a precedent for total retreat on all fronts, including East Jerusalem, and a return to borders which are indefensible against a surprise attack.

The legitimization of the uprooting of Jewish settlements from their land — for the first time in the history of Zionism.

The acceptance of an autonomy plan which paves the way for a Palestinian state in the heart of the Land of Israel.

The negation of our exclusive right to the Land of Israel through the recognition of the so-called "legitimate rights of the Palestinian people and its just demands".

Yet *real peace is possible.* When the State of Israel demonstrates that she possesses the inner strength and resources to resist political pressures and military adventures, only then will the Arab States realize that the People of Israel's return to all of the Land of Israel is a permanent one and that the State of Israel is a fact that they must accept. Only then will they conclude peace for peace's sake and only then will real peace prevail.

We therefore propose *a halt to the retreat from the Sinai peninsula and a reexamination and renegotiation of the Israeli-Egyptian treaty,* along the following lines:

Complete detachment of the Sinai agreement from any agreement concerning other areas of the Land of Israel;

Israel's retention of territories vital to her security;

The continuation of Jewish settlements on their land;

Nullification of the autonomy plan for Judea, Samaria and the Gaza Strip and the proclamation of Israeli sovereignty over these portions of the Land of Israel.

In order to secure our real possession of the Land and to establish Jewish majorities in all its sectors, we further propose that *the government — aided by private initiative, with all the resources and its disposal, engage in a full-scale effort of urban and rural settlement in these areas.* For the sake of this national mission, lands will be allocated and expropriated as the need for such action arises.

The problem of the Arab minority residing within the Land of Israel can be solved through a clear, resolution decision that the Land belongs exclusively to the People of Israel and that no other national entity will be established therein. In light of this, we propose that, after a specified period of time during which a basis for establishing a modus vivendi with the Arab residents is formulated, they be presented with the following alternatives:

Acceptance of citizenship for those wishing to be fully integrated into the State of Israel. This status shall be granted to anyone who pledges his allegiance to the State and accepts the full obligations of citizenship, including payment of taxes and national service.

Acceptance of resident status for those wishing to live in Israel but unwilling to accept citizenship and the obligations to the State that citizenship implies. This status will be granted to anyone who declares his recognition of the State of Israel and his acceptance of her laws. It will endow its possessor with all personal freedoms but will not entitle him to vote or be elected to national institutions.

A program designed to encourage emigration for all Arabs who are unwilling either to accept citizenship or resident status. This emigration will be aided, in a humane and considerate fashion, within a governmental framework designed for this purpose.

The problem of the Arab refugees residing within the Land of Israel and abroad will be solved within the framework of an internationally supported, all-embracing program to rehabilitate them and resettle them in the Arab States who bear full responsibility for the creation and perpetuation of the problem.

3. The Israeli Labour Party, Political Resolutions, 1980 [Excerpts]

1.   The Israel Labour Party will reinforce the effort of the nation to upbuild the independent State of Israel and realise its Zionist aims, based upon the historic right of the Jewish people to establish and uphold its State in its homeland.

The achievement of permanent peace is the central aim of Israeli policy in the days ahead.

2. The repulsion of aggression by the Arab States during the Six Day War, the perseverance during the War of Attrition, the ability of the Israel Defence Forces to overcome the surprise attack in the October 1973 War, the policies leading to the Disengagement Agreements with Egypt and Syria (1974), and the Interim Agreement with Egypt (1975), which were signed in the face of extreme opposition by the Likud, constituted the first breakthrough towards peace; the road was paved for the journey of the President of Egypt to Jerusalem; the Framework Agreements were subsequently reached at Camp David, and the Peace Treaty between Israel and Egypt was signed, and they were confirmed by the Knesset with the support of the Labour Alignment Faction.

3. Israel was always destined to be a Jewish independent and democratic State, maintaining full equality of rights for all her citizens irrespective of religion or nationality. Out of loyalty to this historic mission, Likud policy aiming to annex the whole of the West Bank and Gaza and their inhabitants, must be rejected. This policy leads to turning Israel from a Jewish into a binational State. Also, from the point of view of the social and moral substance of the State of Israel, the Labour Party rejects the imposition of permanent rule over the 1,200,000 Palestinian Arabs inhabiting these territories.

4. The State of Israel needs defensible boundaries which must enable her to defend herself effectively and on her own against any threat of attack. Demilitarization and security arrangements shall be included in peace agreements in addition to, and not instead of, defensible boundaries. Israel will insist upon recognised defensible boundaries which shall be permanent political boundaries, and she will not return to the lines of June 4, 1967, which constituted a temptation to aggression.

5. United Jerusalem under Israeli sovereignty is the capital of the State of Israel.

The rights of all its inhabitants, irrespective of religion or nationality, will be respected and upheld. The special religious status of the places holy to Islam and Christianity under their independent administration, will be safeguarded.

Freedom of worship at the holy places and freedom of access to them will continue to be safeguarded. The arrangements established for the Arab inhabitants of Jerusalem following its reunification, which have made possible co-existence for all its inhabitants, and have provided for the tranquility and prosperity of the City, will be safeguarded and made permanent.

The City's municipal structure will lend expression to its uniqueness, its unity, and the need to grant to all inhabitants expression of increased involvement in the conduct of their lives.

1. The Government of Israel led by the Labour Alignment will be prepared to negotiate for peace with each of her neighbours, without precon-

ditions on any side, on the basis of Security Council Resolutions 242 and 338. Israel will examine any proposal brought before her in negotiations by authorized negotiating partners. The Labour Party will act in accordance with its basic programme as presented in its platform.

7.   The Government of Israel led by the Labour Alignment will act in order to reach peace agreements with Jordan and Syria within defensible boundaries based upon territorial compromise with each of them, which shall meet security considerations.

8.   The Government of Israel will act in order to attain a peace agreement with independent Lebanon according to the existing boundary between the two States.

9.   The Government of Israel led by the Labour Alignment will fulfill — in accordance with the rules of International Law and on the basis of reciprocity — the international obligations undertaken by Israel in the Peace Treaty with Egypt and in the Camp David Agreements, as confirmed by the Knesset.

10.   Implementation of the Peace Treaty with Egypt will be accompanied by an effort to promote the normalization process and to create a network of reciprocal political, economic and development relations. Israel calls for a joint effort to promote cultural and scientific ties and to extend the dialogue between the two peoples. The development of peaceful relations between Israel and Egypt is likely to become a valuable factor in ensuring stability in the Region and in bringing about social and political change in the relations of States and peoples in the Middle East.

11.   The labour Party rejects the policy of "not an inch" in regard to the West Bank and Gaza, which is liable to jeopardize the prospects for peace. In the election campaign for the Tenth Knesset, the Labour Party will call upon the people to grant the Government of Israel a mandate to sign, with the approval of the Knesset, a peace treaty with Jordan based on territorial compromise in accordance with the Labour Party's programme.

12.   In her efforts to attain peace, Israel will be prepared to negotiate interim agreements and such arrangements as will correspond with her policies and security needs and advance the cause of peace.

13.   Israel, aware of the existence of the Palestinian problem, will be prepared to contribute to its solution in the framework of a Jordanian-Palestinian State, in which the self-indentity of the Palestinian Arabs can find its expression and the refugee problem its solution. The Jordanian-Palestinian State will extend over the territorial space of Jordan and specified densely populated areas of the West Bank and Gaza, from which the Israel Defence Forces will withdraw upon conclusion of peace.

Israel rejects the establishment of an additional Palestinian State in the territory between Israel and Jordan, which would be a source of danger and hostility and perpetuate the conflict rather than bring about its solution. The

Palestinian problem cannot be solved in a separate State without the territory and the population of Jordan, which is predominantly Palestinian.

14' The territory of the Jordanian-Palestinian State west of the Jordan River is to be demilitarised and foreign armies shall not cross the Jordan River westwards. Demilitarization shall not rule out agreed security arrangements involving Israeli presence.

15. Peace between Israel and the Jordanian-Palestinian State shall be based upon mutual respect for the sovereignty, structure and internal regime of each of the two States within its boundaries without either interfering with the other's authority or endangering her neighbour's security.

16. Israel will strive to make the peace with Jordan open up an era of fruitful co-operation between them. Efforts shall be made to obtain resources, locally and internationally, to finance development projects, refugee rehabilitation and exploitation of natural resources.

17. Authorized representatives of the Palestinian inhabitants of the West Bank and Gaza shall be incorporated into negotiations on the realization of the Autonomy and into the peace negotiations with Jordan in order to enable them to participate in the determination of their future.

In accordance with its aspiration to put an end to the Israel-Arab conflict, the Labour Party will be prepared, as in the past, to engage in talks with Palestinian personalities and factors recognizing Israel and rejecting the method of terror.

18. The PLO, which denies the right of Israel to exist, and any other organization basing itself on the "Palestinian Covenant" or having recourse to the method of terror, cannot be a partner in peace negotiations. Active defence against the PLO in the domain of security and in the political-ideological domain is the duty of any Israeli Government. Ideological and political activity should be intensified on the public opinion level and among Governments, Parliaments and international organizations against the legitimization of terror and sabotage organizations and against leniency towards their murderous activities.

19. Autonomy as envisaged by the Likud was not, from the outset, the Israel Labour Party's plan, but since it is an inseparable part of the Camp David Agreements, the Government of Israel, led by the Labour Alignment, will consider it as one of the possible arrangements for a transitory period, to the extent that accord as to its implementation is reached between the factors involved. The policies of the Israel Labour Party on the Autonomy issue as approved by its Central Committee on March 18, 1979, remain in force. The Labour Party rejects the tendency of the Likud and other factors to see Autonomy as a stage in the annexation of the West Bank and Gaza into Israel, as well as any tendency to transform the Autonomy into an independent Palestinian State.

20. Even during implementation of the Autonomy, full Israeli control shall be continued in security locations, where the Israel Defence Forces will be deployed, and which will include Jerusalem and the surrounding areas and the settlement areas of the Jordan Valley (including the area to the north-west of the Dead Sea), the Etzion bloc, and the southern section of the Gaza Strip. In these areas, the status and continued development of Israeli settlement are to be safeguarded.

21. The Government of Israel will continue negotiating with Egypt on the Autonomy issue.

22. Israel will be prepared to negotiate with authorized representatives of the inhabitants of the West Bank and Gaza on realization of the Autonomy, even if Jordan does not participate in these negotiations.

23. The negotiations on peace on the Eastern sector will be conducted with the Government of Jordan, with the participation of authorized representatives of the West Bank and Gaza.

24. The Labour Party rejects the policy of perpetuating a situation of no-peace with Jordan, Syria and Lebanon, implied in imposed rule over the inhabitants of the West Bank and Gaza. Its policy will strive to speed up the attainment of full peace or of progress by stages towards this goal.

However, in the absence of peace or interim agreements leading to peace, including realization of the Autonomy Agreement, Israel shall maintain her full authority in the areas held by her since the Six Day War, while respecting the rights and needs of the inhabitants, maintaining internal security, consolidating her security and settlement position in the security locations, preventing acts of sabotage and terror, and repulsing any military or political attempts to create facts and situations apt to endanger the interests and status of Israel.

25. The policies in the territories of the Government of Israel led by the Labour Party will be guided by considerations of security, prevention of attempts at political undermining on the part of the PLO, maintenance of the policy of the open bridges (between the West Bank and Jordan), encouragement of self-government by the inhabitants, safeguarding the rights of the individual, and unceasing concern for the welfare of the population as regards employment and social services.

26. Peace with each and all of the neighbouring States is a basic component in the design for Israel's security. Peace treaties will not relieve Israel of her duty to provide for her own security, nor will they weaken her alertness or her efforts to base her self-defence on reinforcement and up-to-date development of the Israel Defence Forces with modern fighting equipment, continuous training and deployment to enable them to repulse any appearance of aggression.

27. Israel will uphold her right of active defence and of prevention of

sabotage and terror, even if they originate beyond her borders.

28.   The withdrawal of the Israel Defence Forces from sites vital to the security of Israel, such as the airfields in Northern Sinai and in the Eilat sector, and the uprooting of settlements in Sinai shall be no model or precedent when it comes to determining boundaries in other sectors.

29.   Settlement in the Jordan Valley (including the area to the north-west of the Dead Sea), the Etzion bloc, Jerusalem and the surrounding areas, the southern section of the Gaza Strip and also on the Golan Heights — out of considerations of strategic security, and in close co-ordination with the Israel Defence Forces — is vital to the security of the State. It constitutes, as does the whole enterprise of Zionism, an educational, social and pioneering value; and it will prove to be beneficial in the political struggle to shape the boundaries of peace. The Government of Israel, led by the Labour Alignment, will act towards its consolidation and development.

30.   The Government of Israel will insist that the peacetime deployment of the Israel Defence Forces and of the settlements including the Jordan Valley (including the area to the North-West of the Dead Sea), the Etzion bloc, Jerusalem and its surroundings and the southern section of the Gaza Strip, will be included in the sovereign territory of Israel.

31.   The security deployment of the Israel Defence Forces and the settlement network in the Golan are vital for the defence of the State of Israel.

The Government led by the Labour Party will work for consolidation of the Israeli position on the Golan Heights and will insist that the peacetime security and settlement deployment on the Golan shall be under Israeli sovereignty, as an inseparable part of Israel, and a guarantee of security and peace.

32.   Settlements are not to be established which are not expected to remain under Israeli sovereignty and contrary to the authorized decisions of the Government. Settlement shall not be undertaken in the populated areas in the heart of the West Bank and Gaza.

33.   The decisions of the Knesset in regard to the future of settlements as required in the peace treaties shall be complied with.

4. The Liberal Party Platform 1981 [Excerpts]

Zionism

As a Zionist party we believe that Israel's paramount task is the development and safe-guarding of the Jewish State in our ancestral homeland. In concrete terms this means the defense of our country from military threats to our existence; the right of Jews to settle and live in the entirety of the Land of Israel; and the promotion of the ingathering of the Jewish People from its world-wide dispersion.

We, along with our sister parties in the Likud, believe that the peace which we long for can be achieved only through direct, face-to-face negotiations with our Arab neighbors. Such a peace, in our view, means not only the end to Arab military aggression, but recognition of our right to exist as a sovereign, democratic Jewish State; the normalization of diplomatic and trade relations; and a willingness on the part of the Arab States to replace hostility with the spirit of a mutual cooperation and friendship. Until such a peace is concluded, we believe that national defence requires us to remain in our positions along the cease-fire lines.

As regards the Palestinian question, we consider the P.L.O. to be unprincipled terrorists whose announced intention is the destruction of the State of Israel. We categorically reject the notion that the P.L.O. represents anyone other than its own unelected leadership, and oppose any form of contact or negotiation with it. We believe that Mandatory Palestine, which includes both banks of the Jordan River, is large enough for two nations — a Palestinian-Arab State in Eastern Palestine, and the State of Israel with the Jordan River as the natural boundary between them.

5. The Likud Party Platform 1981 [Excerpts]

The Right of the Jewish People to Eretz Israel

A.   The right of the Jewish people to Eretz Israel is an eternal one, which cannot be challenged and is a part of Israel's right to security and peace.

B.   The state of Israel has a right to, and demands, sovereignty over Judea, Samaria and the Gaza District. Following the interim period stipulated in the Camp David Accords, Israel will press its demand and take action to realize this right.

C.   Any program which entails relinquishing part of Western Eretz Israel to foreign rule, as suggested by the Alignment Party, undermines our right to the land; will invevitably lead to the establishment of a "Palestinian" State; harms the security of the civilian population; endangers the existence of the state of Israel; and frustrates all possibilities for peace. A state in which the cities, towns and villages resided in by the majority of the population would be within firing range of the enemy would serve as a perpetual temptation to aggressors who would again try to destroy it.

D.   The autonomy arrangements agreed upon at Camp David are the only guarantee that under no circumstances will a "Palestinian" State be established in part of Western Eretz Israel.

Our Central Objective — True Peace and the Prevention of War

A.   The Likud will give the struggle for peace top priority and spare no effort to further peace. The peace treaty between Israel and Egypt is a result of the Likud Government's policies and is a historic turning point for the status of Israel in the Middle East.

B.   The government will respect the Camp David Accords.

C.   The Likud will act to renew negotiations concerning implementation of the full autonomy agreement for the Arab inhabitants of Judea, Samaria and the Gaza District.

D.   The autonomy agreed upon at Camp David does not signify a state, or sovereignty, or self-determination. The Arab nation enjoys self-determination thanks to the existence ot twenty-one Arab States.

E.   The government will take all necessary measures to prevent the outbreak of a new War. Everyone will remember that the Labor—Mapam Alignment claimed four years ago that if the Likud were to form a government, "war would immediately break out". Reality and the actions of the government have proved this to be deceptive propaganda. The government has prevented war and achieved the first peace agreement between Israel and the largest of its neighbors.

Continuing Protection of Israel Citizens from Harm

The terrorist organization which calls itself 'PLO" seeks to destroy the state of Israel. There will be no negotiations with this murderous organization, which aims its weapons, supplied by the Soviet Union, against men, women and children. The government will act to protect the civilian population from the terrorists. This will be done by initiating offensive action and preventive attacks against their bases and within them. This policy pursued by the Likud government has proved itself to be the best method for protecting the civilian population.

Settlements

Wide-scale settlement activities have been conducted over the past four years in Judea and Samaria: 55 towns were established in Judea and Samaria; 55 posts and towns in the Galilee; five towns in the Golan Heights; six in the Gaza District; five in the Arava; ten in the Besor region; eight on the Negev plateau and the slopes of Mount Hebron. Altogether, 144 towns have been established throughout Eretz Yisrael in the past four years.

Settlement in the Land of Israel is a right and an integral part of the nation's security. We have observed the rule, and will continue to do so, that Jewish settlement shall not cause the removal of a man from his land, his village or his town. The Likud will act to strengthen the development of, and consolidate its hold over, existing settlements.

6. The Mafdal Party Platform 1977 [Excerpts]*

The basic principles which have to guide the Israeli government and its representatives in negotiations for genuine peace with our Arab neighbours are:

1. Our historic-religious rights to the entire promised land.
2. Only one state should exist between the Mediterranean sea and the Jordan river and it should be the State of Israel whose capital is united Jerusalem.
3. The striving for durable peace between us and our neighbours should find its expression in establishing normal relations with the Arab States with all the political and economic components related to such relationships.
4. The State of Israel should be guaranteed defensible borders and sufficient strategic depth.
5. The rejection of any plan which consists of relinquishing any parts of historical Eretz Israel the land of our forefathers.

7. The Mapam Party platform 1981 [Excerpts]*

I. The Palestinian Problem

A. The Path to a Solution

1. In the history of the encounter of Jews and Arabs in their historical, mutual homeland, a reality was created in which only the partition of the land can save the region from the vicious circle of war. A nation's right to self-determination is a basic one limited only by the equal rights of the other nation to sovereignty, peace and security.

2. In order to bring peace to our eastern border and in order to advance toward a solution to the Palestinian problem in all its aspects, Israel must call upon the government of Jordan and to representatives of the Palestinians to join in negotiations for peace based on recognition of the sovereignty and security of the nations in this area and on the right of self-determination of the

---

*   This platform was used in the 1981 election campaign. Mafdal is the National Religious Party
*   Mapam is the United Workers Party and is part of the Alignment bloc.

Palestinian people. This right will be realized under conditions and in stages which will be determined in a peace agreement. In order to bring this about, Israel must cease immediately, all settlement in the territories.

3.   Israel must be prepared to negotiate with any Palestinian factor which recognizes the State of Israel, repudiates the use of terror and acknowledges Israel's right to secure and recognized borders according to Security Council Resolution 242. The basic meaning of these conditions is the revocation of those articles in the P.L.O.'s Palestinian Covenant which call for the destruction of the State of Israel. On the basis of simultaneous, mutual recognition by both peoples, direct negotiations for peace will be undertaken, with no prior conditions.

4.   Mapam warns against the danger of annexing occupied territory as it is planned and carried out by the Likud government. Annexation leads to endless war and distorts our image. If it is carried out, Israel will be able to exist neither as a Jewish State, nor as a democratic one.

5.   The military government in Judea, Samaria and the Gaza Strip has long since ceased any attempt at maintaining a "liberal administration" in the occupied territories. Acts of brutality and persecution which contribute nothing to public security and order have increased in recent years. The "civilian administration" which the Likud government instituted has had no influence in moderating the attitude of the Palestinians. Rather, it has increased ferment and deepened hostility between the two peoples. Therefore, it is urgent that the Israeli presence in the occupied territories be removed as quickly as possible.

B.   A Solution for Peace

1.   Mapam prefers a solution based upon two independent, sovereign countries; one, the State of Israel and the other, a Jordanian-Palestinian State.

The majority of the population of Jordan is made up of Palestinians. They and their brothers and sisters in the West Bank share the same language and tradition and their family ties are many and extended. The expanse of such a Jordanian-Palestinian State would make it possible for the Palestinian people to realize its right to self-determination, to preserve its unity, to absorb its refugees and solve their problems and to observe the right of Israel to secure and recognized borders through security agreements and a demilitarized zone. This would not be possible if a third state were established between Israel and Jordan.

With the accomplishment of peace, Israel will not determine the political life of the Jordanians and Palestinians and she will respect their democratic decisions in everything pertaining to their independence and sovereignty within their borders, provided that all the articles agreed upon and the security arrangements in the peace treaty are fulfilled and observed.

On the basis of an accomplished, stable peace and good, neighborly relations, Israel will also weigh the possibility of a communal solution — federation or confederation.

2.   After border corrections are agreed upon according to her security needs, Israel will return to secure and recognized borders, and the territory evacuated will be demilitarized according to an agreed upon schedule. No military force will cross the Jordan River and the demilitarization will be carried out according to agreed arrangements.

3.   United Jerusalem is the capital of the State of Israel. Israel will guarantee extra-territorial status to the holy sites of Islam and Christianity within the framework of a peace agreement. The national and cultural character of the Arab residents of the city will have full expression in the framework of an autonomous "borough system" and with the protection of their right to choose the citizenship which they prefer. If and when an Israeli-Arab confederation is formed, there will be established within greater Jerusalem a suitable center for its institutions which would be a confederative City Hall. This center would symbolize peace and the desire to deepen the cooperation between both states of the confederation, as detailed in the Hazan Plan for Jerusalem which was adopted by the Central Committee of Mapam in November, 1979.

4.   A rehabilitation plan for the refugees within the borders of the Jordanian-Palestinian State will be included in the peace negotiations. This plan will be executed under the conditions of an overall peace agreement which will include cooperation between the Arab States and Israel with the assistance of international financing. In this framework, agricultural and industrial projects and housing development will be carried out. Israel will do her part in solving this painful problem by absorbing a specific and agreed upon number of refugees within the humanitarian framework of reuniting familiies.

5.   A solution based on these principles and arrangements was proposed by Mapam as long ago as 1967 and reiterated in subsequent party congresses.

8. The Ratz Party Platform 1981 [Excerpts]*

Peace and Security

The State of Israel should strive towards peace with all her neighbors; a peace which would guarantee her physical security and sovereignty as the State of the people of Israel within safe and agreed-upon borders.

The rule over the Occupied Territories is the result of war. There was and

---

*   The movement for Citizens Rights and Peace.

there is room to maintain security forces in them only as a guarantee of peace. However, continued rule over another people as part of an annexation process which ignores their national aspirations, and also settlement of the Occupied Territories with the intention of perpetuating this situation, corrupt our people. In addition, these policies drain the economic resources of the State of Israel, isolate her from other nations, cut her off from world Jewry, and endanger her very existence.

The State of Israel should recognize the right of the Palestinian people to self-determination. It should conduct peace negotiations with any representative body of Palestinians on the basis of mutual recognition, and should call upon the inhabitants of the Territories to further these ends peacefully and through negotiations.

The Camp David accords and the Peace Agreement with Egypt are welcome steps towards peace. They should be pursued, while attempting to gain the participation of Palestinian representatives as well as representatives of all nations involved in the conflict.

The current situation in the Territories makes it difficult to find immediate solutions and necessitates a gradual process of disentanglement and reconciliation whose purpose is to leave options open for future permanent solutions to be agreed upon by both peoples living in Eretz Yisrael.

This process shall be based upon the following principles:

* As long as Israeli rule continues in the Occupied Territories the legal status quo should be maintained. The rights of the inhabitants should be protected by international law, the Geneva Conventions, and the universal principles of justice regulating human rights in Israel.

* Legislation in the Occupied Territories and the activities of the military government should be reviewed in light of these principles.

* Settlement in the Occupied Territories must cease immediately.

* Inhabitants of the Territories shall be insured freedom of political expression and academic freedom.

* A clear distinction should be made between soldiers and citizens. Unauthorized citizens should not be permitted to act as police in the Territories.

Representatives of the MCRP will cooperate with all parties working to advance peace in our region.

United Jerusalem is the capital city of Israel. Any settlement must take into account the national and religious sentiments of the Arab inhabitants of Jerusalem, Christian and Moslem alike. The holy places of the different communities shall be controlled by these communities. The municipal government shall be decentralized into municipal boroughs which will insure independent administration to the inhabitants of each borough under a single municipality.

9. The Hadash Party, Programme for Establishing a Just, Comprehensive and Durable Peace, 1981 [Excerpts] *

Comrades,

The 18th Congress of our party presented before the people of Israel a peace programme which — if it had been realized — would have put an end to bloodshed and granted security to the people, would have helped the country to free itself from the dangerous dependency upon the U.S. monopolies and safeguarded its economic and political independence. The establishment of a just peace would have enabled the country to curtail substantially military expenditure and would have paved the way for solving the grave economic and social problems.

The ruling circles — of the "Ma'arach" and the "Likud" alike — rejected our peace programme out of the reactionary illusion that arms and backing by the U.S.A. would enable them to liquidate the national rights of the Arab Palestinian people and ensure territorial annexations. Life itself has proved that their aggressive-annexationist policy is condemned to failure.

The developments of the last few years enable us to state with utmost certainty that the application of our peace programme, which is based upon respecting the rights of all the peoples and states of our region, including Israel and the Arab Palestinian people, makes it definitely possible to establish the desired peace and sever the chain of wars. We are submitting to the Congress for endorsement our up-to-date programme for establishing a comprehensive, just and durable peace. (Its principles are identical with the peace programme adopted by our 18th Congress.) The programme reads as follows:

— Israel will withdraw from all the territories occupied in the war of 1967. The lines of June 4th, 1967, will be the peace frontiers;

— The right of the Arab Palestinian people to self-determination and the establishment of their own independent state in the West Bank (including Eastern Jerusalem) and the Gaza Strip, alongside of the State of Israel, will be respected;

— To ensure a just solution to the problem of Palestinian refugees, in accordance with the U.N. resolutions which recognize their right to choose between repatriation and receiving compensations.

The right of the State of Israel and of the Arab States to sovereign existence and development in conditions of peace and security will be respected:

— All the sides concerned will annul any contention to belligerency and will respect the sovereignty and territorial integrity of all the states of the region and their right to live in peace within recognized and safe borders, free from any threat or use of violence.

---

* Hadash is the Communist Party of Israel.

The peace conditions will be anchored in treaties between the states. These treaties will constitute the legal basis for peaceful co-existence.

The annexation of occupied Eastern Jerusalem will be null and void. The sovereignty of the independent Palestinian State will be in force in this part of the city. Within the framework of a peace settlement Western Jerusalem will be recognized as Israel's capital, and Eastern Jerusalem as capital of the independent Palestinian State, in conformity with the wishes of each people in its respective state. Within the framework of a peace settlement, agreed upon arrangements can be made so as to ensure cooperation between the Israeli and the Palestinian parts of the city in the municipal sphere, a free approach to the holy places, and free traffic between the respective parts of the city etc.

We have opposed, and we still oppose the annexation of Eastern Jerusalem and the resolution adopted by the Knesset regarding Jerusalem and demand to revoke both of them.

A peace settlement will guarantee Israel, like any other state, freedom of navigation.

A peace settlement will pave the way for voluntary agreements between the State of Israel, on the one hand, and the Palestinian and other Arab States, on the other hand, concerning various matters of common interest.

In the conditions prevailing in the Middle East and in view of the sediments of bitterness, which have accumulated in many years of war and distrust, effective international guarantees are apt to contribute much to securing the existence of a peace settlement. In view of the conditions prevailing today in the world, international guarantees under the auspices of the U.N.O., and with the participation of the U.S.S.R., the U.S.A. and other states, will constitute the firmest safeguard for the peace and security of Israel, of the future independent Palestinian State and of all the states of the region.

In order to establish a comprehensive, just and durable peace it is imperative to nullify the Camp David agreements, which negate the right of the Arab Palestinian people to self-determination and which take the handling of the Middle East crisis out of the hands of the United Nations and out of the detente in international relations. An international conference for peace in the Middle East, under the auspices of the U.N.O., and based on its resolutions should be convened, with the participation of the Soviet Union, the United States and other interested states, as well as all parties involved in the conflict, including the P.L.O., the sole representative of the Arab Palestinian people.

These are the foundations and ways for establishing a comprehensive, just, durable and realistic peace in the Middle East.

10. The "Shinui's" Party platform
Defence and Foreign Affairs Policies, 1983. [Excerpts] *

The main objectives of Israel's foreign policy should be: consolidation of the peace with Egypt, the conclusion of peace agreements with the remaining Arab States and the resolution of the Palestinian problem. To attain these objectives we will act in the following ways:

1) Although the people of Israel have a natural and historical right to the land of Israel, it is incumbent upon it, in the light of the circumstances created by recent history, to agree to give up territory populated by Arabs in Judea, Samaria and the Gaza district. When eventually negotiations are entered into to determine the final borders between Israel and the Arab State to the east of her, the State of Israel must keep in mind its own vital security interests in the now occupied territories. Securing these interests through demilitarization and similar arrangements would form the basis of such a peace agreement. A long-term Israeli military presence along the River Jordan would ensure the efficacy of the demilitarization.

2) The Autonomy agreement, as originally conceived, could provide a suitable interim solution but cannot take the place of a permanent arrangement. The permanent agreement would be obtained through negotiations with the kingdom of Jordan and such elements among the Palestinians as are prepared to recognize the State of Israel and to live in peace with it.

The Autonomy plan, despite its shortcomings, has several advantages: It is the only plan accepted jointly by Egypt, Israel and the United States. It postpones the permanent solution in the West Bank to a time which would be more convenient for Israel. Such Autonomy arrangements would make it possible to test whether in these territories a co-existence of the two peoples is viable. Once the burden of Israeli administration has been removed from the Arab population and suitable security provisions made in the field.

"Shinui — Party of the Center" agrees with the Autonomy idea but has a detailed Autonomy Plan of its own. Its basic principles are:

a) Transfer to a representative body of the local Arab population of full powers of the running of its economy and daily life, the maintenance of law and order and the judicial system.

b) Resettlement of the Arab refugees of 1967.

c) The securing of close ties with both Israel and Jordan which would ensure the local populations' freedom of movement and its work opportunities in both these countries.

---

* Shinui is the Centerist Party for Change

d) Israel's guaranteed right to act in the occupied territories in all matters affecting her security, and to declare the Jordan Valley a zone vital to its security.

e) The stopping of any further Israeli settlement activity in the territories under the Autonomy.

Shinui believes that the creation of a third State between Israel and Jordan would not provide a stable answer to either the Palestinian problem or the refugee problem, but would on the contrary undermine the very foundations of both Israel and Jordan, as well as provide a launching pad for terrorist activities against either.

Shinui believes that a Jordanian-Palestinian State would provide a suitable setting within which the specific characteristics of the Palestinian people could find expression.

If within the 5 year Autonomy period a significant change would appear to have taken place in the attitudes of the Palestinian organizations towards Israel, and in the balance of powers within the Middle East, the whole issue of the fate of the occupied territories would be re-examined.

3) Israel must hold on to the Golan Height to safeguard the population of the Galilee and secure its water resources. When in the future a peace agreement with Syria is concluded, firm security provisions must be made in those areas of the Golan Heights from which Israel withdraws, such as total demilitarization.

4) Re-united Jerusalem shall not ever be divided again and shall forever remain under Israeli sovereignty. However, in view of the importance which Jerusalem holds for the Arab world generally, such importance should be taken into account and appropriate measures adopted.

11. The Tami Party Platform, 1981
Foreign Affairs and Defence Policy [Excerpts] *

Principles and Aims

— The State of Israel is striving to achieve a comprehensive peace with all the nations of the region and will welcome any Arab State ready to follow in Egypt's footsteps and sign a peace treaty.

— This striving for peace must remain anchored in the Israeli nation's right to its historic inheritance and its uncontested right to exist.

— Tami endorses the peace treaty with Egypt and the autonomy plan as the solution to the problem of the Palestinian nation and the problem of the refugees.

— Tami regards the State of Israel as an integral part of the Middle East and recognizes the need for the development of economic, cultural and political ties with every one of the states of the region, on the basis of equality and mutual recognition, in order to promote common regional interests.

— The conclusions deriving from our existence in the Middle East and our human ties with the nations of the region form the essential basis for any future peace treaty.

— Tami sees the solution of social problems as a necessary condition for defence and political security and does not therefore accept the approach which calls for reducing the attention given to internal problems on account of our special security situation.

— Any progress toward the solution of the Palestinian refugee problem must be conditional on parallel progress regarding the problem of compensation and reparations to those who left the Arab countries or those who were forced to flee, leaving behind much property.

— Tami sees the State of Israel as the Jewish State which must accordingly serve as a homeland to all the Jewish communities in the diaspora and as a land of refuge for those Jews who are persecuted because of their religion, their beliefs and their support for the Zionist idea.

— Jerusalem is the eternal capital of the Jewish people. United Jerusalem will never be redivided. The subject of the guarantee of religious rights to all the religions will be anchored in negotiations for peace.

General Policies

Tami sees the IDF as the people's army subject to the government of Israel and service in the IDF as a duty for the guarantee of the existence of the nation residing in Zion.

---

* Tami is the Movement for Israel's Tradition

Tami does not regard the peace treaty with Egypt as a basis for parallel agreements with Jordan and Syria. An agreement with each one of these two states requires direct negotiations without preconditions.

The Jewish settlements in Judea and Samaria will be subject to the following conditions:

— no settlement in a region densely populated by Arabs

— consideration of economic priorities so that social targets will not be harmed

— settlement to be conducted according to security needs

Tami sees the Palestinian problem as a political and humanitarian problem, and regards the autonomy agreements as the path to its solution.

Tami regards the Arab countries as bearing the major responsibility for the painful situation of most of the refugees and considers that any future solution will require efforts both on the part of the Arab countries and of Israel.

Tami regards the Golan Heights as an area vital to the defence of the State of Israel. As part of the peace process Tami would support the delineation of a recognized and secure border with Syria which would not require Israel's leaving the northern slopes of those Heights, although that border would not necessarily be identical with the present cease-fire line.

Tami calls for continuing action against the terrorist organizations whose purpose is the destruction of the State of Israel. Those terrorist organizations are part of an international network of terror and Tami demands co-operation from the international community in action against them.

Tami supports the development of economic and political relations with the States of Africa and the Third World in order to explain Israel's position and to minimize its political isolation.

12. Extra-Parliamentary Groups — Peace Now Platform [Excerpts]

Objectives

Peace Now is a broad-based non-partisan movement. It seeks to further the following objectives:

* The fulfillment by the State of Israel of Zionism as the national liberation movement of the Jewish people in its homeland.

* Israel living in security and peace with all its neighbors.

* Israel as a state of law, freedom, and full equality of rights for all its citizens, regardless of religion or nationality.

* Israel capable of attracting *aliyah* (immigration) and providing a focus of identification for the Jews of the Diaspora.

These objectives will not be attained so long as our rule over the Palestinian population in the West Bank and Gaza continues.

The continuing rule over another people —

*   Involves acts which violate human and Jewish ethics.

*   Leads to the corruption of society, to the undermining of democracy, and to violence.

*   Erodes the wide-based national consensus.

*   Imposes upon the Israel Defense Forces tasks which distort its character as an army defending its people.

*   Escalates the struggle in the territories, causes bloodshed, and increases the danger of war.

*   Creates barriers between Israel and the Jews of the Diaspora, and isolates Israel from the family of nations.

Therefore, peace on all our borders is crucial for us.

This ongoing struggle for the attainment of the true Zionist dream is a struggle of the entire Jewish people.

Peace Now and the War in Lebanon

Before the war began Peace Now opposed an Israeli incursion into Lebanon. A demonstration against the possibility of such an incursion was staged during the missile crisis of May-June 1981. During the intervening year, and up to the very hours prior to the June 1982 invasion, the movement issued numerous statements, lobbied, and pressured in an effort to avert a military confrontation on Israel's northern border.

In the early weeks of the war, with many of its members and leaders in the front lines, Peace Now spearheaded the growing public protest to Israel's involvement in Lebanon. On July 3, 1982 a mass rally of 100,000 people was held in Tel Aviv to protest the war and its aims. Speakers called upon the government to seize the opportunity presented by the new situation, to turn to the Palestinians and initiate negotiations aimed at resolving the problems of the West Bank and Gaza.

Throughout the course of the war Peace Now sustained a continual stream of protest in the form of meetings, symposia, vigils, and demonstrations. These activities gave voice to the views of those Israelis who decried the use of the IDF in a non-defensive action, the attempt to force a new order upon Lebanon, and the reliance upon military strength to settle the conflict with the Palestinians. Peace Now's opposition to the war in Lebanon rests upon the following principles:

*   Military action will not and cannot solve the Palestinian issue. This can only be achieved through negotiations.

*   The invasion of Lebanon was not necessary to Israel's defense, and did not further Israel's legitimate security interests.

* The elimination of the military arm of the PLO does not eliminate the PLO as an effective political force nor does it effect the likelihood of PLO terrorist activity in the future.

* Intervention in the internal affairs of Lebanon involves Israel in a deep political quagmire. Such involvement is detrimental to Israel's security.

* Israel's involvement in a war the aims and conduct of which many Israelis and much of world Jewry reject have created a rift within the nation and between the Israeli government and world Jewry. Moreover, the war has further isolated Israel within the international community.

Peace Now and the Quest for a Just Peace

At this moment, more than ever before, there is a pressing need to find a lasting solution to the Arab-Israel conflict. Peace Now has set forth guidelines for the peace process.

The peace agreement shall be founded on the following principles:

* Readiness by both sides to agree to a partition of *Eretz Yisrael.* While the people of Israel have a bond with the entire land of Israel, the existence of two peoples on this land necessitates partition as the basis for any compromise solution. Herein lies the basic contradiction between realistic Zionism and the conception of a greater Israel.

* Recognition of Israel. The peoples of the region, including the Palestinians, should recognize Israel's right to sovereign existence within secure and agreed-upon borders, and should abandon the road of war and terror.

* Recognition of Palestinian national existence. Israel should recognize the right of the Palestinians to a national existence, which will be realized in a manner to be agreed upon by the parties concerned.

* Peace with security. The interests of Israel's security shall be assured in any peace agreement. Security has many aspects; recognized defensible borders are only one phase of the security for which we strive.

* Jerusalem, the capital of Israel, shall not be redivided. Within its boundaries as one city, proper expression should be given to Jerusalem's unique status in the Moslem and Christian worlds, as well as to the national affinity of its Arab residents.

The Process of Negotiations:

The continuation of the peace process requires that:

* Israel shall take an initiative aimed at breaking the vicious cycle of Israeli-Palestinian hostility. The government of Israel shall declare its readiness to negotiate with those representatives of the Palestinians who recognize negotiations as the only path towards resolution of the conflict.

* Israel shall strive to engage Jordan in the peace process, and so also any other Arab State which seeks to play a constructive part in the peace process.

* Israel shall continue to nurture peaceful relations with Egypt, whose contribution to the process of a comprehensive peace in the region is essential. Continuing confrontation with the Palestinians endangers the existence of the peace which has already been achieved.

* Any temporary arrangement which preceeds a peace treaty must be consistent with the principles of the permanent agreement.

* The Autonomy Plan must not be used as a vehicle for annexation and as an obstacle to any future peace agreements.

Israeli Peace Initiatives

First and foremost, however, Israel must immediately do its part:

* A moratorium should be placed on any further settlement and expropriation of land in the West Bank.

* The settlers, some of whom contribute significantly to the spread of hatred, violence, and friction, should be restrained.

* The restrictions placed upon the Arab population shall be removed, except for those limitations which are clearly required for security reasons. The right of these residents to manage their own affairs and to maintain their own institutions should be preserved.

* The well-being, property, and dignity of the residents of the West Bank and Gaza, currently under Israeli control, should be stringently safeguarded.

* All resources currently channelled towards settlements in the West Bank should be redirected towards solving the problems of the social gap and of deprivation within Israel.

The Reagan Plan

The proposals aired by President Ronald Reagan on September 1, 1982 constitute a basis for negotiations between Israel and her Arab neighbors. Peace Now calls on the government of Israel to reconsider its rejection of the US program and accept it as a starting point for constructive negotiations.

Peace with Egypt has been achieved. The goal which faces us now is to complete the peace process throughout the entire region; to attain peace that will enable all the peoples of this war-torn region to live securely and to flourish.

13. Gush Emunim — Platform

A — Sovereignty and Policy

Recognizing that the whole of the land of Israel is the exclusive property of the Jewish people, and demanding fulfillment of the obligation of the Jewish nation to establish full sovereignty in the land, both as a means of ensuring its existence and the ingathering of the Diaspora, as well as an independent matter connected with the mitzva of settling the land, Gush Emunim will work for the consolidation of a policy establishing the following principles of action:

1.   Full Jewish sovereignty should begin immediately over all areas of the land of Israel which are presently in our hands, including Judea and Samaria, the Golan Heights in their present border, the Gaza Strip and large areas of the Sinai.

2.   By means of education and information, a clear national consciousness should be created which sees all areas of the land of Israel as one land which must not be divided.

3.   We should make clear, in an unambiguous manner, to ourselves and to the nations of the world, that the Jewish people will fight with dedication against any attempt to impose on us a withdrawal from any part of the land of Israel, by military or political means, and we will not abandon this necessary struggle as long as we have the power to continue.

4.   The Arabs of the land of Israel, as well as the other non-Jewish minorities living here, must be granted all the private and legal rights to which every person is entitled, including the right to migrate, the right to own property, to a trial, and all other personal freedoms. These rights must not be denied, except for reasons related directly to security. We must examine the possibility of granting Israeli citizenship to every non-Jewish resident who is prepared to accept all the responsibilities involved (including military service or alternative service). On the other hand, we should, by means of information and economic assistance, encourage those who are not prepared to accept Israel citizenship for nationalistic reasons, to emigrate.

5.   The realization of full Jewish sovereignty in the land of Israel involves absolute independence, with no dependence on foreign countries. Therefore every effort should be made to achieve economic and political independence, and above all we must determine an independent national policy which is not subject to any foreign nation.

6.   We must lay the foundation for relations between Israel and the nations of the world on a moral basis of mutual understanding and aid in every case where any nation shows that it wishes this. But we must stand firm in every meeting with a foreign country on the rights and vital needs of the state of Israel, and we must zealously guard the honor of Israel so that it is not debased in the rest of the world.

Every international organization or framework which reaches decisions that dishonor Israel has no right to exist, and we must leave it with the hope that the day will come when the honor of Israel will grow and truth will be revealed among the nations of the world.

B — Education and Love of Israel

4. Introduction of a sense of mission and the obligation of personal fulfillment.

Gush Emunim is searching for ways to create an atmosphere of openness regarding the love of Israel hidden in the heart of the nation by bringing people together from all walks of life with no regard to differences of opinion and background. For activity of this sort, dedicated work to bring different groups together and reduce the gap between social groups in the nation as a basis for all activities, we must develop moral measures and a personal educational example.

C — Settlement

Gush Emunim sees settlement as a real and deep expression of our tie to the land and a powerful factor in preventing the undermining of our right to the whole land, both from inside the country and from outside.

Therefore, Gush Emunim will work diligently and with no rest to expand settlement of all types and to establish new points in every part of the land, first of all in Judea and Samaria, in the Golan, in the Jordan valley, and in the expanses of the Sinai.

Besides being one of the cornerstones of Zionism, settlement is vital to achieving national goals, to improve the socio-economic system, to help the weaker classes, and mainly to develop the overcrowded coastal plain, to diffuse the population and to bring tens of thousands from the coastal plain to the hills and open places of the country.

14. The Israel Council for Israeli-Palestinian Peace Manifesto, January 1976

We Affirm

1. That this land is the homeland of its two peoples — the people of Israel and the Palestinian Arab people.

2. That the heart of the conflict between the Jews and the Arabs is the historical confrontation between the two peoples of this land, which is dear to both.

3. That the only path to peace is through co-existence between two sovereign states, each with its distinct national identity: the State of Israel for

the Jewish people and a state for the Palestinian Arab people, which will exercise its right to self-determination in the political framework of its choosing.

4. That the establishment of a Palestinian Arab State alongside the State of Israel should be the outcome of negotiations between the government of Israel and a recognized and authoritative representative body of the Palestinian Arab people, without refusing negotiation with the Palestine Liberation Organization, on the basis of mutual recognition.

5. That the border between the State of Israel and the Palestinian Arab State will correspond to the pre-war lines of June 1967, except for changes agreed upon by the parties and after settlement of the problem of Jerusalem.

6. That Jerusalem is the eternal capital of Israel. Being sacred to three religions and inhabited by the two peoples, it deserves a special status. It will remain united under a common municipal roof-organization and will be accessible to people of all nations and faiths. Jerusalem will continue to be the capital of the State of Israel, and the Arab part could become, after the establishment of peace, the capital of the Palestinian Arab State. The Holy Places of all three religions will be administered autonomously by their respective institutions.

7. That the border between Israel and the Palestinian Arabs will be open to the free movement of people and goods throughout the land. Palestinian Arabs will not settle in Israel nor Israelis in the Palestinian Arab State other than by consent of the two governments.

8. That the creation of a Palestinian Arab State will contribute decisively to the solution of the national and humanitarian problem of the refugees. Israel will assist in this solution.

9. That the early stages of Israeli-Palestinian co-existence will require mutually-agreed upon security arrangements. There will be guarantees that foreign military forces will not enter the territory of either of the two states.

10. That the two states will be sovereign in all respects, including matters of immigration and return. The State of Israel will preserve its inalienable Link to Zionism and to the Jewish people throughout the world, and the Palestinian Arab State will maintain the link of its people to the Arab world.

11. That the two states will aim to conduct a continuing dialogue in order to forge closer relations between them, to solve common problems in a spirit of cooperation and for the benefit of both nations. The two states shall not engage in any acts to alter the structure of the co-existence between them, except by mutual agreement.

12. That for the benefit of all nations in the area there should be a system of regional cooperation, in which both the State of Israel and the Palestinian Arab State will participate.

Palestinian Documents

1. Statement Issued by the Palestine Liberation Organization Rejecting U.N. Resolutions 242, Cairo, 23 November, 1967

Having studied the British resolution adopted by the Security Council on the Israeli aggression against Arab territories of June 1967, the Palestine Liberation Organization, in behalf of the Palestinian people, hereby defines its attitude to the said resolution as follows:

1. The resolution as a whole is in the nature of a political declaration of general principles, and is more like an expression of international intentions than the resolution of an executive power. Its treatment of the question of the withdrawal of Israeli forces is superficial, rather than being a decisive demand. It leaves Israel many loopholes to justify her continued occupation of Arab territories, and may be interpreted as permitting her to withdraw from such territories as she chooses to withdraw from and to retain such areas as she wishes to retain.

2. The resolution more than once refers to Israel's right to exist and to establish permanent, recognized frontiers. It also refers to Israel's safety and security and to her being freed from all threats, and, in general to the termination of the state of belligerency with her. All this imposes on the Arab countries undertakings and a political and actual situation which are fundamentally and gravely inconsistent with the Arab character of Palestine, the essence of the Palestine cause and the right of the Palestinian people to their homeland. This resolution completely undermines the foundations of the principles announced by the Khartoum Summit Conference held after the aggression.

3. The resolution ignores the right of the refugees to return to their homes, dealing with this problem in an obscure manner which leaves the door wide open to efforts to settle them in the Arab countries and to deprive them of the

exercise of their right to return, thereby annulling the resolutions adopted by the United Nations over the past twenty years.

4. The resolution recognizes the right of passage through international waterways, by which it means the Suez Canal and the Gulf of Aqaba. Granted that the Canal is an international waterway, this right cannot be exercised by a state which has engaged in usurpation and aggression, especially inasmuch as this usurpation and aggression were directed against an Arab country. The Gulf of Aqaba constitutes Arab internal waters, and its shores include a coastal area belonging to Palestine occupied by Israel through an act of usurpation and aggression. The principle of freedom of innocent passage is not applicable to the Gulf of Aqaba, especially as regards Israel.

5. The resolution includes provisions for the sending on a mission of a personal representative of the Secretary-General of the United Nations. This is no more than a repetition of unsuccessful attempts in the past, beginning with the dispatch of Count Bernadotte and ending with the formation of the International Conciliation Commission. All these attempts provided Israel with repeated opportunities to impose the *fait accompli* and to engage in further aggression and expansion.

6. The resolution as a whole validates Israel's attitude and her demands and disappoints the hopes of the Arab nation and ignores its national aspirations. The conflicting interpretations of the resolution made by members of the Security Council have weakened it even further, and it is not too much to say that the resolution is a political setback at the international level following the military setback which has befallen the Arab homeland.

For these reasons, the most important of which is that the Security Council ignores the existence of the Palestinian people and their right of self-determination, the Palestine Liberation Organisation hereby declares its rejection of the Security Council resolution as a whole and in detail. In so doing it is not only confirming a theoretical attitude, but also declaring the determination of the Palestinian people to continue their revolutionary struggle to liberate their homeland. The Palestine Liberation Organization is fully confident that to achieve this sacred aim the Arab nation will meet its national responsibilities to mobilize all its resources for this battle of destiny, with the support of all forces of liberation throughout the world.

2. The Palestinian National Covenant, 1968

This Covenant will be called The Palestinian National Covenant *(al-mithaq al-watani al-filastini)*.

Article 1: Palestine is the homeland of the Palestinian Arab people and an integral part of the great Arab homeland, and the people of Palestine is a part of the Arab nation.

Article 2: Palestine with its boundaries that existed at the time of the British mandate is an integral regional unit.

Article 3: The Palestinian Arab people possesses the legal right to its homeland, and when the liberation of its homeland is completed it will exercise self-determination solely according to its own will and choice.

Article 4: The Palestinian personality is an innate, persistent characteristic that does not disappear, and it is transferred from fathers to sons. The Zionist occupation, and the dispersal of the Palestinian Arab people as a result of the disasters which came over it, do not deprive it of its Palestinian personality and affiliation and do not nullify them.

Article 5: The Palestinians are the Arab citizens who were living permanently in Palestine until 1947, whether they were expelled from there or remained. Whoever is born to a Palestinian Arab father after this date, within Palestine or outside it, is a Palestinian.

Article 6: Jews who were living permanently in Palestine until the beginning of the Zionist invasion will be considered Palestinians. [For the dating of the Zionist invasion, considered to have begun in 1917.]

Article 7: The Palestinian affiliation and the material, spiritual and historical tie with Palestine are permanent realities. The upbringing of the Palestinian individual in an Arab and revolutionary fashion, the undertaking of all means of forging consciousness and training the Palestinian, in order to acquaint him profoundly with his homeland, spiritually and materially, and preparing him for the conflict and the armed struggle, as well as for the sacrifice of his property and his life to restore his homeland, until the liberation of all this is a national duty.

Article 8: The phase in which the people of Palestine is living is that of national *(watani)* struggle for the liberation of Palestine. Therefore, the contradictions among the Palestinian national forces are of secondary order which must be suspended in the interest of the fundamental contradiction between Zionism and colonialism on the one side and the Palestinian Arab people on the other. On this basis, the Palestinian masses, whether in the homeland or in places of exile *(mahajir)*, organizations and individuals, comprise one national front which acts to restore Palestine and liberate it through armed struggle.

Article 9: Armed struggle is the only way to liberate Palestine and is therefore a strategy and not tactics. The Palestinian Arab people affirms its absolute resolution and abiding determination to pursue the armed struggle and to march forward towards the armed popular revolution, to liberate its homeland and return to it [to maintain] its right to a natural life in it, and to exercise its right of self-determination in it and sovereignty over it.

Article 10: Fedayeen action forms the nucleus of the popular Palestinian war of liberation. This demands its promotion, extension and protection, and the mobilization of all the masses and scientific capacities of the Palestinians, their organization and involvement in the armed Palestinian revolution and cohesion in the national *(watani)* struggle among the various groups of the people of Palestine, and between them and the Arab masses, to guarantee the continuation of the revolution, its advancement and victory.

Article 11: The Palestinians will have three mottoes: national *(wataniyya)* unity: national *(qawmiyya)* mobilization and.liberation.

Article 12: The Palestinian Arab people believes in Arab unity. In order to fulfill its role in realizing this, it must preserve, in this phase of its national *(watani)* struggle, its Palestinian personality and the constituents thereof, increase consciousness of its existence and resist any plan that tends to disintegrate or weaken it.

Article 13: Arab unity and the liberation of Palestine are two complementary aims. Each one paves the way for realization of the other. Arab unity leads to the liberation of Palestine, and the liberation of Palestine leads to Arab unity. Working for both goes hand in hand.

Article 14: The destiny of the Arab nation, indeed the very Arab existence, depends upon the destiny of the Palestine issue. The endeavour and effort of the Arab nation to liberate Palestine follows from this connection. The people of Palestine assumes its vanguard role in realizing this sacred national *(qawmi)* aim.

Article 15: The liberation of Palestine, from an Arab viewpoint, is a national *(qawmi)* duty to repulse the Zionist, Imperialist invasion from the great Arab homeland and to purge the Zionist presence from Palestine. Its full responsibility falls upon the Arab nation, peoples and governments, with the Palestinian Arab people at their head. For this purpose, the Arab nation must mobilize all its military, human, material and spiritual capacities to participate actively with the people of Palestine in the liberation of Palestine. They must especially in the present stage of armed Palestinian revolution, grant and offer the people of Palestine all possible help and every material and human support, and afford it every sure means and opportunity enabling it to continue to assume its vanguard role in pursuing its armed revolution until the liberation of its homeland.

Article 16: The liberation of Palestine, from a spiritual viewpoint, will prepare an atmosphere of tranquillity and peace for the Holy Land in the shade of which all the Holy Places will be safeguarded, and freedom of worship and visitation to all will be guaranteed, without distinction or discrimination of race, colour, language or religion. For this reason, the people of Palestine looks to the support of all the spiritual forces in the world.

Article 17: The liberation of Palestine, from a human viewpoint, will restore to the Palestinian man his dignity, glory and freedom. For this, the Palestinian

Arab people looks to the support of those in the world who believe in the dignity and freedom of man.

Article 18: The liberation of Palestine, from an international viewpoint is a defensive act necessitated by the requirements of self-defence. For this reason the Arab people of Palestine, desiring to befriend all peoples, looks to the support of the states which love freedom, justice and peace in restoring the legal situation to Palestine, establishing security and peace in its territory, and enabling its people to exercise national *(wataniyya)* sovereignty and national *(qawmiyya)* freedom.

Article 19: The partitioning of Palestine in 1947 and the establishment of Israel is fundamentally null and void, whatever time has elapsed, because it was contrary to the wish of the people of Palestine and its natural right to its homeland, and contradicts the principles embodied in the Charter of the UN, the first of which is the right of self-determination.

Article 20: The Balfour Declaration, the Mandate document, and what has been based upon them are considered null and void. The claim of a historical or spiritual tie between Jews and Palestine does not tally with historical realities nor with the constituents of statehood in their true sense. Judaism, in its character as a religion of revelation, is not a nationality with an independent existence. Likewise, the Jews are not one people with an independent personality. They are rather citizens of the states to which they belong.

Article 21: The Palestinian Arab people, in expressing itself through the armed Palestinian revolution, rejects every solution that is a substitute for a complete liberation of Palestine, and rejects all plans that aim at the settlement of the Palestine issue or its internationalization.

Article 22: Zionism is a political movement organically related to world Imperialism and hostile to all movements of liberation and progress in the world. It is a racist and fanatical movement in its formation: aggressive, expansionist and colonialist in its aims; and fascist and Nazi in its means. Israel is the tool of the Zionist movement and a human and geographical base for world Imperialism. It is a concentration and jumping-off point for Imperialism in the heart of the Arab homeland, to strike at the hopes of the Arab nation for liberation, unity and progress.

Article 23: The demands of security and peace and the requirements of truth and justice oblige all states that preserve friendly relations among peoples and maintain the loyalty of citizens to their homelands to consider Zionism an illegitimate movement and to prohibit its existence and activity.

Article 24: The Palestinian Arab people believes in the principles of justice, freedom, sovereignty, self-determination, human dignity and the right of peoples to exercise them.

Article 25: To realize the aims of this covenant and its principles the Palestine Liberation Organization will undertake its full role in liberating

Palestine.

Article 26: The Palestine Liberation Organization, which represents the forces of the Palestinian revolution, is responsible for the movement of the Palestinian Arab people in its struggle to restore its homeland, liberate it, return to it and exercise the right of self-determination in it. This responsibility extends to all military, political and financial matters, and all else that the Palestine issue requires in the Arab and international spheres.

Article 27: The Palestine Liberation Organization will cooperate with all Arab States, each according to its capacities, and will maintain neutrality in their mutual relations in the light of and on the basis of, the requirements of the battle of liberation and will not interfere in the internal affairs of any Arab State.

Article 28: The Palestinian Arab people insists upon the originality and independence of its national *(wataniyya)* revolution and rejects every manner of interference, guardianship and subordination.

Article 29: The Palestinian Arab people possesses the prior and original right in liberating and restoring its homeland and will define its position with reference to all states and powers on the basis of their positions with reference to the issue [of Palestine] and the extent of their support for [the Palestinian Arab people] in its revolution to realize its aims.

Article 30: The fighters and bearers of arms in the battle of liberation are the nucleus of the popular army, which will be the protecting arm of the gains of the Palestinian Arab people.

Article 31: This organization shall have a flag, oath and anthem, all of which will be determined in accordance with a special system.

Article 32: To this covenant is attached a law known as the fundamental law of the Palestine Liberation Organization, in which is determined the manner of the organization's formation, its committees, institutions, the special functions of every one of them and all the requisite duties associated with them in accordance with this covenant.

Article 33: This covenant cannot be amended except by a two-thirds majority of all the members of the National Assembly of the Palestine Liberation Organization in a special session called for this purpose.

3. Palestine National Assembly, Political Resolutions, Cairo, 17 July, 1968 [Excerpts]

II. Political Decisions:

(A)   The Palestinian Cause at Palestinian Level:
Inasmuch as a definition of the objectives of the Palestinian struggle, the

methods it adopts and the instruments it employs, is essential for the unification of that struggle under one leadership, the Assembly, having debated the matter, endorses the following definitions:

First — Objectives:

1. The liberation of the entire territory of Palestine, over which the Palestinian Arab people shall exercise their sovereignty.

2. That the Palestinian Arab people have the right to establish the form of society they desire in their own land and to decide on their natural place in Arab unity.

3. The affirmation of the Palestinian Arab identity, and rejection of any attempt to establish tutelage over it.

Second — Methods:

1. The Palestinian Arab people have chosen the course of armed struggle in the fight to recover their usurped territories and rights. The current phase in their armed struggle started before the defeat of June, 1967 and has endured and escalated ever since. Moreover, despite the fact that this struggle renders a service to the entire Arab nation at the present stage, insofar as it prevents the enemy from laying claim to a *status quo* based on surrender, and insofar as it keeps the flame of resistance alive and maintains a climate of war, preoccupies the enemy and is an object of concern to the entire world community, that struggle is nevertheless a true and distinct expression of the aspirations of the Palestinian Arab people and is inspired by their objectives. In addition, we feel bound to declare quite frankly that this struggle goes beyond the scope of what it has become customary to call "the elimination of the consequences of the aggression", and all other such slogans, for the objectives of this struggle are those of the Palestinian Arab people, as set out in the preceding paragraph. The fight will not cease; it will continue, escalate and expand until final victory is won, no matter how long it takes and regardless of the sacrifices involved.

2. The enemy has chosen *Blitzkrieg* as the form of combat most suitable to him, in view of the tactical mobility at his command which enabled him, at the moment of battle, to unleash forces superior to those deployed by the Arabs. The enemy chose this method in the belief that a lightning victory would lead to surrender, according to the pattern of 1948, and not to Arab armed resistance. In dealing with it, we must adopt a method derived from elements of strength in ourselves and elements of weakness in the enemy.

3. The enemy consists of three interdependent forces:

a) Israel.

b) World Zionism.

c) World imperialism, under the direction of the United States of America.

Moreover, it is incontestable that world imperialism makes use of the forces of reaction linked with colonialism.

If we are to achieve victory and gain our objectives, we shall have to strike at the enemy wherever he may be, and at the nerve centres of his power. This is to be achieved through the use of military, political and economic weapons and information media, as part of a unified and comprehensive plan designed to sap his strength, scatter his forces, destroy the links between them and undermine their common objectives.

4. A long-drawn out battle has the advantage of allowing us to expose world Zionism, its activities, conspiracies, and its complicity with world imperialism and to point out the damage and complications it causes to the interests and the security of many countries, and the threat it constitutes to world peace. This will eventually unmask it, bringing to light the grotesque facts of its true nature, and will isolate it from the centres of power and establish safeguards against its ever reaching them...

5. An information campaign must be launched that will throw light on the following facts:

a) The true nature of the Palestinian war is that of a battle between a small people, which is the Palestinian people, and Israel, which has the backing of world Zionism and world imperialism.

b) This war will have its effect on the interests of any country that supports Israel or world Zionism.

c) The hallmark of the Palestinian Arab people is resistance, struggle and liberation, that of the enemy, aggression, usurpation and the disavowal of all values governing decent human relations.

6. A comprehensive plan must be drawn up to fuse the Arab struggle and the Palestinian struggle into a single battle. This requires concentrated ideological, information and political effort that will make it clear to the Arab nation that it can never enjoy peace or security until the tide of Zionist invasion is stemmed, and that its territory will be occupied piecemeal unless it deploys its resources in the battle, not to mention the extent to which the Zionist presence constitutes a drain on its resources and an impediment to the development of its society.

Palestinian action regards the Arab nation as a reserve fund of political, financial and human resources on which it can draw, and whose support and participation will make it possible to fight the successive stages in the battle.

7. The peoples and governments of the Arab nation must be made to understand that they are under an obligation to protect the Palestinian struggle so that it may be able to confront the enemy on firm ground and direct all its forces and capabilities to this confrontation, fully assured of its own safety and security. This obligation is not only a national duty, it is a necessity deriving from the fact that the Palestinian struggle is the vanguard in the defence of all

Arab countries, Arab territories and Arab aspirations.

8.   Any objective study of the enemy will reveal that his potential for endurance, except where a brief engagement is concerned, is limited. The drain on this potential that can be brought about by a long-drawn out engagement will inevitably provide the opportunity for a decisive confrontation in which the entire Arab nation can take part and emerge victorious.

It is the duty of Palestinians everywhere to devote themselves to making the Arab nation aware of these facts, and to propagating the will to struggle. It is also their duty to endure, sacrifice and take part in the struggle.

Practical Application in the Field of Armed Struggle:

1.   The Palestine Liberation Organization is a grouping of Palestinian forces in one national front for the liberation of the territory of Palestine through armed revolution.

2.   This Organization has its Charter which defines its objectives, directs its course and organizes its activities. The Organization also has a National Assembly and an Executive Command chosen by the National Assembly, which Command forms the supreme executive authority of the Organization, as defined by its constitution.

The Executive Committee shall draw up a unified general plan for Palestinian action at all levels and in all fields. This plan is to be implemented through the instruments of the revolution gathered in this Council, each of which must abide by the role assigned to it by this plan and by the decisions of the Command.

Proposals for the Creation of a Spurious Palestinian Entity:

The Zionist movement along with imperialism and its tool, Israel, is seeking to consolidate Zionist aggression against Palestine and the military victories won by Israel in 1948 and 1967, by establishing a Palestinian entity in the territories occupied during the June, 1967 aggression. This entity would owe its existence to the legitimization and perpetuation of the State of Israel, which is absolutely incompatible with the Palestinian Arab people's right to the whole of Palestine, their homeland. Such a spurious entity would in fact be an Israeli colony and would lead to the liquidation of the Palestinian cause once and for all to the benefit of Israel. The creation of such an entity would, moreover, constitute an interim stage during which Zionism could evacuate the territory of Palestine occupied during the June 5 war of its Arab inhabitants, as a preliminary step to incorporating it in the Israeli entity. In addition, this would lead to the creation of a subservient Palestinian Arab administration in the territories occupied during the June 5 war on which Israel could rely in combating the Palestinian revolution. Also to be considered in this context are imperialist and Zionist schemes to place the Palestinian territories occupied since June 5 under international administration and protection. For these reasons, the National Assembly hereby declares its categorical rejection of the idea of establishing a spurious Palestinian entity in the territory of Palestine occupied since June 5, and of any form of international protection. The Assembly hereby declares, moreover, that any individual or party, Palestinian Arab or non-Palestinian, who advocates or supports the creation of such a subservient entity is the enemy of the Palestinian Arab people and the Arab nation.

(C) — Palestinian Struggle in the International Field:

The Security Council Resolution and the Peaceful Solution:

1. The Security Council resolution of November 22, 1967 is hereby rejected for the following reasons:

a) The resolution calls for the cessation of the state of hostility between the Arab nations and Israel. This entails the cessation of the state of hostility, free passage for Israeli shipping through Arab waterways, and an Arab commitment to put an end to the boycott of Israel, including the abrogation of all Arab legislation regulating that boycott. The cessation of the state of hostility also entails the relaxation of economic pressure on Israel, so that the door would be opened to an invasion of all Arab markets by Israeli goods, inasmuch as such goods could circulate, be traded in and flood the market regardless of whether or not economic agreements were concluded.

b) The resolution calls for the establishment of secure frontiers to be agreed upon with Israel. Apart from the fact that secure and mutually agreed frontiers involves the de facto recognition of Israel, and an encroachment on the unconditional right of the Palestinian Arab people to the whole of Palestine, which is totally unacceptable to the Arab countries, if the Arab countries agreed to secure frontiers for Israel, they would be committed to protecting Israel's security, after having first suppressed commando action, put an end to the Palestinian revolution and prevented the Palestinian Arab people and the Arab masses from discharging their sacred national duty to liberate and recover Palestine and to terminate the Zionist and imperialist presence there.

c) The resolution calls for the establishment of permanent peace between the Arab nations and Israel. This would have the following injurious consequences:

1. It would provide Israel with security and stability at domestic, Arab and international levels. This would throw the doors wide open to the Zionist movement, allowing it to entice large sections of Jewish communities in Western Europe and America into immigrating and settling in Israel. These communities have held back from doing so for the past twenty years because of misgivings about the security, future and continued existence of Israel.

2.   It would eliminate the reasons, including Arab influence, for which friendly nations have so far not allowed their Jewish citizens to immigrate to Israel, notably in the case of the millions of Jews in the Soviet Union.

3.   It would eliminate all reasons for which many countries friendly to the Arabs have refrained from recognising Israel or from dealing with Israel at all levels.

4.   It would strengthen the human and geographic barrier that separates the Arab homeland into east and west. This would be extremely injurious, as it would prevent the achievement of even partial, not to mention total, Arab unity.

5.   It would be a severe blow to the Palestinian armed struggle and to the Arab liberation movement whose objectives are liberation, social progress and unity. The consequence of this would be increased imperialist influence in the Arab homeland, accompanied by increased Zionist influence, in view of the organic political, economic, and other ties linking Zionism to imperialism. Arab policy would, as a result, be forced away from the line of neutrality and non-alignment.

6.   The resolution ignores the Palestine problem, which it does not even mention by name, and ignores the rights of the Arabs of Palestine to their territories and their homeland, referring to both as if the problem was merely a problem of refugees. This presages the final liquidation of the issue of Palestine as an issue of a land and of a homeland.

7.   It was not only territory that the Arab nation lost in June, 1967. Arab dignity and self-confidence were also involved. A peaceful solution might restore some, or even all of those territories to the Arabs, but it would not restore their dignity and self-confidence.

8.   The Arab nation must come to realise that it is under an inescapable obligation to defend its homeland, and not to rely on others for its protection or for the recovery of its territories and its rights. If the Arab countries accept a peaceful solution they will be renouncing the Arab will and agreeing that their destiny should be under the control of the Great Powers.

9.   A peaceful solution might lead the Arab countries to imagine themselves to be secure. Israel would certainly exploit this illusion to strike again, after creating a political situation more to her liking, and thus realize her expansionist designs on the territories of the Arab countries.

For these reasons the National Assembly calls on the newly elected Executive Committee to draft a comprehensive plan operative at Arab popular, official and international levels, designed to frustrate any political solution of the Palestine problem.

The Assembly affirms, moreover, that the aggression against the Arab nation, and the territories of that nation, began with the Zionist invasion of Palestine in 1917, and that, as a consequence "the elimination of the conse-

quences of the aggression" must signify the elimination of all such consequences since the beginning of the Zionist invasion and not merely since the
June, 1967 war. The slogan "the elimination of the consequences of the aggression" is therefore rejected in its present form, and must be replaced by the
slogan, "the destruction of the instrument of aggression". Thus, and thus
alone, will "peace based on justice" be established.

4. Palestinian National Council Statement, Cairo, 13 July, 1971

[Statement issued 13 July by the Palestine National Council on its ninth
session]

The Palestine National Council held its ninth session in Cairo from 7 to 13
July 1971 during extremely difficult conditions and amid increasing plotting
against the Palestine revolution. The council members discussed the demands
of the current stage of the Palestine revolution, at a time when the Jordanian
authorities are attacking the Palestine revolution bases and our heroic fighters
in 'Ajlun, Jarash, and the Ghazzah camp.

In addition to tackling the mission entrusted to it, the council adopted the
measures to deal with the situation. These measures have been announced.

The ninth session of the Palestine National Council was distinguished by
several progressive steps toward national unity. The following are the most
important:

1 — In its new form, the council is more representative of the various sectors
than past councils. All the fedayeen organizations without exception participated in it and representation of the trade union organizations has been increased.

2 — The council has affirmed the national unity formula as approved by the
eighth session and has adopted new practical decisions to achieve unity of the
revolution forces in all fields of command, organization, training, arms, and
combat orders. It has also approved the establishment of a unified council for
information and a unified system of collection and expenditure of funds.

3 — On the basis of and in complete response to these stands, the Executive
Committee was elected as supreme command of the Palestine revolution.
Representation of the various fighting organizations on the committee has
been widened to insure more collective action and bar individual action and
also to insure the participation of all forces in facing the dangerous conditions
threatening the Palestine revolution and people.

The first point the council dealt with was the serious situation facing the
revolution in Jordan. In view of the Jordanian regime's insistence on striking
and foiling the revolution, the council censured the policy of suppression and
terrorization exercised by the Jordanian authorities and the regional
fanaticism resulting from this policy. This policy has produced and continues

to produce serious negative effects on the cause of national unity in the Palestine-Jordanian arena, which in practice lead to the weakening of the masses' unity and the denial of the revolution's right to represent the Palestine people and to seek the realization of their aspirations for the liberation of their usurped land.

The council has censured the successive obstacles that the Jordanian authorities have been placing to prevent the fighters from proceeding to their occupied land. These obstacles include beseiging of the revolution bases and intercepting the revolution's supply convoys and armed men returning from military operations in the occupied territory.

The council condemns the recurrent disregard for the Palestine revolution's right to exercise its basic duty, and declares that several aspects of this duty have been regulated by the Cairo and Amman agreements. The council demands adherence to these agreements. It calls on the Arab States that signed these agreements to take the stands they pledged to take in order to guarantee implementation of the two agreements. It also calls on these states to stop financial aid to the Jordanian authority, which continues to disregard and violate these agreements, and to use this aid for its intended purpose — the liberation of Palestine from the imperialist onslaught against Arab land.

The council supports the efforts by the Jordanian nationalist forces to establish a cohesive nationalist front working to reinforce the march of the Palestine revolution and protect it against anyone plotting against it.

While it finds itself committed to the defense of the national rights of our people in Jordan and seeks to consolidate the unity of the two banks as one of its objectives, the Palestine revolution affirms through its National Council that the consolidation of this unity cannot take place through the practices of the Jordanian authorities, which encourage separatist and regional learnings, but only through strengthening the cohesion of the people and unifying their efforts for the sake of liberation. This cohesion and unity should be based on national and democratic foundations.

The second point the council dealt with was the danger of a political settlement. The council discussed the extensive current efforts to implement a settlement, particularly the activities of U.S. imperialism in imposing itself on the Middle East and creating deceptive conditions leading only to the liquidation of the palestine issue.

The council reaffirms its stand based on the permanent upholding of the Palestine people's full rights to liberate their land through popular armed struggle and on the reaffirmation of categorical rejection of all capitulationist settlements and of plans that harm the natural and historic rights of the Palestine people, including UN Security Council resolution No. 242 of 22 November 1967.

The Palestine National Council expresses the will of the Palestine people and their determination to continue their armed struggle until the achievement of all their national aims, despite the viciousness of the conspiratorial onslaught against the Palestine revolution.

While it is continuing its struggle and sacrifices, the Palestine revolution always looks to the Arab masses and their nationalist forces and the national liberation movements in the world to perform their duty in one of the most ferocious battles waged by a peaceful people against Zionist and imperialist forces and their agents in the Arab area.

5. Palestinian National Council Political Program, Cairo, 12 January, 1973 [Excerpts]

1. The Palestinian Theatre

1. To continue the battle and the armed struggle for the total liberation of the soil of the Palestinian homeland and for the establishment of the democratic Palestinian society in which all citizens will enjoy the right to work and to a decent life, so that they may live in equality, justice and brotherhood, and which will be opposed to all kinds of ethnic, racial and religious fanaticism.

This society will also ensure freedom of opinion, assembly, demonstration, and the freedom to strike and form political and trade union institutions and to practise all religions, inasmuch as this Palestinian society will be part of the comprehensive unified Arab democratic society.

2. To struggle against the settlement mentality and the projects it harbours either for the liquidation of our people's cause as far as the liberation of our homeland is concerned or for the distortion of this cause by proposals for entities and for the establishment of a Palestinian State — in part of the territory of Palestine; and to resist these proposals through armed struggle and through mass political conflict linked with it.

3. To strengthen the links of national unity and unity in struggle between the masses of our countrymen in the territory occupied in 1948 and those in the West Bank, the Gaza Strip and outside the occupied territory.

4. To oppose the policy of evacuating the Arab population of the occupied territory, and to resist with violence the building of settlements and the Judaization of parts of the occupied homeland.

5. To mobilize the masses in the West Bank, the Gaza Strip and the whole of Palestinian territory, to arm them to continue the struggle, and to increase their ability to struggle against Zionist settler colonialism.

6. To assist the organizations of the masses to resist the attempts by the Histadrut to attract Arab workers to join it and strengthen it, and with this end in view to support the trade unions of Palestine and Jordan and to resist

the effort of the Zionist parties to establish Arab branches in the occupied territories.

7.   To support the endurance of workers working in Arab territory and institutions, to provide safeguards to protect them against the temptation to work in enemy projects, and to resist the enemy's attempts to take over or smash Arab production projects.

, 8.   To support the peasant masses and to promote national economic and cultural institutions in the occupied homeland, so as to attach Arab citizens to the land and check the trend to emigrate, and to resist Zionist economic and cultural aggression.

9.   To show concern for the situation of our countrymen in the territory occupied in 1948 and to support their struggle to maintain their Arab national identity, to take up their problems, and to assist them to join the struggle for liberation.

10.   To show concern for the interests of the masses of our people working in different parts of the Arab homeland, and to make every effort to ensure that they obtain economic and legal rights equal to those of the citizens of the societies they live in, especially as regards the right to work, compensation, indemnities, freedom for Palestinian action, both political and cultural, and freedom of travel and movement within the framework of maintaining their Palestinian personality.

11.   To promote and develop the role of the Palestinian woman in the struggle at social, cultural and economic levels and to ensure that she plays her part in all fields of the struggle.

12.   To show concern for the situation of our countrymen in the camps and to make every effort to raise their economic, social and civilizational levels, and to train them to manage their own affairs.

13.   To regard anyone who cooperates with the enemy, joins him in his crimes against the people and the homeland, or neglects the established historical and natural rights of the people and the homeland, as a fit object for attack by the revolution, as regards both his person and his possessions, whether these be money, immovable property or land.

14.   To show concern for the situation of our masses who live abroad as emigrants, and to make every effort to link them with their cause and their revolution.

15.   In its official Arab relations the Liberation Organization concentrates on protecting the interests of Palestinian citizens in the Arab homeland and expressing the political will of the Palestinian people, and the Palestinian revolution, within the framework of the Palestine Liberation Organization, will continue to be the highest command of the Palestinian people; it alone speaks on their behalf on all problems related to their destiny, and it alone, through its organizations for struggle, is responsible for everything related to

the Palestinian people's right to self-determination.

16. Therefore the Palestine Liberation Organization consists of all the sections of the armed Palestinian revolution, of the Palestinian mass organizations, both trade union and cultural, and of all nationalist groups and personalities that believe that armed struggle is the principal and fundamental course to the liberation of Palestine, and that adhere to the Palestinian National Charter.

II.   The Jordanian-Palestinian Theatre

It is the duty of the Jordanian-Palestinian national front to direct the struggle of the two people towards the following strategic objectives:

a)   To establish a national democratic regime in Jordan, and to liberate the whole of Palestinian soil from Zionist occupation and establish a national democratic regime that will ensure the protection of the national sovereignty of the Jordanian and Palestinian peoples and guarantee the renewal and restoration of the unity of the two banks on the basis of regional national equality between the two peoples. In this way it will fully safeguard the historical national rights of the Palestinian people and the established national rights of the two peoples, ensure their joint national development at economic, social and civilizational levels and strengthen brotherly relations and equality between the two peoples through equality of constitutional, legal, cultural and economic rights and by placing the human, economic and civilizational resources of each of the two peoples at the disposal of their joint development.

b)   To weld the struggle of the Palestinian and Jordanian peoples to the struggle of the Arab nation for national liberation and against imperialist projects designed to impose solutions and situations involving surrender of the Arab homeland, the struggle to liquidate the Zionist and imperialist presence in all its forms, economic, military and cultural, and all forces linked thereto, which play the role of go-between for neo-colonialist infiltration.

So that the Jordanian-Palestinian national front may be effectively established and be strengthened and grow, it is essential that an immediate start should be made on activating all kinds of day-by-day mass struggle, so that the movement of the masses on behalf of both their day-by-day- and general demands may lead to the emergence among them of organized leaderships and organizations that will express the interests of their various groups — leaderships and organizations that have been absent from the day-by-day battles of the masses in recent years.

Also, for the objectives of the Jordanian-Palestinian national front to be achieved, there must be a long and hard struggle, so that through day-by-day struggle and partial battles the masses may surmount all regional and social obstacles and be fused in a joint struggle. Such a struggle will enable the masses to play their part as fighters for the national cause, and will expose the subservient royalist regime whose basic support lies in the tribal relationships and regional bigotry which it employs as a mask to disguise its subservience to Zionism and colonialism.

The Jordanian-Palestinian national front which is striving to establish a national democratic regime in Jordan and to liberate Palestine must activate and direct the popular struggle on all the different fronts of the clash between the masses and the Jordanian authorities, employing appropriate slogans in the day-by-day battles, so as to forge a permanent link between these partial battles and its general objectives and so as to direct both the bayonets with which it fights and the consequences it achieves into the channel of the general struggle of the two peoples.

The Palestine Liberation Organization adopts the programme of action in the Jordanian theatre and submits it as a subject for serious comradely dialogue with the organizations in Jordan which are engaged in the struggle for the building of the Jordanian-Palestinian front, and which must engage in struggle:

1. To mobilize and organize the masses with a view to establishing a national democratic regime which will ensure that the revolution in Jordan is provided with all the means necessary for engaging in mass struggle.

2. To bring the members of the Jordanian people into the armed struggle against the Zionist enemy, this being a right at both local and Arab levels, and essential for the protection of Eastern Jordan in particular.

3. To struggle to achieve freedom for the Palestinian revolution to act in and from Jordan and to establish its bases in Jordanian territory, and to expose the conspiracies of the subservient regime and its misrepresentations in this connection, and to ensure protection by the masses of combatants who operate from and return to the territory west of the River.

4. To resist terrorist police measures and all aggressions against the freedoms and rights of citizens to expose and resist imperialist capitalists; to show up and resist the infiltration of Zionist political, economic and cultural domination; to resist all increases in taxes and prices; to expose the laws which disseminate a spirit of separatism between members of the two peoples; to disclose the deliberately repressive role of the army; to show up subservient and hostile elements and plans directed against the masses and other Arab countries instead of such efforts being directed to the battle of liberation; to make every effort to activate mass struggles of all kinds; to encourage the struggle of the workers, the agricultural, industrial, commercial and nationalist sectors, the peasants, the Beduin, the wage-earners, the intellectuals and students.

5. To make every effort to ensure that the Jordanian-Palestinian front has an active share in a single front of struggle to strengthen relations between the Palestinian and Jordanian national struggle and world revolutionary forces.

6. Statements by General Secretary Hawatma of the PDFLP Defending the Establishment of a Palestinial National Authority in Territories Liberated from Israeli Occupation. Beirut, 24 February, 1974

We know that American imperialism seeks a settlement of surrender and liquidation to the detriment of the rights of the people of Palestine, a settlement that would, once again, expose our people to the dangers of dispersal and subjection, caught between Zionism, expansionism and subjection to the Hashimites. Imperialism believes that the interests of the Palestinian people are best served within the framework of Zionist expansion, with Israel not returning to the borders of June 4, 1967, and that they are best served by dissolving the Palestinian people once more in the proposed United Kingdom and in places of their exile in the Arab countries and abroad. Imperialism further presents schemes for dissolution, resettlement and relocation in the countries of the region. Our position with regard to these schemes is clear.

Yes, we are Arabs but we are, at the same time, Palestinians. Just as every Arab people has a full right to an independent national existence, so the Palestinian people too has a full right to an independent national existence and to fight all schemes which agree with American imperialist schemes, for these latter seek to obliterate our national existence and refuse to grant it prior recognition.

Knowing all this, we still find opportunistic currents of thought which at times counsel wisdom and at others call upon us to remain within the framework of nationalist unity, such as took place with the regime of King Hussein. We also find leftist opportunist Palestinian opinions attempting to obscure their true positions, which do not in the least lead to a clash with imperialism, Zionism and Arab and Hashimite reaction, by putting forth bombastic slogans ("The whole of Palestine at once", "Palestinian territories liberated from occupation are to go to the regime of King Hussein"). Our answer to these currents of thought is: They shall not succeed in directing the attention of the revolution from its objectives at this stage. Our people, our revolutionary bases and all the vanguard of the revolution know well that they must submit a pragmatic programme which puts the Palestinian people as a whole, the revolution as a whole and the movement for Arab national liberation against the American-Israeli-Hashimite solution of surrender and liquidation, together with any other solution presented by any Arab country which ignores our people's national and historic rights at this stage.

... We are fighting to end occupation and to stand effectively against imperialist solutions. We are fighting for our people's right to establish their national authority on their own land after the occupation has been ended. We also maintain that the logic of events in the world today demands that we inflict more defeats upon imperialism and racist regimes, whether in Palestine, Rhodesia or South Africa. And while these regimes came into existence at a certain historical stage, our own age is witnessing the end of that stage. We are entering upon a new age whose basic feature is further defeats for imperialism, local reaction and racist regimes. To inflict further defeats upon these regimes, we must follow a correct international policy which enables our people to become self-reliant and stand on its own land. This is a necessary step if the struggle is to continue on the long path ahead, the path of a long popular war of liberation. We know the road well and shall not allow these opportunistic currents, both of the left and the right, both in the Palestinian and in the Arab fields, to lead us astray by endangering the rights of our people and making us surrender.

These opportunistic forces do not have a leg to stand on. At times they claim that a national authority would not have the means necessary for economic subsistence and would not be able to survive on the West Bank and in the Gaza Strip. To these opportunists we answer that we are not at the stage of searching for a homeland. Over there is our homeland, even if it is a desert with nothing but thorn and sand. There is our homeland, whether it has the economic means of survival or not, although we should bear in mind that the economic potentialities of Palestinian territories occupied after 1967 are greater and more promising than those of many African and Asian countries, for example, Democratic Yemen. If we adopt this lunatic theory, half of Africa and the greater part of Asia would have been bound to fight to keep imperialism in their countries until such time as their economic means of subsistence would have allowed them to become independent.

7. Palestinian National Council, Cairo, Political Programme, 8 June, 1974

Proceeding from the Palestinian national charter and the PLO's political programme which was approved during the 11th session held from 3 to 12 January 1973, believing in the impossibility of the establishment of a durable and just peace in the area without the restoration to our Palestinian people of all their national rights, foremost of which is their right to return to and determine their fate on all their national soil, and in the light of the study of the political circumstances which arose during the period between the Council's previous and current sessions, the Council decides the following:

1.   The assertion of the PLO position regarding Resolution 242 is that it obliterates the patriotic [wataniyah] and national [qawmiyah] rights of our people and deals with our people's cause as a refugee problem. Therefore, dealing with this resolution on this basis is rejected on any level of Arab and international dealings, including the Geneva conference.

2.   The PLO will struggle by all means, foremost of which is armed struggle, to liberate Palestinian land and to establish the people's national, independent and fighting authority on every part of Palestinian land to be liberated. This necessitates making more changes in the balance of power in favor of our people and their struggle.

3.   The PLO will struggle against any plan for the establishment of a Palestinian entity the price of which is recognition, conciliation, secure borders, renunciation of the national right, and our people's deprivation of their right to return and their right to determine their fate on their national soil.

4.   Any liberation step that is achieved constitutes a step for continuing [the efforts] to achieve the PLO strategy for the establishment of the Palestinian democratic State that is stipulated in the resolutions of the previous national councils.

5.   To struggle with the Jordanian national forces for the establishment of a Jordanian-Palestinian national front whose aim is the establishment of a national democratic government in Jordan — a government that will cohere with the Palestinian entity to be established as a result of the struggle.

6.   The PLO will strive to establish a unity of struggle between the two peoples [the Palestinian and Jordanian peoples] and among all the Arab liberation movement forces that agree on this programme.

7.   In the light of this programme, the PLO will struggle to strengthen national unity and to elevate it to a level that will enable it to carry out its duties and its patriotic [wataniyah] and national [qawmiyah] tasks.

8.   The Palestinian national authority, after its establishment, will struggle for the unity of the confrontation states for the sake of completing the liberation of all Palestinian soil and as a step on the path of comprehensive Arab unity.

9.   The PLO will struggle to strengthen its solidarity with the socialist countries and the world forces of liberation and progress to foil all Zionist, reactionary and imperialist schemes.

10. In the light of this programme, the revolutionary command will work out the tactics that will serve and lead to the achievement of these aims.

A recommendation has been added to the political programme. The recommendation stipulates that the Executive Committee implement this programme. Should a fateful situation connected with the future of the Palestinian people arise, the Council will be called to hold a special session to decide on it.

During today's meeting, the Council approved by a large majority the political statement that asserted the Palestinian people's rallying around the PLO which is the only legitimate representative of the Palestinian people. The statement says: In the period from the time the Palestinian National Council convened its session from 3 to 12 January 1973 to the current session, from 1 to 8 July 1974, the Arab area witnessed a number of important and fateful events and developments, most prominent of which was the October war and its results which have strengthened the position and role of the Arab nation and which has been a step on the path of defeating the imperialist-Zionist enemy camp. In the wake of this, a sharp contradiction emerged between the Arab liberation movement and the enemies of our Arab nation who are trying to go around the achievements of the October war and to impose a political settlement at the expense of our Palestinian people's rights and jeopardize their future struggle and the struggle of our Arab nation.

On the level of our people's and revolution's movement, the Palestinian revolution emerged as a principal active force during and after the war. The movement of our masses inside and outside the occupied territories assumed important and new dimensions in confronting the imperialist, Zionist and reactionary plots by escalating the political and military struggle, especially after the bases of the Palestinian national front expanded in the occupied territories and after the PLO command expanded its political move resulting in a wide-scale world recognition of the PLO as the only legitimate representative of the Palestinian people. At the same time, the isolation of the Jordanian reactionary monarchical regime intensified, especially after the October war had revealed the regime's role of collusion with the enemies of our people and nation. This regime was not only content with its refusal to participate in the war but it also prevented the Palestinian revolution forces from playing their military role across Jordanian territory and it killed and captured many of our fighters.

In confronting these circumstances, our Palestinian people rally around the PLO, the only legitimate representative of the Palestinian people who adhere to the national charter, the political programme adopted during the 11th session, all the resolutions of the national councils, and the phasic political programme that is approved during this session. Therefore, they are determined to continue the struggle, to escalate the armed struggle and to strongly resist the Zionist occupation, the Jordanian reactionary monarchical regime's plots represented by the united Arab kingdom plan, and the imperialist schemes parallel to it.

Our people also resist any settlement that jeopardizes their rights and cause, and struggle to preserve their revolution's gains. In order to achieve this, the National Council believes that the following must be emphasized:

1. Achieving the unity of the aims of the Palestinian revolution by promoting the formulas for Palestinian national unity and implementing all the resolutions in respect in the various political, military, information and financial fields will be conducive to escalating the armed struggle, to achieving the unity of our Palestinian people inside and outside the homeland and to reinforcing the Palestinian national front inside the homeland so that it will

express our people's struggle and be a framework for all their struggles, especially because this front, as a fundamental base of the PLO inside the occupied territories, has played an effective role during the period following the October war. This calls for giving strong support to it and to all the popular establishments and organizations operating through it.

2. As the Palestinian national movement is part of the Arab liberation movement, this calls for exerting all efforts to achieve greater cohesion between the Palestinian struggle and the Arab struggle and for achieving an advanced form of joint action between them through the Arab front participating in the Palestinian revolution and for translating the requirements of the fateful stage through which it is passing. This also calls for coordination among the nationalist Arab regimes to place them face to face with their responsibilities toward the cause of our Palestinians. It is necessary here to refer to the significance of the Arab solidarity which emerged during the October war and the need for its continuation and for adherence to the resolutions of the Arab summit conference held in Algiers in November 1973.

3. The stand of the socialist countries and the forces of liberation and progress in the world in supporting the cause of our people and nation requires further efforts to achieve stronger cohesion with these forces. In this regard, we should concentrate on expanding the front of our friends.

4. The Lebanese arena, which the Palestinian revolution is eager to keep strong and cohesive by strengthening the form of existing relations between the Lebanese and Palestinian peoples and out of the Palestinian people's care for the need to preserve the peace and security of fraternal Lebanon, requires constant and strong support by all the Arab countries to enable it to continue to stand fast against the enemy's aggression and expansionist ambitions and to enable our brothers in southern Lebanon and our people in their camps to stand fast against the enemy's aggression and his attempts to hit this steadfastness.

5. The reactionary monarchical regime in Jordan, with all the history of its policy which is hostile to our people and nation, and which refused to fight the October war on the side on our Arab nation, is now plotting in complete coordination with Zionism and imperialism with the aim of liquidating and obliterating the Palestinian national character and in order to redominate our people in the occupied territory at any price. To confront this, the struggle must be intensified to isolate this regime and to make national democratic rule in Jordan.

6. The Palestinian National Council appeals to all peoples and governments in the world which love peace and justice and all forces of liberation and progress in the world to struggle against the activities of world Zionism [seeking] further immigration of world Jewry to occupied Palestine which contributes to the strengthening of the colonialist Zionist military establishment,

the achievement of Zionist aggressive and expansionist dreams and the continued Zionist defiance of our people's national rights and of the national [qawni] and patriotic [watani] entity of our people and Arab nation.

At the conclusion of its 12th session, the Council addresses a greeting of esteem to the martyrs of the Palestinian revolution and the Arab nation and a greeting of appreciation to our fighters and strugglers in the enemy prisons and in the prisons in Jordan. The Council hails the Egyptian and Syrian armies, the forces of the Palestinian revolution and the Arab countries which took part in the October war of liberation with their forces or their resources. The Council also values the solidarity of the Palestinian masses who have been under the occupation since 1948, the masses of the Arab nation linked with the struggle of the Arab armies as well as the alliance of the Arab liberation movement with the Palestinian revolution and the Arab front participating in the Palestinian revolution, particularly the Lebanese national and progressive movement.

The Council stresses its appreciation for the role of the socialist camp, particularly the Soviet Union and the PRC, in supporting the struggle of the Palestinian people and the Arab nation. The Council also appreciates the support of the Islamic countries, the nonalined countries, the African countries and the world liberation and progressive movements for the Palestinian people.

The Council regards the victory scored by the Vietnamese people as an incentive to our revolution and to all liberation movements in the world in order to further intensity the struggle to achieve the will of our people in liberation, progress and self-determination.

8. Statement by the PFLP Announcing Its Withdrawal from the Executive Committee of the PLO. Beirut, 26 September, 1974 [Excerpts]

We therefore wish to set before our Arab and Palestinian masses the reasons for our withdrawal from the Executive Committee so that the situation may be absolutely clear and that we may perform our duty of opening up the revolutionary road to the movement of the masses.

1. After the October war an international and Arab situation came into existence which was favourable to a so-called political settlement of the Arab-Israeli conflict. America was the power most enthusiastic for this settlement and made every effort to impose it, relying first and foremost on the approval of Egyptian and Saudi reaction. It was perfectly clear what results this settlement was likely to lead to: As the price for submitting Israel to every American pressure, America would be allowed to increase her influence and safeguard her interests in our territory. The price Israel would be paid for withdrawing

from all Arab territory would be support for her economy and armed forces, the reinforcement of her security and stability and steps towards the consolidation of the legality of her existence in the area. It is no longer possible to dispute this picture now that its consequences have taken tangible form before the eyes of the masses of our people.

In the light of this situation the Palestinian revolution should have submitted to all the Palestinian and Arab masses a precise analysis of this picture and its consequences, insisting that they be laid bare, fought against, and made known to all, so that our revolution might be the torch of the revolution for millions of Arabs rather than a cover for the laxness and surrenderism of certain of their rulers.

Since the October war ended and the picture of the imperialist liquidationist conspiracy has taken shape, the Front has called on the Palestine revolution to announce its analysis of the new political situation, to declare its opposition to the liquidationist settlement and to affirm that it would not permit the Liberation Organization to be used as a cover for the laxness of certain surrenderist Arab regimes. The Palestinian revolution should have revealed the truth about the Geneva conference and the consequences it would lead to. It should have placed itself unambiguously outside the framework of this liquidationist settlement and continued to mobilize the masses to continue fighting for dozens of years, whatever is involved.

The value of the Palestine revolution is that it should provide the pattern in accordance with which the masses of the whole Arab nation can settle their conflict with their enemies by force of arms through a people's war of liberation, rather than through laxness and surrenderism under the auspices of a balance of forces which means that the price paid for every piece of land we recover is higher than the value of the land itself.

The Front has made every effort to ensure that this period should provide an opportunity to strengthen the revolution and consolidate its national unity on the basis of the unambiguous and definitive rejection of the Geneva conference and the liquidationist conspiracy, and of continuing on the line of revolution. But the leadership of the Organization has persistently evaded defining any attitude, on the pretext that they have not been officially invited to attend the Geneva conference, although there has been every indication that many international and Arab forces want to contain the Organization and to frustrate its revolution by forcing it on to the road of surrender.

The Organization has maintained an attitude that is no attitude thereby losing its vigour for revolutionary action and influence in Palestinian, Arab and international circles.

2. On the eve of the twelfth session of the Palestine National Council which was held in Cairo last June, the leadership of the Liberation Organization started talking about national unity and its importance at this stage. It

showed that it was prepared to move from an attitude which was no attitude to an attitude of (temporary) refusal to attend the Geneva conference, employing a deceitful "tactic" aimed at suggesting to the forces that reject the settlement that it knew the truth about the liquidationist conspiracy but that it wanted to frustrate it by cunning rather than by confrontation. Profoundly aware as it is of its responsibility for taking any opportunity to achieve national unity seriously in this critical situation, the Front decided to show that such an opportunity existed and to see what actual consequences it would lead to. This is why it gave its approval to the ten points, although in fact they were a compromise and threadbare formula for national unity, after having placed on record in the minutes of the session our understanding of them to the effect that they involved rejection of the Geneva conference and set the Liberation Organization outside the framework of the liquidationist settlement.

At the end of the twelfth session of the Palestine National Council it was clear what the surrenderist leaderships intended by their acceptance of the ten point programme. They regarded it as legalizing their pursuit of the course of deviation and surrender. They started to interpret it as they wished, later making statements as they wished, in a manner incompatible with the Organization's charter and with the resolutions adopted at the sessions of its National Council, including those adopted at the eleventh and twelfth sessions.

The deception was disclosed and it became clear that what the surrenderist forces were talking of was the tactics misleading fellow-travellers and the masses, rather than misleading the enemy.

We continued to struggle within the framework of the Liberation Organization and the Executive Committee in the hope of establishing a sound understanding of the Organization's charter and the resolutions of its national councils, but it daily became clearer to us that the leadership of the Organization was involved in the settlement operation and hope to impose it on the masses piecemeal and to continue on their course of deviation step by step in the hope of ultimately confronting the masses with a fait accompli.

3. The Leadership of the Liberation Organization started to represent the possibility of its attending the Geneva conference — "the conspiracy" — as a great victory won by it over Jordanian reaction and Israel. They also started to talk of the possibility of coordination with the reactionary subservient regime in Jordan if certain conditions were met, thereby coming into conflict with the resolutions of previous sessions of the National Council which insisted that the regime should be overthrown and a democratic nationalist regime established in its place. At a session of the Executive Committee held before the issue of the Egypt-Jordan joint communique, the Executive Committee decided to coordinate with the subservient regime of Jordan on condition that it recognized firstly the Palestine Liberation Organization as the sole legitimate representative of the Palestinian people and, secondly, the Cairo

Agreements, although these agreements did not prevent the subservient regime from destroying the resistance movement and putting an end to its overt presence. It might have been thought that the Palestine revolution had not had a long history of experience of this regime, and that the National Council had never adopted resolutions calling for the regime to be blockaded until it collapsed totally.

4. It was not long after the National Council had ended its session, and the leadership of the Organization had interpreted its resolutions in so lax a manner that in fact they became the loyal followers of the surrenderist regimes, that the Egyptian-Jordanian communique came as a cruel slap in the face both to the leadership and its policy.

The issue of such a communique gave the leadership of the Organization a chance to face up to all the policies it had pursued since the October war in general and since the twelfth session of the National Council in particular. Three organizations represented on the Executive Committee of the Liberation Organization therefore presented a memorandum to the leadership of the Organization calling on it to conduct an operation of reappraisal and criticism, with a view to learning the lessons taught by past experience and defining its relations with the Arab regimes in the light of their attitudes to the imperialist liquidation proposal, and on the basis of reliance mainly on the masses of our Arab nation rather than on the agents of America in the area. But the leadership of the Organization persisted in its deviationist view of things. Heedless of the truth of the points raised in the memorandum, it refused to accept them, and maintained its previous policy. It conceived the idea that its principle battle was not that against the imperialist liquidation solution with a view to frustrating it and to insisting on the continuation of Palestinian and Arab combat, but a battle over its share in the settlement operation as compared with the share of the subservient regime in Jordan.

5. The leadership of the Liberation Organization is now trying to make our masses forget their essential national battle, which concerns the imperialist liquidationist settlement and the need to frustrate it. It is making every effort to distract the attention of the masses from their principal battle so that they may devote all their attention to the battles of the leadership of the Liberation Organization with the subservient Jordanian regime over its share in the settlement. It wants the masses to rally sympathetically around it if the Jordanian regime gets a larger share at its expense, and to applaud it if it gets a larger share at the expense of the subservient Jordanian regime — and all this within the framework of the imperialist liquidationist settlement.

The leadership of the Liberation Organization is at present making every effort to make out that the battle is exclusively between Israel and Jordan on the one hand and the Liberation Organization on the other and to suggest that in that battle it is entitled to seek any allies and to enjoy the support of the masses. We hereby declare most emphatically that this is a grave distortion of the battle and of the understanding of the conflicts. The battle is a continuous one and is being fought between Israel, Jordan, Arab reaction and the surrenderist forces on the one hand and the Palestinian and Arab revolution on the other, and no power on earth will be able to keep this fact from the masses.

The Palestinian masses do not want the leadership of the Liberation Organization to win their battles against Jordanian reaction within the framework of the settlement, so that it may compete with the subservient regime in negotiating with the Israeli enemy.

The Palestinian masses want the leadership of the Liberation Organization to win their battles against all the forces that are seeking to impose this imperialist liquidation settlement so that they may continue their popular revolution against Israel, the subservient regime in Jordan, imperialism and all reactionary surrenderist forces.

6. The leadership of the Liberation Organization ignored the memorandum of the three organizations, and when it had had time enough to anaesthetize and deceive the masses it attended a tripartite conference in Cairo. This the advocates of a settlement represented as being a major victory for the Liberation Organization, although the communique issued after the conference makes no mention of opposition to disengagement on the Jordanian front; indeed, it stresses the need for coordination with the other Arab countries, including the subservient regime in Jordan.

It was to be expected that the subservient rulers in Amman would make such an outcry and would suspend Jordan's political activities until the Arab summit conference meets. It can be easily understood in the context of the formula of competing over the share each party will obtain as a result of this settlement which America is conducting with the aim of imposing "permanent" stability in the area, while ensuring the continued existence of Israel and safeguarding her security and stability.

Our masses will not allow deceptions and play-acting to be foisted on them again. They are not prepared to allow our battle to be restricted to the framework that the leadership of the Liberation Organization is now establishing so as to ensure sympathy for itself if it gets a smaller share in the settlement and applause if it gets a greater share.

7. Nor is this all. The leadership of the Liberation Organization has denied that any secret contacts have been made with America, the enemy of peoples. But we have established that such secret contacts have been made, without the knowledge of the masses. We submitted these facts to the Central Council of the Liberation Organization at its recent session, and we now place them before the Palestinian and Arab masses.

We regard this as amounting to secret contacts with the imperialist enemy without the knowledge of the masses of the revolution and its forces and bases.

If some commands have started to regard such contacts as normal and natural, we leave it to the masses to decide their own view and understanding and to make their own appraisal of this matter.

The Popular Front for the Liberation of Palestine, having become acquainted with these facts, would be failing in its duty to the masses if it did not place them at their disposal so that they may judge the situation in the light of them. The time is past when the commands could regard the masses of our people and the bases of their revolution as so many sheep.

8.   These are the most important reasons for our withdrawal from the Executive Committee. There are other reasons, but we do not wish, at this juncture, to touch on the organizational and administrative situation of the Liberation Organization. Nor do we wish to consider the repercussions of such a policy on a number of matters, such as the building of shelters, the fortification of the camps in Lebanon, and other issues.

In the light of the above, how can we continue to bear any responsibility within the framework of the Executive Committee?

Our withdrawal from the Executive Committee is now unavoidable.

9. The Speech of Yasser Arafat at the U.N., 13 November, 1974

Yasser Arafat, as the Chairman of the Executive Committee of the Palestine Liberation Organization, addressed the United Nations General Assembly on November 13, 1974, during the debate on Palestine. The following is a translation of the speech, originally delivered in Arabic.

Mr. President, I thank you for having invited the Palestine Liberation Organization to participate in the plenary session of the United Nations General Assembly. I am grateful to all those representatives of United Nations member states who contributed to the decision to introduce the question of Palestine as a separate item on the Agenda of this Assembly. That decision made possible the Assembly's resolution inviting us to address it on the question of Palestine.

This is a very important occasion. The question of Palestine is being reexamined by the United Nations, and we consider that step to be as much a victory for the world organization as it is for the cause of our people. It indicates anew that the United Nations of today is not the United Nations of the past, just as today's world is not yesterday's world. Today's United Nations represents 138 nations, a number that more clearly reflects the will of the international community. Thus today's United Nations is more capable of implementing the principles embodied in its Charter and in the Universal Declaration of Human Rights, as well as being more truly empowered to support causes of peace and justice.

Our people are now beginning to feel that change. Along with them, the peoples of Asia, Africa and Latin America also feel the change. As a result, the United Nations acquires greater esteem both in our people's view and in the view of other peoples. Our hope is thereby strengthened that the United Nations may contribute actively to the pursuit and triumph of the causes of peace, justice, freedom and independence. Our resolve to build a new world is fortified — a world free of colonialism, imperialism, neo-colonialism and racism in all its forms, including Zionism.

Our world aspires to peace, justice, equality and freedom. It hopes that oppressed nations, at present bent under the weight of imperialism, may gain their freedom and their right to self-determination. It hopes to place the relations between nations on a basis of equality, peaceful coexistence, mutual respect for each other's internal affairs, secure national sovereignty, independence and territorial unity on the basis of justice and mutual benefit. This world resolves that the economic ties binding it together should be grounded in justice, parity and mutual interest. It aspires finally to direct its human resources against the scourge of poverty, famine, disease and natural calamities, toward the development of productive scientific and technical capabilities to enhance human wealth — all this in the hope of reducing the disparity between the developing and the developed countries. But all such aspirations cannot be realized in a world that is at present ruled by tension, injustice, oppression, racial discrimination and exploitation, a world also threatened with unending economic disaster, wars and crises.

Many peoples, including those of Zimbabwe, Namibia, South Africa and Palestine, among many others, are still victims of oppression and violence. Their areas of the world are gripped by armed struggles provoked by imperialism and racial discrimination. These, both merely forms of aggression and terror, are instances of oppressed peoples compelled by intolerable circumstances into a confrontation with such oppression. But wherever that confrontation occurs it is legitimate and just.

It is imperative that the international community should support these peoples in their struggles, in the furtherance of their rightful causes and in the attainment of their right to self-determination.

In Indo-China the people are still exposed to aggression. They remain subjected to conspiracies preventing them from the enjoyment of peace and the realization of their goals. Although peoples everywhere have welcomed the peace agreements reached in Laos and South Vietnam, no one can say that genuine peace has been achieved, for the forces responsible in the first place for aggression are determined that Vietnam should remain in a state of disturbance and war. The same can be said of the present military aggression against the people of Cambodia. It is therefore incumbent on the international community to support these oppressed peoples, and also to condemn the oppressors for their designs against peace. Moreover, despite the positive stand taken by the Democratic Republic of Korea with regard to a peaceful and just solution of the Korean question, there is as yet no settlement of that question.

A few months ago the problem of Cyprus erupted violently before us. All peoples everywhere shared in the suffering of the Cypriots. We ask that the United Nations continue its efforts to reach a just solution in Cyprus, thereby sparing the Cypriots further war and ensuring peace and independence for them instead. Undoubtedly, however, consideration of the question of Cyprus belongs within that of Middle Eastern problems as well as of Mediterranean problems.

In their efforts to replace an outmoded but still dominant world economic system with a new, more logically rational one, the countries of Asia, Africa, and Latin America face implacable attacks on these efforts. These countries have expressed their views at the special session of the General Assembly on raw materials and development. Thus the plundering, exploitation, and the siphoning off of the wealth of impoverished peoples must be terminated forthwith. There must be no deterring of these peoples' efforts to develop and control their wealth. Furthermore, there is a grave necessity for arriving at fair prices for raw materials from these countries.

In addition, these countries continue to be hampered in the attainment of their primary objectives formulated at the Conference on the Law of the Sea at Caracas, at the population conference and at the Rome food conference. The United Nations should therefore bend every effort to achieve a radical alteration of the world economic system, making it possible for developing countries to advance rapidly. The United Nations must resolutely oppose forces that are trying to lay the responsibility for inflation on the shoulders of the developing countries, especially the oil-producing countries. The United Nations must firmly condemn any threats made against these countries simply because they demand their just rights.

The world-wide armaments race shows no sign of abating. As a consequence, the entire world is threatened with the dispersion of its wealth and the utter waste of its energies. Armed violence is made more likely everywhere. Peoples expect the United Nations to devote itself single-mindedly to putting an end to the armaments race; to convert the vast sums spent on military technology until the stage is reached where nuclear weapons are destroyed, and resources go into projects for development, for increasing production, and for benefiting the world.

And still, the highest tension exists in our part of the world. There the Zionist entity clings tenaciously to occupied Arab territory; the Zionist entity is holding on to the Arab territories is has occupied and persisting in its aggressions against us. New military preparations are feverishly being made. These anticipate another, fifth war of aggression to be launched against us.

Such signs behoove the closest possble watching, since there is a grave likelihood that this war would forbode nuclear destruction and cataclysmic annihilation.

The world is in need of tremendous efforts if its aspirations to peace, freedom, justice, equality and development are to be realized, if its struggle is to be victorious over colonialism, imperialism, neo-colonialism and racism in all its forms, including Zionism. Only by such efforts can actual form be given to the aspirations of all peoples, including the aspirations of peoples whose states oppose such efforts. It is this road that leads to the fulfillment of those principles emphasized by the United Nations Charter and the Universal Declaration of Human Rights. Were the status quo simply to be maintained, however, the world would instead be exposed to the most dangerous armed conflicts, in addition to economic, human and natural calamities.

Despite abiding world crises, despite the powers of darkness and backwardness that beset the world, we live in a time of glorious change. An old world order is crumbling before our eyes, as imperialism, colonialism, neo-colonialism and racism, the chief form of which is Zionism, ineluctably perish. We are witnessing a great wave of history bearing peoples forward into a new world which they have created. In that world just causes will triumph. Of that we are confident.

The question of Palestine is crucial amongst those just causes fought for unstintingly by masses labouring under imperialism and oppression. I am aware that, if I am given the opportunity to address the General Assembly, so too must the opportunity be given to all liberation movements fighting against racism and imperialism. In their names, in the name of every human being struggling for freedom and self-determination, I call upon the General Assembly urgently to give their just causes the same full attention the General Assembly has so rightly given to our cause. Such recognition once given, there will be a secure foundation thereafter for the preservation of universal peace. For only with such peace will a new world order endure in which peoples can live free of oppression, fear, injustice and exploitation. As I said earlier, this is the true perspective in which to set the question of Palestine. I shall now do so for the General Assembly, keeping firmly in mind both the perspective and the goal of a coming world order.

Even as today we address this General Assembly from an international rostrum we are also expressing our faith in political and diplomatic struggle as complements, as enhancements of armed struggle. Furthermore we express our appreciation of the role the United Nations is capable of playing in settling problems of international scope. But this capability, I said a moment ago, became real only once the United Nations had accommodated itself to the living actuality of aspiring peoples, towards which this international organization owes unique obligations.

In addressing the General Assembly today our people proclaims its faith in the future, unencumbered either by past tragedies or present limitations. If, as we discuss the present, we enlist the past in our service, we do so only to light up our journey into the future alongside other movements of national liberation. If we return now to the historical roots of our cause we do so because present at this very moment in our midst are those who, as they occupy our homes, as their cattle graze in our pastures, and as their hands pluck the fruit of our trees, claim at the same time that we are ghosts without an existence, without traditions or future. We speak of our roots also because until recently some people have regarded — and continue to regard — our problem as merely a problem of refugees. They have portrayed the Middle East question as little more than a border dispute between the Arab States and the Zionist entity. They have imagined that our people claim rights not rightfully their own and fight neither with logic nor legitimate motive, with a simple wish only to disturb the peace and to terrorize others. For there are amongst you — and here I refer to the United States of America and others like it — those who supply our enemy freely with planes and bombs and with every variety of murderous weapon. They take hostile positions against us, deliberately distorting the true essence of the problem. All this is done not only at our expense, but at the expense of the American people and its well-being, and of the friendship we continue to hope can be cemented between us and this great people, whose history of struggle for the sake of freedom and the unity of its territories we honour and salute.

I cannot now forego this opportunity of appealing from this rostrum directly to the American people, asking them to give their support to our heroic and fighting people. I ask them wholeheartedly to endorse right and justice, to recall George Washington to mind — heroic Washington whose purpose was his nation's freedom and independence, Abraham Lincoln, champion of the destitute and the wretched, and also Woodrow Wilson whose doctrine of Fourteen Points remains subscribed to and venerated by our people. I ask the American people whether the demonstrations of hostility and enmity taking place outside this great hall reflect the true intent of America's will? What, I ask you plainly, is the crime of the people of Palestine against the American people? Why do you fight us so? Does this really serve your interests? Does it serve the interests of the American masses? No, definitely not. I can only hope that the American people will remember that their friendship with the whole Arab nation is too great, too abiding, and too rewarding for any such demonstrations to harm it.

In any event, in focusing our discussion of the question of Palestine upon historical roots, we do so because we believe that any question now exercising the world's concern must be viewed radically, in the true sense of that word, if a real solution is ever to be grasped. We propose this radical approach as an antidote to an approach to international issues that obscures historical origins behind ignorance, denial and a slavish obedience to the fait accompli.

The roots of the Palestinian question reach back into the closing years of the nineteenth century, in other words, to that period which we call the era of colonialism and settlement and the transition to the eve of imperialism. This was when the Zionist imperialist plan was born: its aim was the conquest of Palestine by European immigration, just as settlers colonized, and indeed raided, most of Africa. This is the period during which, pouring forth out of the West, colonialism spread into the furthest reaches of Africa, Asia, and Latin America, building colonies everywhere, cruelly exploiting, oppressing, plundering the peoples of those three continents. This period persists into the present. Marked evidence of its totally reprehensible presence can be readily perceived in the racism practised both in South Africa and in Palestine.

Just as colonialism and the settlers dignified their conquests, their plunder and limitless attacks upon the natives of Africa and elsewhere, with appeals to a "civilizing mission", so too did waves of Zionist immigrants disguise their purposes as they conquered Palestine. Just as colonialism used religion, colour, race and language to justify the people's exploitation and its cruel subjugation by terror and discrimination, so too were these methods employed as Palestine was usurped and its people hounded from their national homeland.

Just as colonialism used the wretched, the poor the exploited as mere inert matter with which to build and to carry out settler colonialism, so too were destitute, oppressed European Jews employed on behalf of world imperialism and of the Zionist leadership. European Jews were transformed into the instruments of aggression; they became the elements of settler colonialism and racial discrimination.

Zionist ideology was utilized against our Palestinian people: the purpose was not only the establishment of Western-style settler colonialism but also the severing of Jews from their various homelands and subsequently their estrangement from their nations. Zionism is an ideology that is imperialistic, colonialist, racist; it is profoundly reactionary and discriminatory; it is united with anti-Semitism in its tenets and is the other side of the same coin. For when what is proposed is that adherents of the Jewish faith, regardless of their national residence, should neither owe allegiance to their homeland nor live on equal footing with its other, non-Jewish citizens — when that is proposed we hear anti-Semitism being proposed. When it is proposed that the only solution for the Jewish problem is that Jews must alienate themselves from communities or nations of which they have been a historical part, when it is proposed that Jews solve the Jewish problem by immigrating to and settling the land of another people by terrorism and force, this is exactly the same attitude as that of the anti-Semites to the Jews.

Thus, for instance, we can understand the close connection between

Rhodes, who promoted settler colonialism in Southeast Asia, and Herzl, who had colonialist designs upon Palestine. Having received a certificate of good settler conduct from Rhodes, Herzl then turned around and presented this certificate to the British government, hoping thus to secure a formal resolution supporting Zionist policy. In exchange, the Zionists promised Britain an imperialist base on Palestinian soil so that imperial interests could be safeguarded as the most important chief strategic point in the Middle East.

So the Zionist movement allied itself directly with world colonialism in a common raid on our land. Allow me now to present a selection of historical facts about this alliance.

The Jewish invasion of Palestine began in 1881. Before the first large wave of settlers started ariving, Palestine had a population of half a million, most of these Muslims or Christians, and about 10,000 Jews. Every sector of the population enjoyed the religious tolerance characteristics of our civilization.

Palestine was then a verdant land, inhabited by an Arab people in the course of building its life and enriching its indigenous culture.

Between 1882 and 1917 the Zionist movement settled approximately 50,000 European Jews in our homeland. To do that it resorted to trickery and deceit in order to plant them in our midst. Its success in getting Britain to issue the Balfour Declaration demonstrated the alliance between Zionism and colonialism. Furthermore, by promising to the Zionist movement what was not hers to give, Britain showed how oppressive the rule of colonialism was. As it was then constituted, the League of Nations abandoned our Arab people, and Wilson's pledges and promises came to nought. In the guise of a mandate, British colonialism was cruelly and directly imposed upon us. The mandate document issued by the League of Nations was to enable the Zionist invaders to consolidate their gains in our homeland.

In thirty years the Zionist movement succeeded, in collaboration with its colonialist ally, in settling more European Jews on the land, thus usurping the properties of Palestinian Arabs.

By 1947 the number of Jews had reached 600,000; they owned less than 6 per cent of Palestinian Arab land. The figure should be compared with the [Arab] population of Palestine, which at that time was 1,250,000.

As a result of the collusion between the mandatory power and the Zionist movement and with the support of the United States, this General Assembly early in its history approved a recommendation to partition our Palestinian homeland. This took place on November 30, 1947, in an atmosphere of questionable actions and strong pressure. The General Assembly partitioned what it had no right to divide — an indivisible homeland. When we rejected that decision, our position corresponded to that of the real mother who refused to permit Solomon to cut her child in two when the other woman claimed the child as hers. Furthermore, even though the partition resolution granted the colonialists settlers 54 per cent of the land of Palestine, their dissatisfaction with the decision prompted them to wage a war of terror against the civilian Arab population. They occupied 81 per cent of the total area of Palestine, uprooting a million Arabs. Thus, they occupied 524 Arab towns and villages, of which they destroyed 385, completely obliterating them in the process. Having done so, they built their own settlements and colonies on the ruins of our farms and our groves. The roots of the Palestine question lie here. Its causes do not stem from any conflict between two religions or two nationalisms. Nor is it a border conflict between neighbouring states. It is the cause of people deprived of its homeland, dispersed and uprooted, the majority of whom live in exile and in refugee camps.

With support from imperialist and colonialist powers, headed by the United States of America, this Zionist entity managed to get itself accepted as a United Nations member. It further succeeded in getting the Palestine question deleted from the Agenda of the United Nations and in deceiving world public opinion by presenting our cause as a problem of refugees in need either of charity from do-gooders, or settlement in a land not theirs.

Not satisfied with all this, the racist state, founded on the imperialist-colonialist concept, turned itself into a base of imperialism and into an arsenal of weapons. This enabled it to assume its role of subjugating the Arab people and of committing aggression against them, in order to satisfy its ambitions of further expansion in Palestinian and other Arab lands. In addition to the many instances of aggression committed by this entity against the Arab States, it has launched two large-scale wars, in 1956 and 1967, thereby endangering world peace and security.

As a result of Zionist aggression in June 1967, the enemy occupied Egyptian Sinai as far as the Suez Canal. The enemy occupied Syria's Golan Heights, in addition to all Palestinian land west of the Jordan. All these developments have led to the creation in our area of what has come to be known as the "Middle East Problem". The situation has been rendered more serious by the enemy's persistence in maintaining its unlawful occupation and in further consolidating it, thus establishing a beachhead for world imperialism's thrust against our Arab nation. All Security Council decisions and calls by world public opinion for withdrawal from the lands occupied in June 1967 have been ignored. Despite all the peaceful and diplomatic efforts on the international level, the enemy has not been deterred from his expansionist policy. The only alternative open to our Arab nations, chiefly Syria and Egypt, was to expend exhaustive efforts to prepare, firstly, to resist this barbarous armed invasion by force and, secondly, to liberate Arab lands and to restore the rights of the Palestinian people, after all other peaceful means had failed.

Under these circumstances, the fourth war broke out in October 1973, bringing home to the Zionist enemy the bankruptcy of its policy of occupation and expansion and its reliance on the concept of military might. Despite all this, the leaders of the Zionist entity are far from having learned any lesson from their experience. They are making preparations for the fifth war, resorting once more to the language of military superiority, aggression, terrorism, subjugation and, finally, always to war in their dealings with the Arabs.

It pains our people greatly to witness the propagation of the myth that its homeland was a desert until it was made to bloom by the toil of foreign settlers, that it was a land without a people, and that the settler entity caused no harm to any human being. No, such lies must be exposed from this rostrum, for the world must know that Palestine was the cradle of the most ancient cultures and civilizations. Its Arab people were engaged in farming and building, spreading culture throughout the land for thousands of years, setting an example in the practice of religious tolerance and freedom of worship, acting as faithful guardians of the holy places of all religions. As a son of Jerusalem, I treasure for myself and my people beautiful memories and vivid images of the religious brotherhood that was the hallmark of our Holy City before it succumbed to catastrophe. Our people continued to pursue this enlightened policy until the establishment of the State of Israel and their dispersion. This did not deter our people from pursuing their humanitarian role on Palestinian soil. Nor will they permit their land to become a launching pad for aggression or a racist camp for the destruction of civilization, culture, progress and peace. Our people cannot but maintain the heritage of their ancestors in resisting the invaders, in assuming the privileged task of defending their native land, their Arab nationhood, their culture and civilization, and in safeguarding the cradle of the monotheistic religions.

By contrast, we need only mention briefly some instances of Israel's racist attitudes: its support of the Secret Army Organization in Algeria, its bolstering of the settler-colonialists in Africa — whether in the Congo, Angola, Mozambique, Zimbabwe, Rhodesia or South Africa — and its backing of South Vietnam against the Vietnam revolution. One can also mention Israel's continuing ,support of imperialism everywhere, its obstructionist stand in the Committee of Twenty-four, its refusal to cast its vote in support of independence for the African states, and its opposition to the demands of many Asian, African and Latin American nations, and several other states in the conferences on raw materials, population, the law of the sea, and food. All these facts offer further proof of the character of the enemy who has usurped our land. They justify the honourable struggle which we are waging against it. As we defend a vision of the future, our enemy upholds the myths of the past.

The enemy we face has a long record of hostility even towards the Jews themselves, for there is within the Zionist entity ugly racial discrimination against Oriental Jews. While we were vociferously condemning the massacres of Jews under Nazi rule, Zionist leadership appeared more interested at that time in exploiting them as best it could in order to realize its goal of immigration into Palestine.

If the immigration of Jews to Palestine had had as its objective the goal of enabling them to live side by side with us, enjoying the same rights and assuming the same duties, we would have opened our doors to them, as far as our homeland's capacity for absorption permitted. Such was the case with the thousands of Armenians and Circassians who still live among us in equality as brethren and citizens. But no one can conceivably demand that we submit to or accept that the goal of this immigration should be to usurp our homeland, disperse our people, and turn us into second-class citizens. Therefore, since its inception, our revolution has not been motivated by racial or religious factors. Its target has never been the Jew, as a person, but racist Zionism and aggression. In this sense, ours is also a revolution for the Jew, as a human being. We are struggling so that Jews, Christians, and Muslims may live in equality, enjoying the same rights and assuming the same duties, free from racial or religious discrimination.

a)   We distinguish between Judaism and Zionism. While we maintain our opposition to the colonialist Zionist movement, we respect the Jewish faith. Today, almost one century after the rise of the Zionist movement, we wish to warn of its increasing danger to the Jews of the world, to our Arab peoples and to world peace and security. For Zionism encourages the Jew to emigrate from his homeland and grants him an artificially-made nationality. The Zionists proceed with their destructive activities even though these have proved ineffective. The phenomenon of constant emigration from Israel, which is bound to grow as the bastions of colonialism and racism in the world falls, is an example of the inevitability of the failure of such activities.

b)   We urge the people and governments of the world to stand firm against Zionist attempts at encouraging world Jewry to emigrate from their countries and to usurp our land. We urge them as well firmly to oppose any discrimination against any human being, as to religion, race, or colour.

c)   Why should our people and our homeland be responsible for the problems of Jewish immigration, if such problems exist in the minds of some people? Why do the supporters of these problems not open their own countries, which are much bigger, to absorb and help these immigrants?

Those who call us terrorists wish to prevent world public opinion from discovering the truth about us and from seeing the justice on our faces. They seek to hide the terrorism and tyranny of their acts, and our own posture of self-defence.

The difference between the revolutionary and the terrorist lies in the reason for which each fights. For whoever stands by a just cause and fights for the freedom and liberation of his land from invaders, settler and colonialists would have been incorrectly called terrorist; the American people in their struggle for liberation from the British colonialists would have been terrorists, the European resistance against the Nazis would be terrorism, the struggle of the Asian, African and Latin American peoples would also be terrorism. It is actually a just and proper struggle of the Asian, African, and Latin American peoples, consecrated by the United Nations Charter and by the Declaration of Human Rights. As to those who fight against just causes, those who wage war to occupy the homelands of others, and to plunder exploit and colonize their peoples — those are the people whose actions should be condemned, who should be called war criminals: for the just cause determines the right to struggle.

Zionist terrorism which was waged against the Palestinian people to evict them from their country and usurp their land is on record in your documents. Thousands of our people have been assassinated in their villages and towns; tens of thousands of others have been forced by rifle and artillery fire to leave their homes and the crops they have sown in the lands of their fathers. Time and time again our children, women and aged have been evicted and have had to wander in the deserts and climb mountains without any food or water. No one who in 1948 witnessed the catastrophe that befell the inhabitants of hundreds of villages and towns — in Jerusalem, Jaffa, Lydda, Ramleh, and Galilee — no one who has been a witness to that catastrophe will ever forget the experience, even though the mass blackout has succeeded in hiding these horrors as it has hidden the traces of 385 Palestinian villages and towns destroyed at the time and erased from the map. The destruction of 19,000 houses during the past seven years, which is equivalent to the complete destruction of 200 more Palestinian villages, and the great number of maimed as a result of the treatment they were subjected to in Israeli prisons, cannot be hidden by any blackout.

Their terrorism fed on hatred and this hatred was even directed against the olive tree in my country, which they saw as a symbol of our spirit, a flag, and which reminded them of the indigenous inhabitants of the land, a living reminder that the land is Palestinian. Hence they uprooted or killed it by neglect, or used it for firewood. How can one describe the statement by Golda Meir in which she expressed her disquiet about "the Palestinian children born every day"? They see in the Palestinian child, in the Palestinian tree, an enemy which should be exterminated. For tens of years Zionists have been harassing our people's cultural, political, social and artistic leaders, terrorizing them and assasinating them. They have stolen our cultural heritage, our popular folklore and have claimed it as theirs. Their terrorism even reached our sacred places in our beloved city of peace, Jerusalem. They have endeavored to deprive it of its Arab (Muslim and Christian) character by evicting its inhabitants and annexing it.

I need not dwell on the burning of the al-Aqsa Mosque, the theft of the treasures of the Church of the Holy Sepulchre and the disfiguring of so many aspects of its culture and civilization. Jerusalem, with its beauty, and atmosphere redolent of history, bears witness to successive generations of our people who have lived in it, leaving in every corner of it proof of our eternal presence, of our love for it, of our civilization, of our human values. It is therefore not surprising that under its skies the three religions were born and that under that sky these three religions have shone to enlighten mankind so that it might express the tribulations and hopes of humanity, and that it might mark out the road of the future with its hopes.

The small number of Palestinian Arabs whom the Zionists did not succeed in uprooting in 1948 are at present refugees in their own country. Israeli law treats them as second-class citizens — even as third-class citizens since Oriental Jews are second-class citizens — and they have been subject to all forms of racial discrimination and terror after the confiscation of their land and property. They have been victims of bloody massacres such as that of Kafr Qassim; they have been expelled from their villages and denied the right to return, as in the case of the inhabitants of Iqrit and Kafr Bir'im. For 26 years, our population has been living under martial law and has been denied freedom of movement without prior permission from the Israeli military governor — this at a time when an Israeli law was promulgated granting citizenship to any Jew anywhere who wanted to emigrate to our homeland. Moreover, another Israeli law stipulated that Palestinians who were not present in their villages or towns at the time they were occupied are not entitled to Israeli citizenship.

The record of Israeli rulers is replete with acts of terror perpetrated on those of our people who remained under occupation in Sinai and the Golan Heights. The criminal bombardment of the Bahr al-Baqar School and the Abu Za'bal factory in Egypt are but two such unforgettable acts of terrorism. The destruction of the Libyan aircraft is another unforgettable act. The total destruction of the city of Quneitra is yet another tangible instance of systematic terrorism. If a record of Zionist terrorism in south Lebanon were to be compiled, and this terrorism is still continuing, the enormity of its acts would shock even the most hardened: piracy, bombardments, scorched earth, destruction of hundreds of homes, eviction of civilians and the kidnapping of Lebanese citizens. This clearly constitutes a violation of Lebanese sovereignty and is in preparation for the diversion of the Litani River waters.

Need one remind this Assembly of the numerous resolutions adopted by it condemning Israeli aggressions committed against Arab countries, Israeli violations of human rights and the articles of the Geneva Conventions, as well as the resolutions pertaining to the annexation of the city of Jerusalem and its restoration to its former status?

The only description for these acts is that they are acts of barbarism and terrorism. And yet, the Zionist racists and colonialists have the temerity to describe the just struggle of our people as terror. Could there be a more flagrant distortion of truth than this? We ask those who usurped our land, who are committing murderous acts of terrorism against our people and are practising racial discrimination more extensively than the racists of South Africa, we ask them to keep in mind the United Nations General Assembly resolution that called for the expulsion of South Africa from the United Nations. Such is the inevitable fate of every racist country that adopts the law of the jungle, usurps the homeland of others and oppresses its people.

For the past 30 years, our people have had to struggle against British occupation and Zionist invasion, both of which had one intention, namely the usurpation of our land. Six major revolts and tens of popular uprisings were staged to foil these attempts, so that our homeland might remain ours. Over 30,000 martyrs, the equivalent in comparative terms of 6 million Americans, died in the process.

When the majority of the Palestinian people was uprooted from its homeland in 1948, the Palestinian struggle for self-determination continued in spite of efforts to destroy it. We tried every possible means to continue our political struggle to attain our national rights, but to no avail. Meanwhile we had to struggle for sheer existence. Even in exile we educated our children. This was all a part of trying to survive.

The Palestinian people have produced thousands of engineers, physicians, teachers and scientists who actively participated in the development of the Arab countries bordering on their usurped homeland. They have utilized their income to assist the young and aged amongst their people who could not leave the refugee camps. They have educated their younger brothers and sisters, have supported their parents and cared for their children. All along the Palestinian dreamt of return. Neither the Palestinian's allegiance to Palestine nor his determination to return waned; nothing could persuade him to relinquish his Palestinian identity or to forsake his homeland. The passage of time did not make him forget, as some hoped he would. When our people lost faith in the international community which persisted in ignoring its rights and when it became obvious that the Palestinians would not recoup one inch of Palestine through exclusively political means, our people had no choice but to resort to armed struggle. Into that struggle it poured its material and human resources and the flower of its youth. We bravely faced the most vicious acts of Israeli terrorism which were aimed at diverting our struggle and arresting it.

In the past ten years of our struggle, thousands of martyrs and twice as many wounded, maimed and imprisoned have been offered in sacrifice, all in an effort to resist the imminent threat of liquidation, to regain the right to self-determination and our right to return to our homeland. With the utmost dignity and the most admirable revolutionary spirit, our Palestinian people have not lost their spirit either in Israeli prisons and concentration camps or in the great prison of Israeli occupation. The people struggle for sheer existence and continue to strive to preserve the Arab character of their land. Thus they resist oppression, tyranny and terrorism in their grimmest forms.

It is through the armed revolution of our people that our political leadership and our national institutions finally crystallized and a national liberation movement, comprising all Palestinian factions, organizations and capabilities, materialized in the Palestine Liberation Organization.

Through our militant Palestine national liberation movement our people's struggle has matured and grown enough to accommodate political and social struggle in addition to armed struggle. The Palestine Liberation Organization has been a major factor in creating a new Palestinian individual, qualified to shape the future of our Palestine, not merely content with mobilizing the Palestinians for the challenges of the present.

The Palestine Liberation Organization can be proud of having a large number of cultural and educational activities, even while engaged in armed struggle, and at a time when it faced the increasingly vicious blows of Zionist terrorism. We have established institutes for scientific research, agricultural development and social welfare, as well as centres for the revival of our cultural heritage and the preservation of our folklore. Many Palestinian poets, artists and writers have enriched Arab culture in particular, and world culture generally. Their profoundly humane works have won the admiration of all those familiar with them. In contrast to that, our enemy has been systematically destroying our culture and disseminating racist, colonialist ideologies; in short, everything that impedes progress, justice, democracy and peace.

The Palestine Liberation Organization has earned its legitimacy because of the sacrifice inherent in its pioneering role, and also because of its dedicated leadership of the struggle. It has also been granted this legitimacy by the Palestinian masses, which in harmony with it have chosen it to lead the struggle according to its directives. The Palestine Liberation Organization has also gained its legitimacy by representing every faction, union or group as well as every Palestinian talent, either in the National Council or in people's institutions. This legitimacy was further strengthened by the support of the entire Arab nation which supports it, and further consecrated during the last Arab Summit Conference, which affirmed the right of the Palestine Liberation Organization, in its capacity as the sole representative of the Palestinian people, to establish an independent national authority on all liberated Palestinian territory.

Moreover, the Palestine Liberation Organization's legitimacy has been intensified as a result of fraternal support given by other liberation movements and by friendly, like-minded nations that stood by our side, encouraging and aiding us in our struggle to secure our national rights.

Here I must also warmly convey the gratitude of our revolutionary fighters and that of our people for the honourable attitudes adopted by the non-aligned countries, the socialist countries, the Islamic countries, the African countries and friendly European countries, as well as all our other friends in Asia, Africa and Latin America.

The Palestine Liberation Organization represents the Palestinian people. Because of this, the Palestine Liberation Organization expresses the wishes and hopes of its people. Because of this, too, it brings these very wishes and hopes before you, urging you not to shirk a momentous historic responsibility towards our just cause.

For many years now, our people have been exposed to the ravages of war, destruction and dispersion. They have paid with the blood of their sons that which cannot ever be compensated. They have borne the burdens of occupation, dispersion, eviction and terror more than any other people. And yet all this has made our people neither vidictive nor vengeful. Nor have they caused us to resort to the racism of our enemies. Nor have we lost the true method by which friend and foe are distinguished.

For we deplore all those crimes committed against the Jews; we also deplore all the open and veiled discrimination suffered by them because of their faith.

I am a rebel and freedom is my cause, I know well that many of you present here today once stood in exactly the same position of resistance as I now occupy and from which I must fight. You once had to convert dreams into reality by your struggle. Therefore you must now share my dream. I think this is exactly why I can ask you now to help, as together we bring out our dream into a bright reality, our common dream for a peaceful future in Palestine's sacred land.

As he stood in an Israeli military court, the Jewish revolutionary Ehud Adiv said: "I am no terrorist; I believe that a democratic state should exist in this land." Adiv now languishes in a Zionist prison among his co-believers. To him and his colleagues I send my heartfelt good wishes.

And before those same courts there stands today a brave prince of the church, Archbishop Capucci. Raising his fingers to form the same victory sign used by our freedom-fighters, he said: "What I have done, I have done that all men may live in peace in this land of peace." This princely priest will doubtless share Adiv's grim fate. To him we send our salutations and greetings.

Why therefore should I not dream and hope? For is not revolution the making real of dreams and hopes? So let us work together that my dream may be fulfilled, that I may return with my people out of exile, there in Palestine to live with this Jewish freedom-fighter and his partners, with this Arab priest and his brothers, in one democratic state where Christian, Jew and Muslim live in justice, equality, fraternity.

Is this not a noble goal and worthy of my struggle alongside all lovers of freedom everywhere? For the most admirable thing about this goal is that it is Palestinian, from the land of peace, the land of martyrdom, heroism, and history.

Let us remember that the Jews of Europe and here in the United States have been known to lead the struggles for secularism and the separation of church and state. They have also been known to fight against discrimination on religious grounds. How can they reject this humane and honourable programme for the Holy Land, the land of peace and equality? How can they continue to support the most fanatic, discriminatory and closed of nations in its policy?

In my capacity as Chairman of the Palestine Liberation Organization and commander of the Palestinian revolution I proclaim before you that when we speak of our common hopes for the Palestine of tomorrow we include in our perspective all Jews now living in Palestine who choose to live with us there in peace and without discrimination.

In my capacity as commander of the forces of the Palestine Liberation Organization I call upon Jews to turn away one by one from the illusory promises made to them by Zionist ideology and Israeli leadership. They are offering Jews perpetual bloodshed, endless war and continuous thralldom.

We invite them to emerge into a more open realm of free choice, far from their present leadership's efforts to implant in them a Masada complex and make it their destiny.

We offer them the most generous solution — that we should live together in a framework of just peace in our democratic Palestine.

In my formal capacity as Chairman of the Palestine Liberation Organization I announce here that we do not wish one drop of either Jewish or Arab blood to be shed; neither do we delight in the continuation of killings for a single moment, once a just peace, based on our people's rights, hopes, and aspirations has been finally established.

In my capacity as Chairman of the Palestine Liberation Organization and commander of the Palestinian revolution I appeal to you to accompany our people in its struggle to attain its right to self-determination. This right is consecrated in the United Nations Charter and has been repeatedly confirmed in resolutions adopted by this august body since the drafting of the Charter. I appeal to you, further, to aid our people's return to its homeland from an involuntary exile imposed upon it by force of arms, by tyranny, by oppression, so that we may regain our property, our land, and thereafter live in our national homeland, free and sovereign, enjoying all the privileges of nationhood.

I appeal to you to enable our people to set up their national authority and establish their national entity in their own land.

Only then will our people be able to contribute all their energies and resources to the field of civilization and human creativity. Only then will they be able to protect their beloved Jerusalem and make it, as they have done for so many centuries, the shrine of all religions, free from all terrorism and coercion.

Today I have come bearing an olive branch and a freedom-fighter's gun. Do not let the olive branch fall from my hand. Do not let the olive branch fall from my hand. Do not let the olive branch fall from my hand.

War flares up in Palestine, and yet is is in Palestine that peace will be born.

10. Palestinian National Council, Political Declaration, Cairo, 22 March, 1977

Proceeding from the Palestine National Charter and the previous national council's resolutions; considering the decisions and political gains achieved by the PLO at the Arab and international levels during the period following the 12th session of the PNC; after studying and debating the latest developments in the Palestine issue; and stressing support for the Palestinian national struggle in the Arab and international forums, the PNC affirms the following:

1. The PNC affirms that the Palestine issue is the essence and the root of the Arab-Zionist conflict. Security Council Resolution 242 ignores the Palestinian people and their firm rights. The PNC therefore confirms its rejection of this resolution, and rejects negotiations at the Arab and international levels based on this Resolution.

2. The PNC affirms the stand of the PLO in its determination to continue the armed struggle, and its concomitant forms of political and mass struggle, to achieve our inalienable national rights.

3. The PNC affirms that the struggle, in all its military, political and popular forms, in the occupied territory constitutes the central link in its programme of struggle. On this basis, the PLO will strive to escalate the armed struggle in the occupied territory, to escalate all other concomitant forms of struggle and to give all kinds of moral support to the masses of our people in the occupied territory in order to escalate the struggle and to strengthen their steadfastness to defeat and liquidate the occupation.

4. The PNC affirms the PLO's stand which rejects all types of American capitulationist settlement and all liquidationist projects. The Council affirms the determination of the PLO to abort any settlement achieved at the expense of the firm national rights of our people. The PNC calls upon the Arab nation to shoulder its pan-Arab responsibilities and to pool all its energies to confront these imperialist and Zionist plans.

5. The PNC stresses the importance and necessity of national unity, both political and military, among all the contingents of the Palestine Revolution

within the framework of the PLO, because this is one of the basic conditions for victory. For this reason, it is necessary to co-ordinate national unity at all levels and in all spheres on the basis of commitment to all these resolutions, and to draw up programmes which will ensure the implementation of this.

6.   The PNC affirms the right of the Palestine Revolution to be present on the soil of fraternal Lebanon within the framework of the Cairo agreement and its appendices, concluded between the PLO and the Lebanese authorities. The Council also affirms adherence to the implementation of the Cairo agreement in letter and in spirit, including the preservation of the position of the Revolution and the security of the camps. The PNC refuses to accept any interpretation of this agreement by one side only. Meanwhile it affirms its eagerness for the maintenance of the sovereignty and security of Lebanon.

7.   The PNC greets the heroic fraternal Lebanese people and affirms the PLO's eagerness for the maintenance of the territorial integrity of Lebanon, the unity of its people and its security, independence, sovereignty and Arabism. The PNC affirms its pride in the support rendered by this heroic fraternal people to the PLO, which is struggling for our people to regain their national rights to their homeland and their right to return to this homeland. The PNC strongly affirms the need to deepen and consolidate cohesion between all Lebanese nationalist forces and the Palestine Revolution.

8.   The PNC affirms the need to strengthen the Arab Front participating in the Palestine Revolution, and deepen cohesion with all forces participating in it in all Arab countries, as well as to escalate the joint Arab struggle and to further strengthen the Palestine Revolution in order to contend with the imperialist and Zionist designs.

9.   The PNC has decided to consolidate Arab struggle and solidarity on the basis of struggle against imperialism and Zionism, to work for the liberation of all the occupied Arab areas, and to adhere to the support for the Palestine Revolution in order to regain the constant national rights of the Palestinian Arab people without any conciliation [*sulh*] or recognition [of Israel].

10.   The PNC affirms the right of the PLO to exercise its responsibilities in the struggle at the pan-Arab level and through any Arab land, in the interest of liberating the occupied areas.

11.   The PNC has decided to continue the struggle to regain the national rights of our people, in particular the right of return, self-determination and establishing an independent national state on their national soil.

12.   The PNC affirms the significance of cooperation and solidarity with socialist, non-aligned, Islamic and African countries, and with all the national liberation movements in the world.

13.   The PNC hails the stands and struggles of all the democratic countries and forces against Zionism as one form of racism, as well as against its aggressive practices.

14.   The PNC affirms the significance of establishing relations and coordinating with the progressive and democratic Jewish forces inside and outside the occupied homeland, since these forces are struggling against Zionism as a doctrine and in practice. The PNC calls on all states and forces who love freedom, justice and peace in the world to end all forms of assistance to and cooperation with the racist Zionist regime, and to end contacts with it and its instruments.

15.   Taking into consideration the important achievements in the Arab and international arenas since the conclusion of the PNC's 12th session, the PNC, which has reviewed the political report submitted by the PLO, has decided the following:

a.   The Council confirms its wish for the PLO's rights to participate independently and on an equal footing in all the conferences and international forums concerned with the Palestine issue and the Arab-Zionist conflict, with a view to achieving our inalienable national rights as approved by the UN General Assembly in 1974, namely in Resolution 3236.

b.   The Council declares that any settlement or agreement affecting the rights of our Palestinian people made in the absence of this people will be completely null and void.

11. Six-point Programme Agreed to by the Various Palestinian Organizations Calling for the Formation of a "Steadfastness and Confrontation Front" in Opposition to Sadat's Negotiations with Israel, Tripoli, 4 December, 1977

In the wake of Sadat's treasonous visit to the Zionist entity, all factions of the Palestinian Resistance Movement have decided to make a practical answer to this step. On this basis, they met and issued the following document:

We, all factions of the PLO, announce the following:

First: We call for the formation of a "Steadfastness and Confrontation Front" composed of Libya, Algeria, Iraq, Democratic Yemen, Syria and the PLO, to oppose all capitulationist solutions planned by imperialism, Zionism and their Arab tools.

Second: We fully condemn any Arab party in the Tripoli Summit which rejects the formation of this Front, and we announce this.

Third: We reaffirm our rejection of Security Council resolutions 242 and 338.

Fourth: We reaffirm our rejection of all international conferences based on these two resolutions' including the Geneva Conference.

Fifth: To strive for the realization of the Palestinian people's rights to return and self-determination within the context of an independent Palestinian national state on any part of the Palestinian Revolution.

Sixth: To apply the measures related to the political boycott of the Sadat regime.

In the name of all the factions, we ratify this unification document:

— The Palestinian National Liberation Movement, Fatah: Abu Ayyad [Salah Khalaf].

— The Popular Front for the Liberation of Palestine: Dr. George Habbash.

— The Democratic Front for the Liberation of Palestine: Nayef Hawatmeh.

— The P.F.L.P. — General Command: Ahmad Jabril.

— Vanguards of the People's Liberation War, Saiqa: Zuhair Muhsin.

— Arab Liberation Front: Abdul-Rahim Ahmad.

— Palestinian Liberation Front: Talaat Ya'qoub.

— P.L.O.: Hamed Abu-Sitta.

12. Statement by West Bank Mayors on Sadat's Visit to Israel, 21 December, 1977 [Excerpts]

We state our dissatisfaction with this step taken by President Sadat, because of the results and dangers likely to arise from it and because in his speech to the Knesset he made no mention of the PLO as the sole legitimate representative of the Palestinian people. We also declare that the PLO had every right, and indeed the duty, to adopt the attitude it has taken to this visit. In adopting this attitude it was clearly expressing the view and the attitude of the Palestinian people. However, our sense of responsibility prompts us to record that President Sadat has committed himself not to resort to a separate solution with "Israel" and that he has declared that he insists on the Arab character of Jerusalem, "Israel" withdrawing from all the occupied territories, on the refugees returning to their homes and on the Palestinian people being granted their right to self-determination and to establish their independent state.

While recalling the world's commitment to the resolutions of the United Nations and, in particular, General Assembly resolution 3236, adopted on November 22, 1974 and the resolutions of the Algiers and Rabat summits which regarded the PLO as the sole legitimate representative of the Palestinian people wherever they may be, we affirm our adherence to these resolutions, as also to the resolutions of the Thirteenth Palestine National Council held in Cairo. We call on all quarters to respect the commitment of the peoples of the world, including our Palestinian people, and we condemn any attempt to prejudice the legitimate rights of our people and, first and foremost, their right to self-determination. In the light of the above we assert the following principles:

1. While stating our attitude to President Sadat's visit to "Israel" we affirm our belief in the role Egypt has played and the sacrifices she has made on behalf of the Palestinian cause and the problems of Arab struggle. We stress the strength of the alliance between our people and the people of Egypt, and our unshakable belief in the central role occupied by Egypt in the battle of Arab liberation, and we salute the struggle and great sacrifices of her people.

2. The ferocity of the battle that is being fought to counter the present imperialist attack on the achievements of our people and the Arab people requires the establishment of a broad Arab front comprising all the Arab countries that reject the imperialist attack on the area in all its forms. This front should also include the Arab popular organizations and the PLO. Also required is the mobilization of all economic, political and military resources to resist this attack and to put an end to the conspiracy against all the national gains in Arab lands, and to strengthen the alliance of this front with all forces opposed to imperialism and Zionism.

3. The Palestinian people in the occupied territories unambiguously affirm their belief in the unity of the Palestinian people inside and outside the country. They also stress that all Palestinians are represented by the PLO alone, which is the only quarter entitled to speak on behalf of the Palestinian people. We condemn any attempt to establish an alternative or parallel leadership.

4. The rights of the Palestinian people, as affirmed by the various resolutions of the UN, are not subject to bargaining, and first and foremost among these rights is their legitimate right to self-determination in their land and in full freedom.

We therefore reject any form of tutelage, whatever its source, and all kinds of solutions which detract from the independence of the Palestinian people and the independence of their will.

We therefore cannot agree that the Palestinian state should be forcibly linked to any other quarter, as such a trend is incompatible with our people's freedom to decide their own destiny.

5. From the occupied territories we salute the struggle of all the Arab peoples. We also salute all the forces that have provided support for our just struggle. Above all we salute the struggle of our people outside the country under the leadership of the PLO and we call for resolute resistance to all attempts to shake the Arab solidarity which is based on the will of the Arab nation for delivery from the imperialist attack and Zionist aggression.

13. Statement by the West Bank National Conference, Beit Hanina, Jerusalem, 1 October, 1978

On this day Sunday, October 1, 1978, in the professional unions' centre in Jerusalem, Muslim and Christian religious leaders, mayors and city council members, representatives of the unions, clubs and national institutions, and leading personalities in Jerusalem and the rest of the occupied territories held a national conference and studied the results of the Camp David conference, its agreements, explanations, letters and the declarations of those who signed it. All those present have unanimously decided the following:

1. To totally reject and oppose these agreements, and all the documents, explanations and annexes related to them.

2. The Camp David agreements are in contradiction to the all-Arab character of our battle, as they actually constitute a separate treaty between Egypt and Israel, which will take Egypt out of the Arab arena in order to strike at the Arab and African liberation movements.

3. The above-mentioned agreements are a clear deviation from the resolutions of the Arab summit conferences in general and the Algiers and Rabat summits in particular, which clearly opposed separate solutions and demanded that the confrontation forces work jointly in all fields.

4. The above-mentioned agreements contradict the UN General Assembly resolutions on the Palestinian issue and are an open defiance on the international will and an attack on the Palestinian people's natural rights.

5. The above-mentioned agreements have denied the rights of the Palestinian people and ignored their just cause, which is the crux of the conflict in the Middle East, and ignored their usurped rights and their right of self-determination on their land. The agreements have also ignored the PLO, which is the sole legitimate leadership of the Palestinian people, and attempt to create an alternative leadership to the PLO under the auspices of occupation by establishing self-rule which time after time all sectors of our people have absolutely rejected.

6. The struggle of the Palestinian people was and still is an integral part of the struggle of the Arab peoples for freedom, unity and progress, and is part of the world liberation movement. And the Palestinian people inside and outside the occupied territory are a unified, inseparable whole.

7. No peace is possible in the area without the complete and genuine withdrawal of Israeli forces from all the occupied territories, nor without securing for the Palestinian people the right of return, self-determination and the creation of their own independent state on their land, with Jerusalem as its capital.

8. We reject the self-government plan both in its form and content. It is a plan to consolidate the occupation, to continue the oppression of our people

and the usurping of our legitimate rights. It is an open plot to bypass the ambitions of our people and our right to our own homeland and to self-determination.

9. From our beloved Jerusalem, the throbbing heart of Palestine, we appeal to our Arab people everywhere to retain their national unity, confirm their allegiance to their legitimate leadership, the Palestine Liberation Organization, and stand united in the face of all efforts to implement the proposed self-government plan and other capitulationist solutions.

On this occasion we salute our Palestinian people inside and outside [Palestine], the memory of our martyrs who sacrificed their lives for their country and the resisters in the Israeli prisons. We salute the Steadfastness and Confrontation Front and the resolutions of its summits in Tripoli and Damascus. These are an extension of the Arab people through their struggles. And we salute all friendly nations for their clear position in support of our national rights.

[96 signatories]

14. Palestinian National Council, Political and Organizational Programme, Damascus, 23 January, 1979

The US settlement of the Arab-Zionist conflict embodied in the Camp David agreements poses grave threats to the cause of Palestine and of Arab national liberation. That settlement condones the Zionist enemy's continued usurpation of the national soil of Palestine, abrogates the inalienable right of the Palestinian Arab people to their homeland, Palestine, as well as their right to return to it and their right to self-determination and to the exercise of their national independence on their soil. It dissipates other Arab territories and overrides the PLO, the leader of our people's national struggle and their sole legitimate representative and spokesman expressing their will.

In addition, these agreements violate Palestinian, Arab and international legitimacy and pave the way for tighter imperialist and Zionist control over our Arab region and Africa, employing the Egyptian regime, in the context of its alliance with imperialism and Zionism, as a tool for the repression of the Arab and African national liberation movements.

Motivated by our awareness of the gravity of this new conspiracy and its implications and by our national responsibilities in the PLO, which represents our Palestinian Arab people with all their national groups and forces, we are obliged to reject this new conspiratorial scheme, to confront it and to defend our people and their inalienable national rights to their homeland, Palestine, as well as to safeguard our Palestinian revolution.

The courageous position adopted by our Palestinian masses inside and outside the occupied homeland and by the masses of our Arab nation through their rejection of the Camp David agreements and their open determination to confront this new conspiracy against our people and their inalienable national rights and our Arab nation strengthens our resolve to resist this conspiracy and our faith in defeating it.

At the same time, we shoulder a great responsibility which can be carried out only by adopting a united national and popular stand, within the framework of the PLO.

In response to the will of our people and to the challenges that we face, and motivated by our faith in national unity within the PLO as the sole means to achieve victory; basing ourselves upon the Palestine National Charter, the resolutions of the Palestine National Councils and the Tripoli document which established unity among the various organizations of the Palestinian revolution; believing in the right of our people to establish a democratic state on the whole of our national soil and in order to confront this critical and dangerous stage in the struggle of our people, we, the representatives of all organizations of the Revolution and Palestinian national forces, declare the following:

In the Palestinian Sphere

1. [That we] adhere to the inalienable national rights of our people to their homeland, Palestine, and to their right to return and to self-determination on their soil without foreign interference, and to their right to establish their independent state on their soil unconditionally.

2. [That we shall] defend the PLO and adhere to it as the sole legitimate representative of our people, as leader of their national struggle and as their spokesman in all Arab and international forums; resist all attempts to harm, override or circumvent the PLO, or to create alternatives or partners to it as regards representation of our Palestinian people; adhere to the resolutions of the Arab summits of Algiers and Rabat and to UN resolutions — especially resolutions 3236 and 3237 — which affirm our inalienable national rights as well as Arab and international recognition of the PLO as the sole legitimate representative of the Palestinian people.

3. [That we] resolve firmly to continue and escalate the armed struggle and use all other forms of political and mass struggle, especially inside the occupied homeland which is the principal arena of conflict with the Zionist enemy, in order to achieve the inalienable and non-negotiable national rights of the Palestinian Arab people.

4. [That we] affirm that the problem of Palestine is the crux and the basis of the Arab-Zionist conflict, and [we] reject all resolutions, agreements and

settlements that do not recognize or that impinge upon the inalienable rights of our people to their homeland, Palestine, including their right to return, to self-determination and to the establishment of their independent national state. This applies in particular to Security Council resolution 242.

5. [That we] reject and resist the self-rule scheme in the occupied homeland, which entrenches Zionist settler colonization of our occupied land and denies the rights of our Palestinian people.

6. [That we] affirm the unity of our Palestinian Arab people inside and outside the occupied homeland, and their sole representation through the PLO; [we shall] resist all attempts and schemes that seek to divide our people or to circumvent the PLO; work to support the struggle of our people in the occupied territories and to fortify their unity and their steadfastness.

7. [That we shall] consolidate the framework of the Palestinian National Front inside Palestine since it is an integral part of the PLO, and [shall] furnish it with all means of political and financial aid so that it can mobilize our masses inside to face the Zionist occupation, its schemes and its projects which are inimical to our people and to their inalienable national rights.

8. [that we] cling to Palestine as the historic homeland of the Palestinian people for which there can be no substitute; resist all schemes for resettlement or for an "alternative homeland", which the imperialist and Zionist enemy is proposing in order to liquidate the Palestinian cause and Palestinian national struggle, and to circumvent our right to return.

In the Arab Sphere

1. [that we] emphasize that the task of confronting the Camp David agreements, their annexes and their consequences, with the fateful dangers they pose to the cause of Arab struggle, is the responsibility of all the Arab masses and their national and progressive forces, that the Arab Front for Steadfastness and Confrontation, with Syria and the PLO as its central link, is the primary base from which to confront the US-Zionist conspiratorial settlement.

2. [That we must] work to fortify and strengthen the Arab Front for Steadfastness and Confrontation and to expand its scope on the basis of resistance to imperialist and Zionist settlement schemes; adhere to the objective of liberating the occupied Palestinian and Arab territories and to the inalienable national rights of the Palestinian people, and not dissipate or infringe upon these rights; [we must] furnish all possible mass and financial support to the Arab Front for Steadfastness and Confrontation, especially to the PLO and the Syrian Arab region.

3. The PLO calls upon all national and progressive parties, movements and forces in the Arab homeland to support the Arab Front for Steadfastness

and Confrontation and to furnish it with all possible mass and financial aid. It further calls upon them to unite and to struggle on the basis of resistance to the imperialist and Zionist schemes for settlement.

4. a) The PLO asserts its firm commitment to the unity, Arab character and independence of Lebanon, its respect for Lebanese sovereignty and its adherence to the Cairo Agreement and its sequels which regulate relations between the PLO and Lebanon's legitimate authority.

b) The PLO highly values the role that has been and is being played by the Lebanese people and their national, progressive and patriotic forces in support of and in defence of the struggle of the Palestinian people. In expressing its pride in the solidarity between our Palestinian people and the people of Lebanon and their national, progressive and patriotic forces in defence of Lebanese territory and of the Palestinian revolution against Zionist aggression, its schemes and its local agents, the PLO emphasizes the importance of continuing and strengthening this solidarity.

5. a) The PLO affirms the special character of the relationship linking the two fraternal peoples, Palestinian and Jordanian, and its concern that the solidarity between these two fraternal peoples should continue.

b) The PLO declares its adherence to the resolutions of the Arab summits of Algiers and Rabat which affirm that the PLO is the sole legitimate representative of the Palestinian people and that our people have a right to establish their national and independent state. The PLO considers that the commitment of the Jordanian regime to these resolutions, its rejection of the Camp David agreements and their aftermath as well as its refusal to be involved in them and its role in enabling the PLO to exercise its responsibility for militant and mass struggle against the Zionist enemy, constitute the basis that governs relations between the PLO and the Jordanian regime.

6. The PLO affirms its right to exercise its responsibility for struggle on the Arab and national levels, and across any Arab territory, in order to liberate the occupied Palestinian territories.

7. The PLO declares that its policies toward and its relations with any Arab regime are determined by the policy of that regime as regards adherence to the resolutions of the summits of Algiers and Rabat and to the rejection of and the opposition to the Camp David agreements with their annexes and their consequences.

8. The PLO calls upon all Arab and national forces and all national and friendly regimes to support and aid the Egyptian people and their national movement to enable them to confront the Sadat conspiracy and to foil the Camp David agreement and its effect upon the Egyptian people, their Arabism and their history of struggle against Zionism and imperialism.

In the International Sphere

1. The role played by the US against our Palestinian people and their national struggle and against the Arab national liberation movement and its objectives of liberation and independence, whether this is manifested in its support of the Zionist entity or through its agents in the Arab region, constitutes a naked aggression against our people and their national cause. The PLO, by acting in solidarity with all groups in the Arab national liberation struggle and their national and progressive forces and regimes, declares its determination to resist the policy, objectives and actions of the US in the region.

2. The PLO affirms the importance of alliance with the socialist countries, and first and foremost with the Soviet Union, since this alliance is a national necessity in the context of confronting American-Zionist conspiracies against the Palestine cause, the Arab national liberation movement and their achievements.

3. The PLO affirms the importance of consolidating its cooperation with the non-aligned, Islamic, African and friendly states which support the PLO and its struggle to achieve the national rights of the Palestinian people to return to their homeland, to self-determination and to establish their independent national state.

4. The PLO, as a national liberation movement, expresses its solidarity with national liberation movements throughout the world, especially with Zimbabwe, Namibia and South Africa, and its determination to consolidate relations of struggle with them since the fight against imperialism, Zionism and racism is a joint cause for all forces of liberation and progress in the world.

5. The PLO declares its firm adherence to the achievements won by Palestinian struggle in the international sphere, such as the wide international recognition accorded to the PLO and to the inalienable right of the Palestinian Arab people to their homeland, Palestine, their right to return, to self- determination and to the establishment of their independent national state on their national soil. These are the achievements embodied in UN resolutions adopted since 1974 and up to the present, especially resolutions 3236 and 3237. It underlines the right of the PLO to participate in all meetings and conferences that discuss the Palestine question on these bases and considers that any discussion or agreement that takes place in its absence about matters related to the Palestine question are totally invalid.

In the Sphere of Organization

1. All the organizations of the Revolution and all Palestinian national forces participate in all institutions of the PLO, and principally in the National

Council and the Central Council and the Executive Committee, on a representative basis and in a democratic manner.

2. Palestinian leadership is a collective one. This means that decisions are the responsibility of all, both through participation in the adoption of decision and in its execution. This takes place in a democratic manner where the minority adheres to the view of the majority, in accordance with the political and organizational programme and with the resolutions of the National Councils.

3. [The PLO will work] to ensure that the departments, institutions and organs of the PLO carry out their functions in full, each within its own specific sphere as defined in the basic regulations of the PLO. The Executive Committee will form higher organs, composed on a representative basis, which will undertake to formulate the plans for the various institutions of the PLO and supervise their execution by them, especially in the military, informational and financial spheres.

4. The Executive Committee and the Central Council are composed in accordance with what is agreed upon as stated in the basic regulations of the PLO and the resolutions of the National Council.

5. The next Executive Committee undertakes as soon as it commences its activity to lay down the necessary plans to implement the interim programme and to review the departments and organs of the PLO in a manner that would take merit and quality into account in order to achieve optimal performance from these departments and organs.

15. Letter from PLO Executive Committee to Delegate Walter Fauntroy, 5 October, 1979

Walter Fauntroy,   Washington, D.C.
Chairman, SCLC,   October 5, 1979
Washington, D.C.

In response to Dr. Joseph Lowery and Congressman Walter Fauntroy and the Southern Christian Leadership Conference peace initiative as well as Reverend Jesse Jackson's People United to Save Humanity (PUSH) appeal, PLO Chairman Yasser Arafat after meeting with members of the Executive Committee of the Palestine Liberation Organization issued the following 6 point programme. (1) The PLO reaffirms its rejection of the Camp David process and the autonomy plan which only legitimizes the occupation and oppression of the Palestinian people.   (2) The PLO reaffirms the resolution of the Palestine National Council including the Palestinian people's right of self determination, their right of return, and their right to an independent state. (3) The PLO commits itself to a cease fire in Lebanon in line with the safety and security of Lebanon, at a time when Israel continues its ceaseless attacks by air, land and sea which have resulted in 600,000 refugees. (4) The PLO reaffirms its right to an independent state on any land Israel evacuates or is liberated. (5) The PLO reaffirms its respect for Judaism and the right of Jews to live in peace and its commitment to full equality of Jews, Moslems, and Christians and its opposition to all forms of racism. (6) The PLO appeals to all people to support the legitimate rights of the Palestinian people.

Chairman Arafat sends his best wishes to the SCLC delegation members and to the PUSH delegation.

16. The Fourth General Conference of the Palestinian Liberation Movement, Fatah, Political Programme, Damascus, 31 May, 1980

I. At the Palestinian Level

In the light of the unity of the Palestinian people, and the unity of their territory and their political representation, and in affirmation of their independent national will for the continuation and victory of their revolution;

Inasmuch as armed popular revolution is the sole and inevitable road to the liberation of Palestine, and inasmuch as the road to liberation is the road to unity; and in confirmation of the principle that democracy governs relations in the Palestinian arena and that democratic dialogue is the proper way to develop these relations, the Conference affirms the following:

1. Ceaseless efforts to consolidate Palestinian national unity at all levels inside and outside the occupied territory under the leadership of our Movement and within the framework of the PLO, so as to ensure the continuing escalation of all forms of Palestinian struggle.

2. The importance of stepping up our Movement's participation — with its proper weight — in the PLO, so as to ensure that it plays an effective role and so as to develop its internal regulations and organs in such a way as to guarantee the independence of all its institutions.

3. The escalation of armed struggle inside the occupied territory and via all lines of confrontation with the Zionist enemy.

4. Increasing concern for the organization of our people wherever they may reside, and expansion of the framework of the activities of popular and professional organizations and federations; protection of our people in their places of temporary residence and defence of them against persecution, exploitation or absorption.

5. Support at all levels for the steadfastness of our people inside the occupied territory, and provision of the necessary material support to enable them to maintain their steadfastness, escalate their struggle and develop all their national institutions and, in particular, efforts to strengthen the links

with the Palestinian masses in the territories occupied in 1948 to enable them to resist the plans to fragment their unity and suppress their Arab identity.

6. Stress on the necessity of independent Palestinian decision-making, and efforts to develop the ability of all organizations of the Palestinian revolution to abide by the independent Palestinian decision.

7. In conformity with the leading position occupied by our Movement in the PLO, with what the political programme outlines on this subject and with the legitimacy of the PLO in the Arab and international arenas, the resolutions of the PLO's Palestinian National Council currently in force are to be regarded as complementing the Movement's Political Programme, since they do not conflict with the goals and principles of our Movement and its political programmes.

8. Consolidation of the role of the Palestinian woman in all the fields of struggle, and efforts to ensure that she participates effectively in all frameworks and at all levels.

II. At the Arab Level

A. At the Mass level:

Inasmuch as Palestine is part of the Arab homeland, and the Palestinian people are part of the Arab nation and their struggle part of its struggle, and inasmuch as the Palestinian revolution is the vanguard of the Arab nation in the battle for the liberation of Palestine, [the Conference affirms that:]

1. The relationship with the Arab masses is a strategic relation that enjoins more extensive participation by these masses in the protection of the revolution and in the conduct of all forms of struggle against the imperialist Zionist base in Palestine and against all the enemies of our people and our nation, and in the liquidation of imperialist and colonialist interests in the region.

2. There must be closer cohesion with the Arab national liberation movements and the Arab nationalist and progressive forces for the joint battle for the liberation of Palestine, and the achievement of the objectives of the Arab nation in the liberation of its regions and the building of a unified progressive Arab society.

4. [There must be] consolidation of the militant cohesion with the Lebanese national movement and all other nationalist forces that are valiantly fighting in the same trench as the Palestinian revolution against the enemies of the Palestinian and Lebanese peoples and the Arab nation, and participation with them in the struggle to protect Lebanon's unity, Arab character and territorial integrity. This requires strenuous efforts [both] to eliminate all negative manifestations that threaten relations with the masses, and to consolidate our relations with them by all ways and means.

4. The cohesion of the Lebanese masses with, and heroice support for, the Palestinian revolution in confronting the war of liquidation and annihilation

must be safeguarded, supported and developed so that it may become a model for relations with the masses throughout the Arab homeland on the basis of kinship ties; this requires further support with all our energies and resources.

5. The special importance of the Jordanian arena requires that special attention be devoted to its recovery as one of the principal bases of support in the struggle against the Zionist enemy; the energies of the masses must be harnessed for the achievement of this goal.

6. [It is necessary to] reinforce the common struggle with the Egyptian people, represented by their nationalist and progressive forces, to abort the Camp David conspiracy and its consequences, and to bring Egypt back into Arab ranks to assume its natural position in the Arab struggle.

B. At the level of Relations with Arab Regimes:

Inasmuch as the aim of relations with the Arab regimes is to develop their positive aspects, these relations must be governed by the following principles:

1. The principles, goals and methods of the Movement.

2. These relations must not conflict with the strategic relations with the masses.

3. The position of each regime with regard to the cause of Palestine and the armed revolution of its people and, in particular, recognition of and commitment to the PLO as the sole legitimate representative of the Palestinian people, and rejection of any attempt from any quarter to prejudice this.

4. No interference in our internal affairs, and confrontation of any attempts to impose tutelage on or to subjugate our people, or to persecute or exploit them, also confrontation of any attempt to settle [our people] in any land other than their homeland, Palestine.

5. Confrontation of any attempt to deny the revolution freedom of action within the ranks of our people, wherever they reside.

6. The revolution exercises its responsibilities at the pan-Arab level and via any Arab territory for the sake of [regaining] the occupied Palestinian Arab territories, and every effort must be made to mobilize the human and material resources of the Arab nation, in particular its oil wealth, as a weapon for the achievement of this goal.

7. Efforts to develop the Steadfastness and Confrontation Front so that it may become a primary instrument of action based on supporting the PLO, continuing the struggle against the Zionist enemy and confronting and thwarting all liquidationist solutions; efforts to harden Arab positions with a view to confronting and foiling the settlement in whatever form and under whatever name, and resolute resistance to any attempt to provide the Camp David agreements with a cover of legitimacy.

8. Efforts to create a broad Arab front, as stipulated by the resolutions of Steadfastness and Confrontation Front, for the confrontation of all imperialist and Zionist conspiracies, and first and foremost, the Camp David

conspiracy in all its forms.

III. At the International Level

Inasmuch as the cause of Palestine is the central cause of the Arab nation in its just struggle against the Zionist-imperialist enemy;

And inasmuch as the Middle East area is of international strategic importance, the cause of Palestine, in addition to its justice and the struggle of its people, has always had an important international dimension and [has always] been the focus of world conflict that has led to the emergence of two camps: that of the enemies, and that of the friends of the cause and the struggle of our people.

Our Movement is part of the international liberation movement in the common struggle against imperialism, Zionism, racism and their agents, and we establish our alliances with all international parties in conformity with our principles and with the Palestinian National Charter.

A. International Organizations:

[The Conference affirms the need for:]

1. Efforts through the PLO to secure the adoption of more comprehensive resolutions on the rights of the Palestinian Arab people in all international forums and organizations — in particular the UN — so as to increase the isolation of the Zionist-American enemy in these organizations and in the international arena.

2. Efforts to embody the UN General Assembly resolution condemning Zionism as a form of racism and racial discrimination in measures and sanctions against the imperialist and settler Zionist base in Palestine, as stipulated by the UN Charter.

3. Intensification of efforts to maintain the UN positions rejecting the Camp David agreements, and to develop these positions to involve the rejection of all forms of settlement reached at the expense of our people and their cause.

B. Friendly Forces:

[The Conference affirms the importance of:]

1. Consolidating the strategic alliance with the socialist countries, headed by the USSR, since this alliance is essential for the serious and effective confrontation of American and Zionist conspiracies against the cause of Palestine and liberation causes in the world.

2. Consolidating our relations with the world liberation movements that are fighting in the same trench with us against American imperialism, Zionism, racism, Fascism and reaction; Fatah supports the struggle of all liberation movements and all freedom-fighters against injustice, coercion and tyranny.

3. Consolidating our Movement's external relations and intensifying its

political activity on the basis of the Movement's principles and programmes, for the establishment of alliances with democratic and progressive political forces that support our just struggle and our legitimate rights.

4. Consolidating relations with the Islamic revolution in Iran which has swept away the most arrogant fortress of American imperialism in the region, and which supports us in our struggle for the liberation of Palestine.

5. Strengthening relations with the peoples and governments of the Islamic, African and the non-aligned countries, with a view to developing their positions towards greater support of the Palestinian cause and our struggle, and to winning greater recognition of the PLO as the sole legitimate representative of the Palestinian people.

C. The American Position:

The US heads the enemies of our people and our nation in that it pursues a policy hostile to our people, our revolution and the Arab nation, and to all Arab and international forces of liberation; it supports the Zionist enemy and its agents in the area, and establishes military pacts with the aim of subjecting the area to its military influence so that it may continue to plunder the wealth of our nation. It is, therefore, imperative to consolidate the international front opposed to US policy, to fight against it and abort it, and to strike at American interests in the area.

D. The Positions of Western Europe (EEC), Japan and Canada:

1. [The Conference affirms the need to] intensify political activity in these countries and benefit from the support of democratic and progressive political forces in them to reduce and then halt support for the Zionist entity, and achieve its isolation through the recognition by these forces of the PLO as the sole legitimate representative of the Palestinian people, and [the need to] achieve maximum political and material support for our cause, our struggle and our national rights.

2. Many of the Western European countries and Canada still pursue a policy that does not recognize the national rights of our people, and they provide support at all levels to the Zionist enemy. They are following a policy in conformity with that of the US and its schemes in the area, and Japan's policy is not dissimilar. Therefore, efforts must be intensified to resist and thwart any plan or initiative that conflicts with the national rights of our people.

In conclusion, the General Conference of our Movement stresses the need to safeguard and consolidate the political gains that have been achieved in the international political arena, and that have kept the cause of Palestine a living cause that enjoys such extensive international support that it is now the vanguard and standard-bearer of the world liberation movement.

17. Palestinian National Council Political Statement, Damascus, 21 April, 1981

The Palestine National Council [PNC] held its 15th session in Damascus, the capital of the Arab Republic of Syria, from 11-16 April 1981. His Excellency President Hafiz al-Assad, the president of the Syrian Republic, inaugurated the session with a speech in which he affirmed the cohesion of the Arab Syrian people with the struggle of the Arab people of Palestine and Syria's commitment to wage a struggle to liberate Palestine. President al-Assad pointed out the uniqueness of the Palestinian revolution in the Arab struggle movement and expressed Syria's intention to continue its support for the PLO in its confrontation with the Zionist-imperialist aggression and the Camp David designs and its signatories.

Ninety-two delegations representing Arab fraternal countries as well as friendly countries participated in the conference. Also attending were delegations from national liberation movements and from political organizations of a number of countries. These delegations delivered speeches expressing their countries' support for the Arab Palestinian people's struggle and its just cause. Also attending were a large number of observers representing the Palestinian people from various areas of their residence who are contributing to various spheres of the struggle; these observers interacted with the activities of the conference.

This session was convened at a time when the Palestinian struggle was waging an escalating struggle under the leadership of the PLO in various arenas inside and outside Palestine's soil in order to confront the imperialist-colonialist-Zionist aggression and to pursue its march along the path of liberation and return [to the homeland].

This aggression has been embodied by many forms represented by daily attacks that are being carried out by the Zionist enemy forces by land, sea and air against southern Lebanon and in which these forces are using the most deadly U.S. arms. This aggression is also embodied in the policies of persecution, despotism and settlement being practiced by the Zionist occupation in the Palestinian people's homeland. Another form of this aggression is represented by U.S. attempts to impose its domination and control over the Arab nation and the areas surrounding it by various means, foremost among which is the establishment of military bases and the call to sign pacts while brandishing the so-called Soviet threat.

The PNC conducted its activities in a democratic atmosphere, an atmosphere which the Palestinian people are very keen on and which the PLO adheres to and which the Palestinian revolution takes pride in.

The council debated the political and financial reports that were submitted by the Executive Committee and studied, by means of its committees, the various dimensions of the current situation in the Palestinian, Arab and international arenas. The PNC committees adopted the necessary organizational, military, political and financial resolutions with regard to various issues.

The PNC affirmed the organizational and political programs adopted in its previous session, the democratic bases and the collective leadership in various levels related to the PLO's activities and its bodies. The PNC also affirmed the need to have the PLO's offices and organizations exercise their full powers and establish specialized supreme councils on factional bases in order to draw up plans for the PLO's institutions in the military, information and financial spheres and to supervise their implementation.

The council expressed the need to work for completing national unity through the participation of the revolutionary squads and all the Palestinian national forces in all the institutions and in the various popular national organizations — inasmuch as this will constitute the basis for unifying the people's efforts. The council also called for developing the unified military activities under the responsibility of the Supreme Military Council and the Executive Committee in order to ensure the proper confrontation of the current perilous circumstances and as a step along the road to full military union.

The council stressed the importance of establishing consultative committees which will interact with the organization's offices wherever they may be and wherever Palestinian communities and aggregations exist.

The PNC also approved the proposal to declare a general military mobilization that will include the various sectors of our people in their places of congregation outside the occupied homeland. The council also called on the Arab and friendly countries to facilitate the implementation of the above and to enable the Palestinians residing in their countries to join the Palestinian revolutionary forces.

The council affirmed that the only alternative for resolving the Palestinian problem is the Palestinian alternative. The council rejected and denounced those alternative solutions proposed for solving the Palestinian problem by the imperialist-Zionist and those worked out by agents.

The PNC also affirmed that no country has the right to allege that it represents the Palestinian people or to negotiate the Palestinian problems — whether this refers to the Palestinian soil, people or rights. Anyone who violates this is taking a decision that is null and void and has no legal standing. The PLO alone has the right to choose the just and overall solution that will fully ensure the Palestinian people's firm national rights.

The council affirmed that the occupied city of Jerusalem is the capital of Palestine and that the council regards the Zionist occupation of Jerusalem as a violation of the Palestinian people's rights and a defiance of international laws as well as a provocation of all the believers in the world. The council called on all the world countries and organizations to refuse to carry out anything that will entail an implicit recognition of the Zionist aggression against Jerusalem or its actions therein.

In its debates and resolutions the council expressed its deep admiration for the standard of struggle which has been attained by our people's uprising in the occupied homeland, as well as their solid unity and their complete cohesion with the PLO. The council saluted the heroic struggle of our people in the Galilee, the triangle and the Negev as well as in Jerusalem, the West Bank and the Gaza Strip against the Zionist designs that aim at expanding the settlements, Judaization and the destruction of the national economy and education and the holy places.

The council also expressed its admiration for the steadfastness of those who are interned in the enemy's prisons and who are setting an example in their sacrifice in defending their people's right to liberate and return to their homeland. The council affirmed the exceeding importance of building the PNC inside the occupied homeland, considering that the PNC is a vital arm of the PLO and stressed the role of the national guiding committee and the various popular bodies and organizations in their national struggle against occupation and its designs.

The council stressed the importance of supporting the organizations encompassing students, unions and women as well as various vocational unions and municipal councils to enable them to carry out their tasks in enhancing the steadfastness of our people on their own soil and in bolstering their unity in the face of the Zionist enemy's practices and its expansionist policies.

The council considers the development and escalation of the armed struggle against the Zionist enemy as being the cardinal task that rests on the shoulders of the Palestinian revolution inside and outside [Palestine]. The council reiterated the importance of opening the various Arab fronts to the heroic fighters of our revolution.

The council debated social, economic, educational and health issues related to our people in their places of residence and the appropriate solutions for these issues. In this respect the council affirmed the importance of supporting the role of the institutions working within the framework of the organization which are dealing with the aforementioned problems.

the council also considered the continuation of UNRWA an international responsibility until the times comes for our refugees to practice their unshaken right in returning to their houses and taking over their properties. The council called for putting an end to the political blackmail being practiced by some Western countries, particularly the United States, which is embodied by threats of curbing the UNRWA services. The council affirmed the Arab League's resolution to work for integrating UNRWA's budget with the UN's regular budget.

The council also affirmed the importance of enhancing Arab solidarity by pledging enmity toward imperialism, Zionism and by rejecting the Camp David agreements and the Egyptian-Israeli pact and by implementing the Palestinian people's firm national rights, including their right to return to their homeland, their right to self-determination and the establishment of their independent state on their national soil under the leadership of the PLO.

The PNC also denounced Somalia, Oman and Sudan, which deviated from the Arab summit resolutions in Baghdad and Tunis. The council stressed the importance of the alliance between Syria and the PLO considering them the basic foundation of the Arab nation's struggle and its confrontation against its enemies. The council emphasized the importance of enhancing these fateful relations and providing the means that will achieve the joint national struggle.

The PNC stressed the importance of the deep-rooted struggle in the relations between the Palestinian and Jordanian fraternal people and the PNC's support for the Jordanian national movement in various spheres, particularly in its national struggle against any attempt to make Jordan deviate from the Arab and Islamic summit resolutions with regard to the Palestinian problem and the rejection of the Camp David agreements and the autonomy conspiracy. The council declared the PLO's adherence to the Arab summit resolutions in Algeria, Rabat, Baghdad and Tunis. The council regards the Jordanian regime's adherence to these resolutions — such as enabling the PLO to assume its popular responsibilities of struggle in the Jordanian arena — as the basis governing bilateral relations. The council also placed the blame on the Jordanian regime for not attaining positive results [with the PLO] that would practically enhance the PLO's role as the sole legal representative of the Palestinian people in their various places of residence.

The PNC also discussed the joint coordination committee's activities in bolstering steadfastness and stressed the need to work on the Arab level to let the PLO assume its full responsibility in this respect. The council also stressed the role of the Palestinian side in the committee and the need to draw a comprehensive plan, in accordance with predetermined priorities, in order to bolster the steadfastness of our people and their national institutions with the participation of the revolutionary squads as well as with national gatherings inside and outside the homeland.

Considering the fateful cohesion between the Lebanese and Palestinian people, the National Council stressed the importance of a unified political and military stance between the Palestinian revolution and the Lebanese National Movement and various other Lebanese forces as well as the importance of the joint struggle to thwart all the attempts that aim at sapping the strength of the Palestinian revolution in the Lebanese arena, at fragmenting Lebanon, and at endangering its security and Arab character.

The PNC saluted the Lebanese and Palestinian masses and the joint forces, which are standing fast in southern Lebanon, for their sacrifices and acts of heroism in their confrontation against the Zionist enemy and the separatist forces, which are armed to the teeth by the most modern U.S. weapons of destruction. The PNC also considers the Arab summit resolutions and the bases of national accord that were announced by President Ilyas Sarkis as the starting points for ensuring Lebanon's stability and for preserving the Palestinian revolution. The council also affirmed the continuation of the struggle, side by side with the heroic Lebanese people, under the leadership of their national movement and the various other national forces for the sake of the unity of Lebanon's territory, and their people's Arab character and democratic development.

The PNC affirmed its support for the Lebanese National Movement, which rejects all forms of outside intervention and the internationalization projects that aim at harming the Palestinian revolution's steadfastness, the Lebanese National Movement and Syria.

The PNC praised the efforts to unify the forces that are opposed to the separatist-Zionist designs into a broad Lebanese national front. The council affirmed the importance of the national role being played by the Arab Deterrent Forces in order to preserve Lebanon's security, Arab character, territorial safety and unity and in order to foil the partition plans. The council also expressed its rejection of all the resettlement plans and affirmed its full adherance to our people's right to return to their homeland — Palestine.

The PNC has also highly praised the patriotic and progressive forces in Arab Egypt for their heroic struggle waged to abort the Camp David accords and the Egyptian-Israeli treaty. The PNC emphasized its support for the patriotic forces and its belief in the inevitable triumph of the will of our Arab people in Egypt so that Egypt would resume its role of leading the Arab struggle against imperialism and Zionism and for the sake of liberating Palestine.

Regarding the Iraqi-Iranian war, the PNC called for the need to halt this war forthwith. The PNC blessed the efforts that the PLO command has exerted, and which it is still exerting, to halt this war so that the full potential of the two countries could be channeled toward buttressing the struggle that is being waged against the imperialist-Zionist aggression against our area and to liberate Palestine and holy Jerusalem. The reason is that the continuation of this war harms our cause and serves the enemies of our Arab nation and the Muslim peoples.

The PNC emphasized the importance of boosting the efficacy of the National Front for Steadfastness and Confrontation and the need to develop the existing relations among the members of this front in a way that would facilitate achieving its objectives to check all the imperialist conspiracies which are facing this area — first and foremost the Camp David designs and the parties to these designs. The PNC also stressed the basic role of the PLO and Syria, within the framework of the National Front for Steadfastness and

Confrontation, in seeking to discharge the national and pan-Arab objectives of the struggle prescribed by the resolutions passed by the steadfastness and confrontation summit conference.

The PNC expressed the importance it attaches to the Arab people's conference and the need to work to develop the formula for this conference so that this conference can constitute the framework for a popular Arab front dedicated to the achievement of the objectives of our Arab people and nation — liberation, unity and advancement.

The PNC affirmed that imperialist military provocations that are being made in the Arab Gulf and Red Sea areas are an integral part of the imperialist strategy geared to striking the national liberation movements, controlling the destinies and resources of the area and imposing political, military and economic mobilization against it.

The PNC also emphasized that it is imperative to use the Arab homeland's oil resources to ensure the prosperity and progress of the Arab nation and to serve this nation's present causes, particularly the Palestine cause.

The PNC delineated the importance of a strong alliance among the world's revolutionary forces. It expressed its desire to consolidate the relations of friendship and solidarity with the socialist countries — with the friendly Soviet Union in the forefront — with the national liberation movements and with the democratic and progressive forces hostile to imperialism and Zionism in the capitalist countries.

The PNC welcomed the announcement made by President Brezhnev at the 26th CPSU Congress on the Middle East crisis. In this announcement President Brezhnev emphasized the basic role the PLO is playing in the achievement of a just solution to the crisis, the need to put into practice the Palestinian people's inalienable national rights, including their right to set up their independent national state as confirmed by the UN resolutions passed on the Palestine question and the UN role in the resolution of this issue.

The council expressed its appreciation of the political and moral support extended by the socialist countries to the Palestinian revolution and the Palestinian people's struggle.

The PNC emphasized its interest in the unity of the Non-aligned, Movement on the basis of the movement's principles opposed to imperialism, Zionism and racism. It expressed its appreciation of the non-aligned states' solidarity with our people's struggle for their inalienable national rights and their confrontation with aggression. The council lauded the resolutions adopted by the non-aligned sixth summit conference in Havana and the recent resolutions of the foreign ministers in New Delhi on the Palestine and Middle East questions.

The council commended Arab-African solidarity in the struggle against the enemy and its ally the racist regime in South Africa. It also expressed its appreciation of the African states' solidarity with our people's struggle and it saluted the triumph scored by the people of Zimbabwe against racism and the emergence of the Zimbabwe nationalist state. The PNC expressed its full support for the struggle of the people of Namibia against the racist regime in South Africa and for freedom and independence.

The council underscored its firm support for the struggle of the peoples of Latin America and the Caribbean region. It condemned the aggressive practices of the U.S. Government in that region.

The council emphasized the importance of widening the circle of recognition for the PLO. It discussed the moves carried out by the EC states. It expressed its conviction that it is the right and the duty of the Palestinian revolution to continue its political and diplomatic moves and activity at the international level, including the states of Western Europe.

The PNC decided that the soundness of any initiative is measured by its nonrecognition of the Camp David accords and agreements as a basis of a settlement and the recognition of the PLO as the sole legitimate representative of the Palestinian people as well as our people's right to repatriation, self-determination and to their independent state on their national soil.

The PNC called on the Arab and Islamic States, especially the oil states among them, to use their capabilities and resources to make the industrial and capitalist states recognize the PLO and all the inalienable national rights of the Palestinian people.

The council saluted all the democratic and progressive forces opposed to imperialism, Zionism, recial discrimination, and fascism in the states of Western Europe as well as all the capitalist states.

The PNC strongly condemned terrorism and international terrorism, especially the Zionist official and organized terrorism against the Palestinian people, the PLO and the people of Lebanon, as well as American imperialist terrorism against the world liberation movements.

The council affirmed its adherence to the UN Charter and international legitimacy which has recognized the Palestinian people's national rights which are non-negotiable.

At the end of its meetings the PNC accepted the resignation of the Executive Committee in accordance with the basic laws. It elected a new Executive Committee manifesting national unity. The Executive Committee unanimously elected Brother Yasser Arafat as its chairman.

The council extended the term of the present National Council until the meeting of the 16th National Council and specified the way in which it is to be formed.

18. Committee for the Occupied Homeland Report on Contact with Jews. Damascus 21 April, 1981

The Committee discussed various subjects related to the development of activities within the occupied land, in all the military, economic and social spheres. . .

A number of most important matters were decided upon regarding the mobilization and concentration of all the potentials of our masses in the occupied homeland *(al-watan al-muhtall)*, in order to intensify the armed struggle, and to confirm their commitment to the PLO. . .

The recommendations made a special point of saluting the heroic struggle of the Palestinian masses in that part of Palestine occupied since 1948, which thwarted the enemy plans for the liquidation of their identity, the Judaization of their land and the annihilation of their national culture. . .

Regarding the necessities of strengthening the steadfastness and intensifying the national struggle within the occupied land *(al-ard al-muhtall)*, the Council emphasized the need for the mobilization and concentration of the masses' potentials, for the intensification of the armed struggle and the supplying of its necessities, insuring that the PLO is the sole party responsible for the matters concerning the strengthening of our people and its steadfastness in the occupied homeland. . .

The recommendations also confirmed the positive role which the democratic and progressive Jewish anti-Zionist forces play, both ideologically and practically, within the occupied homeland and their recognition of the PLO as the sole legitimate representative of the Palestinian people. . .

The recommendation condemned any contacts which would be held with the parties which follow the way of Zionism, both ideologically and practically. . .

19. Palestinian National Council Political Resolutions, Algiers, 22 February, 1983

On the Palestinian Front

1. Palestinian National Unity:

The steadfast and heroic battle in Lebanon and Beirut embodied Palestinian national unity at its best. From the vantage point of the experience of struggle, the PNC affirms the strengthening of national unity between the factions of the revolution within the PLO and affirms the work to advance the structure of organizational relations in all PLO institutions and bodies on the basis of united front work and collective leadership and on the basis of the political and organizational programme approved by the fourteenth session of the PNC.

(A)   The Independent National Decision:

The PNC affirms the continued adherence to and protection of independent Palestinian decisions and resistance to all pressures from any side, aimed at influencing this independence.

(B)   Armed Palestinian Struggle:

The PNC affirms the need to develop and intensify armed struggle against the Zionist enemy. It also affirms the right of the Palestinian revolutionary forces to carry out military actions against the Zionist enemy from all Arab fronts. It also affirms the need to unite the Palestinian revolutionary forces within the framework of a united Palestinian national liberation army.

2.   The Occupied Homeland:

(a)   The PNC salutes our masses, steadfast in the occupied territories in the face of occupation, settlement and uprooting. It salutes their total national consensus and adherence to the PLO, the sole legitimate representative of the Palestinian people, *inside* and *outside* (the country).

(b)   The PNC denounces and condemns all suspicious American and Israeli attempts to strike at the Palestinian national consensus and calls on the masses to resist and confront them.

(c)   The PNC affirms the strengthening of the unity of popular, social and national institutions and unions and affirms the need to work to build and develop a national front *inside*.

(d)   The PNC affirms the need to double efforts to strengthen the steadfastness of our people inside the occupied homeland and to offer all the requisites for this steadfastness. Thus, to put an end to enforced emigration and to preserve the land and develop the national economy.

(e)   The PNC salutes the steadfastness of our people inside the areas occupied in 1948 and is proud of their struggle and stand, in the face of Zionist racism, to confirm their national identity as an inseparable part of the Palestinian people. The PNC also affirms the need to provide them with all means of support and to strengthen their unity and the unity of their national forces and institutions.

(f)   The council sends greetings of esteem and pride to prisoners and detainees in enemy prisons inside the occupied homeland and in South Lebanon.

3.   Our People in the Diaspora:

The PNC affirms the need to mobilize the energies of our people in all places outside our occupied land and to strengthen their adherence to the PLO as the sole legitimate representative of our Palestinian people. The council charges the executive committee to work to safeguard their (the Palestinian people's) economic and social interests and to defend their acquired rights and their basic freedom and safety.

Relations with Jewish Forces

Affirming resolution 14 of the political declaration issued by the PNC at its thirteenth session held on December 3, 1977, the PNC calls on the executive committee to study action in this framework, insofar as it is in keeping with and in the interest of the Palestinian cause and the national Palestinian struggle.

On the Arab Front

1. Arab Relations:

(a) Deepening the cohesion between the Palestinian revolution and the Arab national liberation movement in the whole Arab nation, in order to actively confront Zionist and imperialist conspiracies and plans of annihilation, especially the Camp David accords and the Reagan plan, and in order to end the Zionist occupation of Arab lands.

(b) Relations between the PLO and Arab States to be built on the following basis:

(i) Commitment to the cause of Arab struggle, headed by the Palestinian cause and struggle for its sake;

(ii) Adherence to the right of the Palestinian people, including the right of return, of self-determination and to establish an independent state under the leadership of the PLO. These are the rights endorsed by Arab summits' resolutions.

(iii) Determination on the unity of representation and national unity and respect for independent Palestinian national decision.

(iv) Rejection of all plans aimed at encroaching upon the right of the PLO as sole legitimate representative of the Palestinian people in any form such as power-of-attorney or agent or participant in the right of representation.

(v) The PNC calls for the strengthening of Arab solidarity on the basis of Arab summit conferences' resolutions and in the light of the above-mentioned principles.

2. Resolutions of the Fez Summit: "The Arab Peace Plan"

The PNC considers the resolutions of the Fez Summit as the minimum for political action by the Arab States which must be complimented by military action in all that it entails, in order to redress the balance of power in favour of the struggle and Arab and Palestinian rights.

The council affirms that its understanding of these resolutions does not contradict commitment to the political programme of the PNC resolutions.

3. Jordan

(i) Affirmation of the special and distinctive relations linking the Palestinian and Jordanian peoples. Affirmation of the need to work to develop this harmony and the national interest of the two peoples and the Arab nation to attain the firm national rights of the Palestinian people, including the right of return, self-determination and the establishment of an independent Palestinian State.

(ii) Adherence to the resolutions of the PNC concerning relations with Jordan, starting with the PLO as the sole legitimate representative of the Palestinian people, *inside* and *outside* the occupied territories.

The PNC sees future relations with Jordan developing on the basis of a confederation between two independent states.

4. Lebanon

(i) Strengthening relations with the Lebanese people and their national forces and offering support to their brave struggle in resisting Zionist occupation and its tools.

(ii) At the forefront of current tasks facing the Palestinian revolution is participation with the Lebanese masses and their democratic national forces in fighting and ending the Zionist occupation.

(ii) The PNC calls on the executive council to work for holding talks between the PLO and the Lebanese government to achieve safety and security for Palestinian residents living in Lebanon and to ensure their rights to residency, freedom of movement, work opportunity and freedom of social and political activity.

(iv) Work to stop the random collective and individual arrests on political bases and the release of detainees from prisons of the Lebanese authorities.

5. Relations with Syria

Relations with Syria are based on PNC resolutions, in successive sessions, which affirm the importance of strategic relations between the PLO and Syria, in the service of patriotic and national goals of struggle in confronting the Zionist-imperialist enemy, and regarding the PLO and Syria — the front line before the common danger.

6. Steadfastness and Confrontation Front

The PNC empowers the executive committee of the PLO to hold talks with all parties of the Steadfastness and Confrontation Front to discuss its revival on actual, clear and sound bases, considering that the front did not meet the tasks required from it during the Zionist invasion of Lebanon.

7. *Egypt*

The PNC affirms its rejection of the Camp David accords and related plans for autonomy and civil administration. From its deep-rooted belief in the role of Egypt and its great people in the Arab struggle, the council affirms its stand alongside the struggle of the Egyptian people and their national forces to end the policy of Camp David, so that Egypt can return to its position of struggle at the heart of the Arab nation. The council calls on the executive committee to develop the PLO's relations with the Egyptian popular democratic national forces struggling against the normalization of relations with the Zionist enemy in various forms. It regards this (struggle) as expressing the basic interests of the Arab nation and supporting the struggle of our Palestinian people for their national rights. The council calls on the executive committee to define relations with the Egyptian regime on the basis of the latter's abandoning the Camp David policy.

8. *The Iraq-Iran War*

The PNC holds in esteem the efforts of the PLO executive committee to end the Iraq-Iran war through the committees of the non-aligned countries and the Islamic countries. The council calls on the executive committee to continue its efforts to end this war, after Iraq declares the withdrawal of its forces from Iranian territory in response to the call of the Palestinian revolution, to mobilize all forces in the battle for the liberation of Palestine.

On the International Front

1. *The Brezhnev Plan*

The PNC expresses its esteem and support for the proposals contained in the plan of President Brezhnev published on September 16, 1980 and which affirm the inalienable national rights of our Palestinian people, including those of return, self-determination and the establishment of an independent Palestinian State under the leadership of the PLO, the sole legitimate representative of the Palestinian people. The council also expresses its esteem for the stand of the socialist bloc countries on the just cause of our people as affirmed by the Prague declaration on the Middle East situation, published on January 3, 1983.

2. *The Reagan Plan*

The Reagan plan, in form and content, does not fulfill the inalienable national rights of the Palestinian people because it denies the right of return, self-determination, the establishment of an independent Palestinian State and that the PLO is sole legitimate representative of the Palestinian people and it contradicts international law. For these reasons, the PNC declares its refusal to consider the plan as a proper basis for a lasting and just solution to the Palestinian cause and the Zionist-Arab conflict.

3. International Relations

(i) Deepening and developing relations of the alliance and friendship between the PLO and the socialist countries, primarily the Soviet Union, and various international progressive and liberation forces opposed to racism, colonialism, Zionism and imperialism;

(ii) Deepening relations with non-aligned countries and Islamic and African countries for the sake of the Palestinian cause and other national liberation causes;

(iii) Strengthening relations with friendly countries in Latin America and working to widen the sphere of friendship there;

(iv) Activating political work with the countries of Western Europe and Japan, with the aim of developing their stand and widening the recognition of the PLO and the right of the Palestinian people to establish an independent Palestinian State.

The PNC salutes all progressive and democratic forces hostile to racial discrimination, Zionism and imperialism in Western European countries and various capitalist countries, considering them a basic ally in these countries. (The council) calls on the executive committee to work jointly with these forces for their countries to recognize the firm national rights of the Palestinian people and the PLO.

(v) Continuing the struggle to achieve the isolation of the Zionist entity in the United Nations in various fields;

(vi) Confronting American imperialism and its policy, regarding it as standing at the head of the camp hostile to our just cause and the causes of struggling peoples.

(vii) The council affirms the importance of continuing the struggle against racial discrimination which remains the prevailing practise in a number of regimes, especially South Africa, which has established the firmest relations with the Zionist enemy. The council salutes the struggle of the developing people, led by the SWAPO organization, for freedom and independence. The council also salutes the struggle of the people of South Africa against racial discrimination and oppression.

(viii) The PNC strongly condemns terrorism and international terrorism, particularly the organized and official terrorism of Israel and the US, against the Palestinian people, the PLO, the Lebanese people, the Arab nation and various national liberation movements.

(ix) The PNC affirms its adherence to the principles, charter and resolutions of the United Nations, which confirm the non-negotiable, inalienable national rights of the Palestinian people to establish a lasting and just peace in the Middle East and the right of all peoples subjugated by occupation to practice all forms of struggle for national independence and liberation. The council also affirms its decisive condemnation of all Zionist and imperialist practises which violate international law and the International Declaration of Human Rights and the principles and resolutions of the United Nations Charter.

(x) The PNC values the activities and achievements of the special UN committee in enabling the Palestinian people to exercise their inalienable rights in Palestine. (The council) salutes the efforts of its members, especially the decision of the UN General Assembly to organize an international conference in the summer of 1983 to support the Palestinian people in achieving their inalienable rights.

The council likewise values the achievements of the secretariat of the international conference of the United Nations in preparing for the success of this conference. The council calls on all brother Arab countries and friendly countries to participate effectively in the work of the conference and likewise, in preparatory and regional meetings, to secure the success of the work of the international conference.

There is no doubt that the people's victory will come. The solidarity of peace-loving peoples is a solidarity we cherish and adhere to. The PNC sends salutations to all the heroic masses of our people, *inside* and *outside* (the occupied territories) and to our brave fighters who have preserved the honour of their revolution, arms and nation. (The council also salutes) the souls of the martyrs and fighters of our Palestinian people and of the Lebanese people who irrigated the national soil with blood and who affirmed that the cause of freedom will not die in our country.

The PNC also salutes our brothers in the Syrian forces who participated in the heroic battle in Beirut and other areas, and their martyrs. The PNC also values all the Arab and Muslim volunteers and friends who came to participate with the joint forces in the battles of Beirut and Lebanon. We salute their heroic martyrs.

The PNC values all countries and friendly forces who offered the support of weapons, money and military effort through equipment and training, particularly the Arab and Islamic States, the non-aligned countries, the African countries and the socialist countries.

— Long live the victorious Palestinian revolution.

— Long live the PLO, the unified framework of our people and leader of their struggle.

— Long live the unity of the struggle of our Arab peoples and the peoples of the world for the sake of freedom and national independence the defeat of Zionism, racism and imperialism.

— Honour and eternal glory to our martyrs.
Revolution Until Victory.

In conclusion, the council warmly thanks and deeply appreciates the people, party, government and president of Algeria for hosting the council and its guests and for its great care for the success of (the council's) work. (We also thank them) for their effort to ensure the coverage of (the council's) activities in the mass media and in providing a suitable atmosphere for the progress of its discussions and ensuring the safety and comfort of its members and guests. The council especially thanks our brother, President Chadhli Ben Jadid, president of the republic and general secretary of the party, for his officially declared stand concerning the independence of Palestinian decision, and Algeria's readiness to support and further this decision by supporting the Palestinian struggle until it achieves victory and the establishment of an independent Palestinian State.

The council sends thanks and esteem to all popular and official delegations who participated in the work of our council and who declared their support for the PLO and the cause of the Palestinian people.

This international support of our revolution is, without doubt, one of the basic elements in the success of our march, in which the free peoples prove their solidarity in face of the joint enemy of Zionism and imperialism for the sake of the progress, independence and freedom of peoples.

As for our brother Arab delegations who have participated with our council, while thanking and saluting them for their presence and support, we also thank them in particular for their role and action in the Arab arena in creating more favourable conditions for supporting our struggle and for confronting Israeli plans.

The PNC, at the conclusion of its work, promises the Arab and Palestinian masses and all international forces for freedom and struggle, to continue the struggle in all political and military forms and to pursue them towards our people's goals. It considers this international, Arab and Palestinian cohesion to be one of the effective weapons of support and solidarity between peoples whose certain result must be the attainment of praiseworthy goals.

Arab Documents

1. The Arab League Summit Conference Resolutions, Khartoum, Sudan, 1 September, 1967

Public Resolutions. On 1 Sept, Sudanese PM Mahjub read out the following resolutions adopted by the Conference:

1) The Conference has affirmed the unity of Arab ranks, the unity of joint action and the need for co-ordination and for the elimination of all differences. The Conference affirmed the Arab Solidarity Charter which was signed at the Third Arab Summit Conference held in Casablanca, and undertook to implement it.

2) The Conference has agreed on the need to consolidate all efforts to eliminate the effects of the aggression on the basis that the occupied lands are Arab lands and that the burden of regaining these lands falls on all the Arab States.

3) The Arab heads of state have agreed to unite their political efforts at the international and diplomatic level to eliminate the effects of the aggression and to ensure the withdrawal of the aggressive Israeli forces from the Arab lands which have been occupied since the aggression of 5 June. This will be done within the framework of the main principles by which the Arab States abide, namely no peace with Israel, no recognition of Israel, no negotiations with it, and insistence on the rights of the Palestinian people in their own country.

4) The Conference of the Arab Ministers of Finance, Economy and Oil recommended that suspension of oil pumping be used as a weapon in the battle. However, after thoroughly studying the matter, the Summit Conference has come to the conclusion that the pumping of oil can itself be used as a positive weapon, since oil is an Arab resource which can be used to strengthen the economy of the Arab States directly affected by the aggression, so that these states will be able to stand firm in the battle. The Conference has,

therefore, decided to resume the pumping of oil, since oil is a positive Arab resource that can be used in the service of Arab goals. It can contribute to the efforts to enable those Arab States which were exposed to the aggression and thereby lost economic resources to stand firm and eliminate the effects of the aggression.

The oil-producing states have, in fact, participated in the efforts to enable the states affected by the aggression to stand firm in the face of any economic pressure.

5)　The participants in the Conference have approved the plan proposed by Kuwait to set up an Arab Economic and Social development Fund on the basis of the recommendation of the Baghdad Conference . . .

6)　The participants have agreed on the need to adopt the necessary measures to strengthen military preparation to face all eventualities.

7)　The Conference has decided to expedite the elimination of foreign bases in the Arab States.

PM Mahjub then read the following additional resolution: "The Kingdom of Saudi Arabia, the State of Kuwait and the Kingdom of Libya have each agreed to pay the following annual amounts which are to be paid in advance every three months beginning from mid-October until the effects of the aggression are eliminated: Saudi Arabia, £ 50 m; Kuwait £ 55 m; Libya £ 30 m. In this way, the Arab nation ensures that it will be able to carry on this battle, without any weakening, till the effects of the aggression are eliminated."

2. Jordanian King Hussein's Peace Plan, 28 April, 1969 [Excerpts]

Speech at the National Press Club, Washington D.C.

1. The end of all belligerency; 2. Respect for, and acknowledgement of, the sovereignty, territorial integrity and political independence of all states in the area; 3. Recognition of the rights of all to live in peace within secure and recognized boundaries free from threats or acts of war; 4. Guarantees of freedom of navigation through the Gulf of Aqaba and the Suez Canal for all states; 5. Guaranteeing the territorial inviolability of all states in the area through whatever measures that were necessary, including the establishment of demilitarized zones; 6. Accepting a just settlement of the refugee problem.

In return for these considerations, Hussein said, the "sole demand upon Israel is the withdrawal of its armed forces from all territories occupied in June 1967 war, and the implementation of all the other provisions of Res. 242."

3. The Cairo and Melkart Agreements: Regulation of the P.L.O. Presence in Lebanon

The Cairo Agreement, 3 November 1969

On Monday, 3 November 1969 the Lebanese delegation headed by Army Commander Emile Bustani and the PLO delegation headed by Yasser Arafat met in Cairo ... It was agreed to re-establish the Palestinian presence in Lebanon on the basis of:

1) The right of Palestinians presently living in Lebanon to work, reside and move freely;

2) The establishment of local committees from Palestinians living in the camps to look after the interests of the Palestinians there, in cooperation with the local authorities and within the context of Lebanese sovereignty;

3) The presence of command centres for the Palestine Armed Struggle Command inside the camps to cooperate with the local authorities and guarantee good relations. These centres will handle arrangements for the carrying and regulation of arms within the camps, taking into account both Lebanese security and the interests of the Palestinian revolution;

4) Permission for Palestinian residents in Lebanon to join the Palestinian revolution through armed struggle within the limits imposed by Lebanese security and sovereignty.

Commando Operations

It was agreed to facilitate operations by [Palestinian] commandos through:

1) Assisting commando access to the border and the specification of access points and observation posts in the border region;

2) Ensuring the use of the main road to the Arqub region;

3) Control by the Palestine Armed Struggle Command of the actions of all members of its organisations and to prevention of any interference in Lebanese affairs;

4) The pursuit of mutual cooperation between the Palestine Armed Struggle Command and the Lebanese army;

5) An end to media campaigns by both sides;

6) A census of the complement of the Palestine Armed Struggle Command through its leadership;

7) The appointment of representatives of the Palestine Armed Struggle Command to the Lebanese High Command;

8) Study of the distribution of suitable concentration points in the border regions to be agreed upon with the Lebanese High Command;

9) Organization of the entry, exit and movement of Palestine Armed Struggle elements;

10) Abolition of the Jainoun base;

11)   Assistance by the Lebanese army in the work of medical centres, and evacuation and supply for commando operations;

12)   Release of all internees and confiscated arms;

13)   Acceptance that the civil and military Lebanese authorities will continue to exercise effective responsibility to the full in all regions of Lebanon and under all circumstances;

14)   Confirmation that the Palestine Armed Struggle acts for the benefit of Lebanon as well as for the Palestinian revolution and for all Arabs.

The Melkart Agreement, 17 May 1973

Both parties eagerly agree to serve the Palestinian cause and to continue its struggle, and to preserve the independence of Lebanon and its sovereignty and stability, and in the light of contracted agreements and Arab decisions, comprising: the Cairo agreement and all its annexes; agreements concluded between Lebanon and the leadership of the resistance forces; and decisions taken at the Joint Arab Defence Council; it was agreed on all points as follows:

Presence in the Camps of Personnel

1)   No commando presence;

2)   Formation of permanent Palestine Armed Struggle Command units;

3)   Confirmation of militia presence for the guarding and internal protection of the camps. By militia is understood Palestinians residing in the camps who are not members of the resistance force and who practice normal civilian duties;

4)   Establishment of a guardpost for Lebanese internal security forces at a location to be agreed upon close to each camp.

Presence in the Camps of Arms

1)   The militia will be permitted to carry light arms individually;

2)   No medium or heavy weapons will be permitted within the camps (e.g. mortars, rocket launchers, artillery, anti-tank weapons, etc.).

Presence in the Border Regions

1)   Western sector: presence and concentration outside the camps is forbidden . . .

2)   Central sector: According to agreements made at the meeting between the Lebanese High Command and the resistance forces leadership on 8 October 1972: Presence will be permitted outside Lebanese villages in certain areas by agreement with the local Lebanese sector commander. Resistance forces are not permitted east and south of the line running Al-Kusair/Al-Ghandouriya/Deir   Kifa/Al-Shihabia/Al-Salasel/Al-Saltania/Tabnin/Haris/Kafra/Sadikin/Qana. This prohibition applies to all these points

inclusively. Concentration of resistance forces at a guardpost south of Hadatha is permitted. The number allowed is between five and ten men in civilian clothes, with all military appearance to be avoided. They will be supplied by animal transport. At all these places the total number permitted must not exceed 250.

3) Eastern sector: According to decisions taken by the Lebanese High Command and the resistance forces leadership, three bases will be permitted in the southern Arqub at Abu-Kamha Al-Kharbiya (Al-Shahid Salah base) and Rashaya al-Fakhar (Jabal al-Shahr). Each base will contain no more than 30 to 35 men each. Supply for these bases will be by motor-transport. Elements at these bases will be forbidden to proceed in the direction of Marjayoun unless they have a permit. The carrying of arms in Marjayoun is forbidden . . . In the northern Arqub and at Rashaya al-Wadi, presence is permitted at a distance from the villages, but not west of the Masnaa-Hasbaya road . . . At Baalbeck no commando presence is permitted except at the Nabi Sbat training base.

Note: Medium and light arms are permitted in these sectors; commando presence inside Lebanese villages is not allowed; all units which have been reinforced in Lebanon from abroad will be adjusted.

Movement [in the camps]
    Movement will be allowed without arms and in civilian dress.

Movement in the [frontier] areas
    Movement will be allowed by arrangement with local Lebanese commanders and according to agreement.

Movement of Civilian and Military Leaders
    Military leaders will be allowed to move freely provided they are above the rank of lieutenant, carrying no more than a personnel weapon and are accompanied by a driver only. Civilian leaders will be supplied with numbered permits signed by the responsible joint liaison committee. The number of permits issued to area leaderships will be determined by the Lebanese liaison centre and supplied under the request of the Palestinian Political Committee in Lebanon.

Military Training
    [Military] training is forbidden in the camps, but allowed at the training base at Nabi Sbat. Technical military training is permitted at points to be agreed upon by arrangement with the Lebanese High Command liaison centre. Practising with arms is forbidden outside the training base.

Operations
    All [commando] operations from Lebanese territory are suspended according to the decisions of the Joint Arab Defence Council. Departure from Lebanon for the purpose of commando operations is forbidden.

Command

The Palestinian side reaffirms that the chief command base is Damascus, and that the Damascus office has representatives in other countries including Lebanon. The Palestinian side pledged to reduce the number of offices [in Lebanon].

Information

The Palestinian side affirmed that the resistance in Lebanon only produces:

a)   *Filastin al-Thawra;* b) Wafa news agency, in addition to certain cultural and educational publications issued by Palestinian organizations publicly or for their own use;   c) The Palestinian side pledged that these publications would not touch upon the interests and sovereignty of Lebanon;   d) the Palestinian side adheres to the abstention from broadcasting in Lebanon; e) the Palestinian side pledges not to involve Lebanon in any of its publications or broadcast news items or announcements emanating from resistance sources in Lebanon.

Controlling Contraventions and Offences

Lebanese laws will be implemented on the basis of Lebanese sovereignty and offenders will be referred to the responsible courts.

1)   Contraventions in military sectors will be submitted to local liaison committees. In cases where no result is achieved, they will be referred to the Higher Coordination Committee which will give an immediate decision.

2)   Contraventions inside the camps will be the charge of the internal security forces in cooperation with the Palestine Armed Struggle Command, regarding the pursuit of all crimes, civil or criminal, which occur within the camps whoever the offender. They will also be responsible for delivering all legal notices and orders pronounced against persons residing in the camps. Incidents occurring in the camps between the commandos which have a bearing on the security and safety of the Palestinian revolution will be excluded from this procedure and be the responsibility of the Palestine Armed Struggle Command.

3)   Contraventions outside the camps shall be subject to Lebanese law. The Palestine Armed Struggle Command will be informed of detentions and the procedures taken against offenders. In the case of commandos being apprehended in an offence and where the Lebanese authorities deem necessary the cooperation of the Palestine Armed Struggle Command, contact will be made through the liaison committee and the decision on the offender will be left to the Lebanese authority.

The Palestinian side condemned detention of any Lebanese or foreigners and the conduct of any investigation by resistance forces and pledged no repetition of such matters.

Regarding traffic offences, it has been agreed previously that a census would be taken of cars with Lebanese number plates under the auspices of the Internal Security Forces, and cars entering Lebanese territory under temporary licensing regulations of the customs authorities. Therefore any commando vehicle on Lebanese territory will be prohibited unless it carries a legal license according to Lebanese traffic regulations.

Foreigners

By the term foreigners it meant not Arab commandos.

The Palestinian side pledges to deport all foreigners with the exception of those engaged in non-combatant work of a civilian or humane nature (including doctors, nurses, translators and interpreters).

Coordination

Implementation will be supervised by the Liaison Committee and its branches in coordination with the Palestinian side.

Highly Confidential
Aspirations of the Palestinian Side After the Joint Meetings

— Re-establishment of the atmosphere to its state before the incidents of 9 May 1973;

— Gradual easing of armed tension;

— Reduction of barriers of suspicion;

— Aspirations towards the cancellation of the emergency situation;

— Dealing with the matter of fugitives from the law, particularly those persons pursued as a result of the incidents of 23 April 1969;

— Freeing of those persons detained as a result of the incidents of 2 April 1973;

— Return of arms confiscated since 1970;

— Facilitation of employment for Palestinians resident in Lebanon.

For the Palestinian side
Lt Col Abal Zaim
Abu Adnan
AlSayyid Salah Salah

For the Lebanese side
Lt Col Ahmad al-Hajj
Col Nazih Rashid (Col Salim Moghabghab)
Col Dib Kamal

4. Jordanian King Hussein's Federation Plan, 15 March, 1972

We are happy to declare that the bases of the proposed formula for the new phase are as follows:

(1) The Hashimite Kingdom of Jordan will become the United Arab Kingdom and will bear this name [applause].

(2) The United Arab Kingdom will consist of two regions: (a) The Palestine region which will consist of the West Bank and any other Palestinian territories which are liberated and whose inhabitants desire to join it [applause]. (b) The Jordan region which will consist of the East Bank.

(3) Amman will be the central capital of the kingdom as well as capital of the Jordan region.

(4) Jerusalem will be the capital of the Palestine region [applause].

(5) The Head of State will be the king, who will assume the central executive authority with the help of a central cabinet. The central legislative authority will be vested in the king and an assembly to be known as the National Assembly. Members of this assembly will be elected by direct secret ballot. Both regions will be equally represented in this assembly.

(6) The central judicial authority will be vested in a central supreme court.

(7) The kingdom will have unified armed forces whose supreme commander is the king [applause].

(8) The responsibilities of the central executive authority will be confined to affairs connected with the kingdom as an international entity to guarantee the kingdom's security, stability and prosperity.

(9) The executive authority in each region will be assumed by a governor general from among its sons and a regional cabinet also from among its sons.

(10) Legislative authority in each region will be assumed by a council to be called the People's Council (Arabic: majlis ash-sha'b). It will be elected by a direct secret ballot. This council will elect the region's governor general.

(11) The judicial authority in the region will be in the hands of the region's courts and nobody will have power over them.

(12) The executive authority in each region will assume responsibility for all the affairs of the region except such affairs as the Constitution defines as coming under the jurisdiction of the central executive authority.

Naturally, the implementation of this formula and its bases must be according to the constitutional principles in force. It will be referred to the [Jordanian] National Assembly to adopt the necessary measures to prepare a new constitution for the country.

The new phase which we look forward to will guarantee the reorganization of the Jordanian-Palestinian house in a manner which will provide it with more intrinsic power and ability to work to attain its ambitions and aspirations. Proceeding from this fact, this formula will bind the two banks with ties of stronger fibre and with closer bonds and will strengthen their brotherhood and march as a result of enhancing man's responsibility in each bank on bases more suitable for serving their national aspirations without prejudice to any of the rights gained by any citizen, whether he be of Palestinian origin living in the Jordanian region or of Jordanian origin living in the Palestinian region.

This formula gathers and does not disperse, strengthens and does not weaken, unites and does not divide. It does not contain anything to change anything gained by any person during a unity of 20 years [applause].

Every attempt to cast doubt on any of this or discredit it is treason against the unity of the kingdom, the cause, the people and the homeland. The experience, vigilance and ability gained by our people make them capable of facing the forthcoming responsibilities with greater confidence and more determination. If ability is a debt for a person to use for himself and others and if vigilance is a weapon to be used for his and other's welfare, then the time has come for that person to stand up and face his responsibilities, perform them sincerely and faithfully and practice them bravely and with dignity. For this reason this formula is the title for a new bright, shining and confident page in the history of this country in which each citizen has a part and responsibility. It is partly based on sound allegiance to his faithful country and sincere devotion to his glorious nation.

The armed forces which from the very beginning marched under the banner of the great Arab revolution [applause] and which includes and will always include in its ranks the best sons of the people in both banks, will always be prepared to welcome more sons of both banks. They will always be at peak efficiency, ability and organization, and will remain open to anyone anxious to serve the homeland and the cause with absolute loyalty to homeland and the cause and to the sublime aims.

This Arab country is the country of the cause, just as it is from the Arabs and for all the Arabs. The record of its sacrifices for the nation and the cause is long and well known. This record was written by its brave armed forces and free and loyal people with their blood and honourable sacrifices. Inasmuch as the attitudes toward this country change to attitudes of fraternity, assistance and support, this country will continue on the path of sacrifice with strength and hope until it and its nation regain their rights and achieve their objectives.

This Arab country belongs to all, Jordanians and Palestinians alike. When we say Palestinians we mean every Palestinian throughout the world [applause], provided he is Palestinian by loyalty and affinity. When we call on every citizen to rise to play his part and carry out his responsibilities in the new stage, we call on every Palestinian brother outside Jordan to respond to the call of duty — unaffected by appearances and attempts to outdo others and free from weaknesses and deviations — to proceed with his relatives and brothers in a march whose basis is this formula and to be united in rank and clear in aim in order that all may participate in attaining the aim of liberation and establishing the cherished edifice and strong structure.

If God helps you, none can defeat you. For God is mighty and strong. Peace be with you.

5. Arab League Summit Conference, Secret Resolutions, Algiers, 4 December, 1973 [Excerpts]

a. The Current Goals of the Arab Nation

The Conference resolves that the goals of the current phase of the common Arab struggle are:

1. The complete liberation of all the Arab territories conquered during the aggression of June 1967, with no concession or abandonment of any part of them, or detrimental to national sovereignty over them.

2. Liberation of the Arab city of Jerusalem, and rejection of any situation which may be harmful to complete Arab sovereignty over the Holy City.

3. Commitment to restoration of the national rights of the Palestinian people, according to the decisions of the Palestine Liberation Organization, as the sole representative of the Palestinian nation. (The Hashemite Kingdom of Jordan expressed reservations.)

4. The Palestine problem is the affair of all the Arabs, and no Arab party can possibly dissociate itself from this commitment, in the light of the resolutions of previous Summit Conferences.

b. Military

In view of continuation of the struggle against the enemy until the goals of our nation are attained, the liberation of the occupied territories and the restoration of the national rights of the Palestinian people, the Conference resolves:

1. Solidarity of all the Arab States with Egypt, Syria and the Palestinian nation, in the common struggle for attainment of the just goals of the Arabs.

2. Provision of all means of military and financial support to both fronts, Egyptian and Syrian, to strengthen their military capacity for embarking on the liberation campaign and standing fast in face of the tremendous amount of supplies and unlimited aid received by the enemy.

3. Support of Palestinian resistance by all possible measures, to ensure its active role in the campaign.

6. Arab League Summit Conference Communique, Rabat, Morocco, 29 October, 1974

The Seventh Arab Summit Conference after exhaustive and detailed discussions conducted by their Majesties, Excellencies, and Highnesses, the Kings, Presidents and Amirs on the Arab situation in general and the Palestine problem in particular, within their national and international frameworks; and after hearing the statements submitted by His Majesty King Hussein, King of the Hashemite Kingdom of Jordan and His Excellency Brother Yasser Arafat, Chairman of the Palestine Liberation Organization, and after the statements of their Majesties and Excellencies the Kings and Presidents, in an atmosphere of candour and sincerity and full responsibility; and in view of the Arab leaders' appreciation of the joint national responsibility required of them at present for confronting aggression and performing duties of liberation, enjoined by the unity of the Arab cause and the unity of its struggle; and in view of the fact that all are aware of Zionist schemes still being made to eliminate the Palestinian existence and to obliterate the Palestinian national entity; and in view of the Arab leaders' belief in the necessity to frustrate these attempts and schemes and to counteract them by supporting and strengthening this Palestinian national entity, by providing all requirements to develop and increase its ability to ensure that the Palestinian people recover their rights in full; and by meeting responsibilities of close cooperation with its brothers within the framework of collective Arab commitment;

And in light of the victories achieved by Palestinian struggle in the confrontation with the Zionist enemy, at the Arab and international levels, at the United Nations, and of the obligation imposed thereby to continue joint Arab action to develop and increase the scope of these victories; and having received the views of all on all the above, and having succeeded in cooling the differences between brethren within the framework of consolidating Arab solidarity, the Seventh Arab Summit Conference resolves the following:

1. To affirm the right of the Palestinian people to self-determination and to return to their homeland;

2. To affirm the right of the Palestinian people to establish an independent national authority under the command of the Palestine Liberation Organization, the sole legitimate representative of the Palestinian people in any Palestinian territory that is liberated. This authority, once it is established, shall enjoy the support of the Arab States in all fields and at all levels;

3. To support the Palestine Liberation Organization in the exercise of its responsibility at the national and international levels within the framework of Arab commitment;

4. To call on the Hashemite Kingdom of Jordan, the Syrian Arab Republic, the Arab Republic of Egypt and the Palestine Liberation Organiza-

tion to devise a formula for the regulation of relations between them in the light of these decisions so as to ensure their implementation;

5.   That all the Arab States undertake to defend Palestinian national unity and not to interfere in the internal affairs of Palestinian action.

7. Statement by President Bourguiba of Tunisia Calling for a Settlement of the Arab-Israeli Conflict on the Basis of the 1947 UN Partition Resolution. Tunis, 26 October, 1976

It was intolerable that we should be blamed for the misdeeds of others and that the atrocities of Nazism should be atoned for in the heart of our land, our homes and our fields.

We therefore decided that we must fight to recover our usurped rights and to put an end to this injustice which is without precedent in modern history.

After nearly a third of a century we realized that this was impossible without exposing the security of the area — and perhaps world peace — to the gravest dangers.

We therefore decided that the maintenance of peace must be preferred to the cause of the homeland, to our love of it and our passionate attachment to it.

Therefore I have come to you today bearing an olive branch in both hands, calling for the implementation of the resolution adopted in 1947, hoping that the passage of time may gradually bring about detente between the two communities, that as the years go by links of mutual exchange and cooperation may be established between them and that rapprochement in one form or another may lead to the two groups coexisting in a single community. This at any rate is the one wager to which we should direct our hopes and energies. This is what I have said to the international community, although I know how heavy is the responsibility involved in this decision, and the reactions it may give rise to in certain circles of the Palestine revolution. In the past I staked all on just such a wager as regards Tunisia, thereby risking my reputation and my life.

But the leader must not be afraid to take decisions leading to peace which, although they appear to indicate weakness, are really, and in the sight of history, revolutionary decisions.

If Abu Ammar did this he would be entitled to as prominent a place in the register of freedom fighters as those who daily lay down their lives in Nablus, Acre and Jerusalem.

If he did this he would open up to Palestine a new era of hope for the building of honour and self-respect.

If he did this it would also be the prelude to many benefits for the Eastern Arab countries which have been trying since the fifties to achieve a reconciliation between two irreconcilable things, between war against Israel and war against backwardness, between the cost of armaments and planning for development. One of them is certainly important, but the second is vital as regards our destiny and it is therefore in my view more important, as without it the other goals and objectives cannot be achieved.

The most important of our duties as Arabs, in both the East and the West, is to give priority to organized and planned development so that we may rescue our peoples from backwardness and promote them to the ranks of the nations that are developing, growing and becoming strong enough to control not only their political destiny, but also, and in particular, their economic destiny, because in our times economic capacity is the key to political capacity.

8. Arab League Summit Conference Declaration, Tripoli, Libya, 5 December, 1977, [Excerpts]

In the name of God, the Merciful, the Compassionate: An Arab summit conference was held in Tripoli, the capital of the Socialist People's Libyan Arab Jamahiriyah, from 2 to 5 December 1977 at the invitation of Brother Colonel Mu'ammar al-Quadhafi. It was attended by the following:

1. President Houari Boumediene for the Algerian Democratic and Popular Republic;

2. President Hafiz al-Assad for the Syrian Arab Republic;

3. Col. Mu'ammar al-Quadhafi, secretary general of the General People's Congress of the Socialist People's Libyan Arab Jamahiriyah;

4. Brother 'Abd al-Fattah Isma'il, secretary general of the Unified Political Organization — National Front, for the FDRY;

5. Brother Taha Yasin Ramadan, for the Iraqi Republic;

6. Brother Yasser 'Arafat, chairman of the PLO Executive Committee and commander of the Palestinian revolution forces.

With a sense of complete pan-Arab responsibility, the conference discussed the dimensions of the current phase through which the Arab cause in general and the Palestinian question in particular are passing and the American-Zionist plans aimed at imposing capitulatory settlements on the Arab nation, prejudicing the established national rights of the Palestinian people, liquidating the national Arab accomplishments and striking at the Arab liberation movement as a prelude to subduing the Arab area and controlling its destiny and tying it to the bandwagon of world imperialism.

The conference also discussed the visit made by President el-Sadat to the Zionist entity as being a link in the framework of the implementation of the hostile schemes. The conference reviewed the results of the visit, which constituted a flagrant violation of the principles and objectives of the pan-Arab struggle against the Zionist enemy, a squandering of the rights of the Palestinian Arab people, a departure from the unity of the Arab ranks, a grave violation of the Arab League Charter and the resolutions of the Arab summit conferences and the withdrawing of Arab Egypt from the front of conflict with the Zionist enemy — a matter which the conference considered a great service by President el-Sadat to Zionism and American imperialism and their designs and a consecretion of the Zionist entity, which is their tool and base in the Arab area.

Those attending the conference studied the current situation with all of its dimensions and concluded that the objectives of the plot are as follows:

1. To undermine the possibility of the establishment of a just and honorable peace which would safeguard the national rights of the Arab nation and guarantee for it the liberation of its occupied territories, the foremost of which is Jerusalem, and for the Palestinian people their established national rights.

2. To isolate the Arab nation from its allies and friends on the African Continent who have adopted a historic stand in support of the Arab issue and exposed the organic link between the Zionist entity and the racist regime in South Africa.

3. To isolate the Arab nation from the group of non-aligned states and Islamic states which have supported the Arab issue in all of its stages and stood on the side of the just struggle of the Palestinian people.

4. To harm the relations of friendship and cooperation between the Arab States on the one hand and the Soviet Union and the countries of the socialist camp, which have given support and backing to the Arab nation in its historic struggle against the imperialist-Zionist enemy.

5. To enable the forces hostile to the Arab nation, headed by the United States, to realize gains that will upset the international balance in favor of the Zionist imperialist forces and Zionism and undermine the national independence of the Afro-Asian and Latin American countries.

6. To establish an alliance between the Zionist enemy and the current Egyptian regime aimed at liquidating the Arab issue and the issue of Palestine, split the Arab nation and forfeit its national interests.

Out of its belief in the nature of the Zionist and imperialist challenges aimed at weakening the Arab will for liberation and harming the firm national rights of the Palestinian people which have been confirmed by international legitimacy — the foremost of which is their right to return and decide their own destiny and build their independent state on the soil of their homeland under the leadership of the PLO, which is the sole legitimate representative of the Palestinian people — and proceeding from the reality of pan-Arab and historic responsibility, the summit conference decided the following:

1.   To condemn President el-Sadat's visit to the Zionist entity since it constitutes a great betrayal of the sacrifices and struggle of our Arab people in Egypt and their armed forces and of the struggle, sacrifices and principles of the Arab nation. While appreciating the role of the great Egyptian people in the national struggle of the Arab nation, the conference stresses that Egypt is not the beginning nor the end and that if the Arab nation is great with Egypt, the latter's greatness is only possible within the Arab nation, without which it can only diminish in importance.

2.   To work for the frustration of the results of President el-Sadat's visit to the Zionist entity and his talks with the leaders of the Zionist enemy and the subsequent measures including the proposed Cairo meeting. The conference warns that anyone who tries to pursue a similar line or to have any dealings with the said results shall be held responsible for his deed nationally and on the pan-Arab level.

3.   To freeze [tajmid] political and diplomatic relations with the Egyptian Government, to suspend dealings with it on the Arab and international level and to apply the regulations, provisions and decisions of the Arab boycott against Egyptian individuals, companies and firms which deal with the Zionist enemy.

4.   To decide not to take part in Arab League meetings which are held in Egypt and to undertake contacts with the Arab League member states to study the question of its headquarters and organs and the membership of the Egyptian regime.

5.   The conference salutes the Palestinian Arab people, who are standing fast in the occupied homeland, including all of their national and other popular organizations which are struggling against the occupation and which reject the visit of el-Sadat to occupied Palestine. The conference also warns against any attempt to prejudice the legitimacy of the PLO representation of the Palestinian people.

6.   The conference takes satisfaction in recording the preliminary positions taken by the Arab States which have denounced the visit and rejected its consequences. Out of its responsibility and in compliance with its commitment and collective resolutions, the conference calls on these states to adopt practical measures to face the serious character of this capitulatory policy, including the suspension of political and material support. The conference also condemns the disgraceful stands adopted by those who praise this visit or support it and warn them of the consequences of their despondent and defeatist policies.

7. The conference appeals to the Arab nation on the official and popular levels to provide economic, financial, political and military aid and support to the Syrian region, now that it has become the principal confrontation state and the base of steadfastness for dealing with the Zionist enemy and also to the Palestinian people represented by the PLO.

8. The conference greets our Arab people in sisterly Egypt and particularly their national and progressive forces, which have rejected the capitulatory policy being pursued by the Egyptian regime as being a betrayal of the sacrifices of the people and their martyrs and an insult to the dignity of their armed forces.

9. In asserting the importance of the relationship of struggle and nationalism between Syria and the Palestinians, the Syrian Arab Republic and the PLO announce the formation of a unified front to face the Zionist enemy and combat the imperialist plot with all its parties and to thwart all attempts at capitulation. The Democratic and Popular Republic of Algeria, the Socialist People's Libyan Arab Jamashiriyah and the PDRY have decided to join this front, making it the nucleus of a pan-Arab front for steadfastness and combat which will be open to other Arab countries to join.

10. Members of the pan-Arab front consider any aggression against any one member as an aggression against all members.

The conference pledges to the Arab nation that it will continue the march of struggle, steadfastness, combat and adherence to the objectives of the Arab struggle. The conference also expresses its deep faith and absolute confidence that the Arab nation, which has staged revolutions, overcome difficulties and defeated plots during its long history of struggle — a struggle which abounds with heroism — is today capable of replying with force to those who have harmed its dignity, squandered its rights, split its solidary and departed from the principles of its struggle. It is confident of its own capabilities in liberation, progress and victory, thanks to God.

The conference records with satisfaction the national Palestinian unity within the framework of the PLO.

Done at Tripoli on 5 December, 1977.

9. Summit of Anti-Sadat "Steadfastness and Confrontation Front". Algeria, Libya, South Yemen and the P.L.O. Damascus, 23 September, 1978

Four-point Agreement

There was agreement on four main points:

1. Economic and political relations with Egypt to be severed, and en-

couragement to be given to "progressive and nationalist forces" within Egypt to overthrow the Sadat government;

2.   The Arab League headquarters to be removed from Cairo or, failing that, a new league to be set up elsewhere in the Arab world;

3.   Closer relations with the Soviet Union, to which end Syrian President Assad would go to Moscow to strengthen co-operation between the front and the Soviet Union;

4.   A joint political and military command to be set up to co-ordinate moves against Israel and Egypt.

Front as Basis for Arab Unity

The conference also voiced its wish to transform the Steadfastness and Confrontation Front into "a base for the Arab national struggle", a base which would be committed to the following goals:

1.   Arab unity and "support of all efforts aimed at removing obstacles in the way of ultimate unity of the Arab world".

2.   Recognition of the fact that the Palestinian problem is "the basic concern of all the Arabs and, consequently, no single Arab party may bargain on or undermine this commitment or take any action that would cause damage to the Palestine case and the national rights of the Palestinian people."

3.   Complete liberation of all Arab and Palestinian lands, no concession or abandonment of any part of these lands, and "no-one may undermine Arab sovereignty" over them.

4.   Commitment to the restoration of the "inalienable national rights of the Palestinian people, including its right to repatriation, self-determination and statehood."

5.   Support for the Palestinian people's struggle "under the leadership of the PLO, the sole legitimate representative of the Palestine people."

10. Arab League Summit Conference, Final Statement, Baghdad, Iraq, 5 November, 1978

The Arab summit conference issued a final statement at the conclusion of its meetings, which lasted for 4 days. The following is the text of the final statement:

By the initiative of the Government of the Republic of Iraq and at the invitation of President Ahmad Hasan al-Bakr, the ninth Arab summit conference convened in Baghdad 2-5 November 1978.

In a high spirit of pan-Arab responsibility and joint concern about the unity of the Arab stand, the conference studied confrontation of the dangers and challenges threatening the Arab nation, particularly after the results of the

Camp David agreements signed by the Egyptian Government and the effects of these agreements on the Arab struggle to face the Zionist aggression against the Arab nation.

Proceeding from the principles in which the Arab nation believes, acting on the unity of Arab destiny and complying with the traditions of joint Arab action, the Arab summit conference has emphasized the following basic principles:

First: The Palestinian question is a fateful Arab issue and is the essence of the conflict with the Zionist enemy. The sons of the Arab nation and all the Arab countries are concerned with it and are obliged to struggle for its sake and to offer all material and moral sacrifices for this cause. The struggle to regain Arab rights in Palestine and in the occupied Arab territory is a general Arab responsibility. All Arabs must share this responsibility, each in accord with his military, economic, political and other abilities.

The conflict with the Zionist enemy exceeds the framework of the conflict of the countries whose territory was occupied in 1967, and it includes the whole Arab nation because of the military, political, economic and cultural danger the Zionist enemy constitutes against the entire Arab nation and its substantial and pan-Arab interests, civilization and destiny. This places on all the countries of the Arab nation the responsibility to share in this conflict with all the resources it possesses.

Second: All the Arab countries must offer all forms of support, backing and facilities to all forms of the struggle of the Palestinian resistance, supporting the PLO in its capacity as the sole legitimate representative of the Palestinian people inside and outside the occupied land, struggling for liberation and restoration of the national rights of its people, including their right to return to their homeland, to determine their future and to establish their independent state on their national soil. The Arab States pledge to preserve Palestinian national unity and not to interfere in the internal affairs of the Palestinian action.

Third: Commitment is reaffirmed to the resolutions of the Arab summit conferences, particularly the sixth and seventh summit conferences of Algiers and Rabat.

Fourth: In light of the above principles it is impermissible for any side to act unilaterally in solving the Palestinian question in particular and the Arab-Zionist conflict in general.

Fifth: No solution shall be accepted unless it is associated with a resolution by an Arab summit conference convened for this purpose.

The conference discussed the two agreements signed by the Egyptian Government at Camp David and considered that they harm the Palestinian people's rights and the rights of the Arab nation in Palestine and the occupied Arab territory. The conference considered that these agreements took place outside the framework of collective Arab responsibility and are opposed to the resolutions of the Arab summit conferences, particularly the resolutions of the Algiers and Rabat summit conferences, the Arab League Charter and the UN resolutions on the Palestinian question. The conference considers that these agreements do not lead to the just peace that the Arab nation desires. Therefore, the conference has decided not to approve of these two agreements and not to deal with their results. The conference has also rejected all the political, economic, legal and other effects resulting from them.

The conference decided to call on the Egyptian Government to go back on these agreements and not to sign any reconciliation treaty with the enemy. The conference hopes that Egypt will return to the fold of joint Arab action and not act unilaterally in the affairs of the Arab-Zionist conflict. In this respect the conference adopted a number of resolutions to face the new stage and to safeguard the aims and interests of the Arab nation out of faith that with its material and moral resources the Arab nation is capable of confronting the difficult circumstances and all challenges, just as it has always been throughout history, because it is defending right, justice and its national existence.

The conference stressed the need to unify all the Arab efforts in order to remedy the strategic imbalance that has resulted from Egypt's withdrawal from the confrontation arena.

The conference decided that the countries that possess readiness and capability will coordinate participation with effective efforts. The conference also stressed the need to adhere to the regulations of Arab boycott and to tighten application of its provisions.

The conference studied means to develop Arab information media beamed abroad for the benefit of the just Arab issues. The conference decided to hold annual meetings for the Arab summit conferences and decided that the month of November will be the date.

After studying the Arab and international situation, the conference asserts the Arab nation's commitment to a just peace based on the comprehensive Israeli withdrawal from the Arab territories occupied in 1967, including Arab Jerusalem, the guaranteeing of the inalienable national rights of the Palestinian Arab people including the right to establish their independent state on their national soil.

The conference decided to embark on large scale international activity to explain the just rights of the Palestinian people and the Arab nation. The conference expressed appreciation to the Syrian Arab Republic and its heroic army, and to the Hashemite Kingdom of Jordan and its heroic army, and expressed its pride in the struggle of the Palestinian people and its steadfastness inside and outside the occupied territories, under the leadership of the P.L.O., the sole legitimate representative of the Palestinian people.

The conference praised the "charter for joint national action" signed by fraternal Syria and Iraq, and the conference regarded the charter as a great achievement on the way to Arab solidarity. The conference also expressed its great appreciation for the initiative of the Iraqi Government using President Hasan al-Bakr in calling for the convening of an Arab summit conference in Baghdad so as to unify Arab ranks and to organize Arab efforts to face the threats to which the Arab nation is currently exposed. The conference expressed its thanks for President Al-Bakr's efforts to make the conference a success.

11. Arab League Summit Conference Resolutions, Baghdad, 31 March, 1979

As the Government of the Arab Republic of Egypt has ignored the Arab summit conferences' resolutions, especially those of the sixth and seventh conferences held in Algiers and Rabat; as it has at the same time ignored the ninth Arab summit conference resolutions — especially the call made by the Arab kings, presidents and princes to avoid signing the peace treaty with the Zionist enemy — and signed the peace treaty on 26 March 1979;

It has thus deviated from the Arab ranks and has chosen, in collusion with the United States, to stand by the side of the Zionist enemy in one trench; has behaved unilaterally in the Arab-Zionist struggle affairs; has violated the Arab nation's rights; has exposed the nation's destiny, its struggle and aims to dangers and challenges; has relinquished its pan-Arab duty of liberating the occupied Arab territories, particularly Jerusalem, and of restoring the Palestinian Arab people's inalienable national rights, including their right to repatriation, self-determination and establishment of the independent Palestinian State on their national soil.

In order to safeguard Arab solidarity and the unity of ranks in defense of the Arabs' fateful issue; in appreciation of the Egyptian people's struggle and sacrifices for Arab issues and the Palestinian issue in particular; in implementation of the resolutions adopted by the ninth Arab summit conference that convened in Baghdad 2-5 November 1978, and at the invitation of the Government of the Republic of Iraq, the Arab League Council convened in Baghdad from 27 March 1979 to 31 March 1979 on the level of Arab foreign and economy ministers.

In light of the ninth Arab summit conference resolutions, the council studied the latest developments pertaining to the Arab-Zionist conflict, especially after the signing by the Government of the Arab Republic of Egypt of the peace [as-sulh] agreement with the Zionist enemy on 26 March 1979.

The Arab League Council, on the level of Arab foreign ministers, has decided the following:

1.   A.   To withdraw the ambassadors of the Arab States from Egypt immediately.

B.   To recommend the severance of political and diplomatic relations with the Egyptian Government. The Arab governments will adopt the necessary measures to apply this recommendation within a maximum period of 1 month from the date of issuance of this decision, in accordance with the constitutional measures in force in each country.

2.   To consider the suspension of the Egyptian Government's membership in the Arab League as operative from the date of the Egyptian Government's signing of the peace treaty with the Zionist enemy. This means depriving it of all rights resulting from this membership.

3.   A.   To make the city of Tunis, capital of the Tunisian Republic, the temporary headquarters of the Arab League, its General Secretariat, the competent ministerial councils and the permanent technical committees, as of the date of the signing of the treaty between the Egyptian Government and the Zionist enemy. This shall be communicated to all international and regional organizations and bodies. They will also be informed that dealings with the Arab League will be conducted with its secretariat in its new temporary headquarters.

B.   To appeal to the Tunisian Government to offer all possible aid in facilitating the settlement of the temporary Arab League headquarters and its officials.

C.   To form a committee comprising representatives of Iraq, Syria, Tunisia, Kuwait, Saudi Arabia and Algeria, in addition to a representative for the General Secretariat. The aim of this committee will be to implement this resolution's provisions and to seek the aid it requires from the member-states. The committee will have all the authorization and responsibilities from the Arab League Council necessary to implement this resolution, including the protection of the Arab League's properties, deposits, documents and records. It is also entitled to take necessary measures against any action that may be taken by the Egyptian Government to hinder the transfer of the Arab League headquarters or to harm the Arab League's rights and possessions.

The committee will have to accomplish its task of transfer to the temporary headquarters within 2 months from the date of this resolution. This period of time may be extended another month if the committee so decides. The committee shall submit a report on its accomplishments to the first forthcoming meeting of the Arab League Council.

D.   A sum of $5 million shall be placed at the committee's disposal to cover the transfer expenses. This sum shall be drawn from the credit accounts of various funds. The committee has the right to spend more than that amount if required. Expenditures for this purpose shall come under the supervision of the committee or of those it authorizes. The expenses shall be paid by the member-states, each according to the percentage of its annual contribution to the Arab League budget.

E. To transfer the Arab League General Secretariat officials who are employed at the time of the issuance of this resolution from the permanent headquarters to the temporary one during the period defined in paragraph 3C of this resolution. The committee referred to in the above-mentioned paragraph 3 will have the responsibility of paying them financial compensation compatible with the standard of living in the new headquarters and for settling their affairs until a permanent system is drafted for this purpose.

4. The competent and specialized Arab organizations, bodies, establishments and federations named in the attached list No. 1 will take the necessary measures to suspend Egypt's membership. They will transfer their headquarters from Egypt to other Arab States on a temporary basis, similar to the action that shall be taken regarding the Council General Secretariat. The executive councils and boards of these bodies, organizations, establishments and federations shall meet immediately following the implementation of this decision within a period not to exceed the period specified in Paragraph 3C above.

5. To seek to suspend Egypt's membership in the non-aligned movement, the Islamic conference organization and OAU for violating the resolutions of these organizations pertaining to the Arab-Zionist conflict.

6. To continue to cooperate with the fraternal Egyptian people and with Egyptian individuals, with the exception of those who cooperate with the Zionist enemy directly or indirectly.

7. The member-States shall inform all foreign countries of their stand on the Egyptian-Israeli treaty and will ask these countries not to support this treaty as it constitutes an aggression against the rights of the Palestinian people and the Arab nation as well as a threat to world peace and security.

8. To condemn the policy that the United States is practicing regarding its role in concluding the Camp David agreements and the Egyptian-Israeli treaty.

9. To consider the measures in this decision to be temporary and subject to cancellation by an Arab League Council decision as soon as the circumstances that justified their adoption are eliminated.

10. The Arab countries will pass legislation, decisions and measures necessary for the implementation of this resolution.

The Arab League Council, on the level of Arab foreign and economy ministers, has also decided the following:

1. To halt all bank loans, deposits, guarantees or facilities, as well as all financial or technical contributions and aid by Arab governments or their es-

tablishments to the Egyptian Government and its establishments as of the treaty signing date.

2. To ban the extension of economic aid by the Arab funds, banks and financial establishments within the framework of the Arab League and the joint Arab cooperation to the Egyptian Government and its establishments.

3. The Arab governments and institutions shall refrain from purchasing the bonds, shares, postal orders and public credit loans that are issued by the Egyptian Government and its financial foundations.

4. Following the suspension of the Egyptian Government's membership in the Arab League, its membership will also be suspended from the institutions, funds and organizations deriving from the Arab League. The Egyptian Government and its institutions will cease to benefit from these organizations. The headquarters of those Arab League departments residing in Egypt will be transferred to other Arab States temporarily.

5. In view of the fact that the ill-omened Egyptian-Israeli treaty and its appendices have demonstrated Egypt's commitment to sell oil to Israel, the Arab States shall refrain from providing Egypt with oil and its derivatives.

6. Trade exchange with the Egyptian State and private establishments that deal with the Zionist enemy shall be prohibited.

7. The Economic Boycott.

A. The Arab boycott laws, principles and provisions shall be applied to those companies, foundations and individuals of the Arab Republic of Egypt that deal directly or indirectly with the Zionist enemy. The boycott office shall be entrusted with following up the implementation of these tasks.

B. The provisions of paragraph A shall include the intellectual, cultural and artistic activities that involve dealing with the Zionist enemy or have connection with the enemy's institutions.

C. The Arab States stress the importance of continued dealings with those private national Egyptian institutions that are confirmed not to be dealing with the Zionist enemy. Such institutions will be encouraged to work and maintain activities in the Arab countries within the framework of their fields of competence.

D. The Arab countries stress the importance of caring for the feelings of the Egyptian people's sons who are working or living in the Arab countries as well as looking after their interests and consolidating their pan-Arab affiliation with Arabism.

E. To consolidate the role of the Arab boycott and to enhance its grip at this stage, in affirmation of Arab unanimity, the assistant secretary general for economic affairs will be temporarily entrusted with the task of directly supervising the major boycott office in Damascus. He will be granted the necessary powers to reorganize and back the said department and to submit proposals on developing the boycott in method, content and scope. He shall submit a report in this regard to the first meeting of the Arab League Council.

8. The United Nations will be asked to transfer its regional offices, which serve the Arab region, from the Arab Republic of Egypt to any other Arab capital. The Arab States will work collectively toward this end.

9. The Arab League General Secretariat will be assigned the task of studying the joint Arab projects so as to take the necessary measures for protecting the Arab nation's interests in accordance with the aims of these resolutions. The General Secretariat shall submit its proposals to the Arab League Council in its first forthcoming meeting.

10. The Zionist plot must be faced by drafting an Arab strategy for economic confrontation. This will lead to utilizing the Arabs' own strength and will emphasize the need for realizing Arab economic integration in all aspects.

The strategy will strengthen joint Arab development and regional development within the pan-Arab outlook and will expand the establishment of joint Arab projects — projects that serve the aims of emancipating, developing and intergrating the Arab economy — and will promote the projects already in operation. The strategy will also develop the methods, systems and substance of the Arab boycott of Israel and will diversify and promote international relations with the developing countries. The Arab League General Secretariat shall rapidly submit studies relevant to the strategy of joint Arab economic action to the forthcoming session of the Arab Economic Council. This will be a prelude to the convention of a general Arab economic conference.

11. The above-mentioned committee shall be assigned the task of supervising the implementation of these decisions and of submitting a follow up report to the Arab League Council in its first forthcoming meeting.

12. The Arab States will issue the decisions and legislations pertaining to these decisions and will take the necessary measures to implement them.

13. These measures taken by the Arab and economy ministers are considered a minimal requirement to face the threats of the treaty. Individual governments can take whatever measure they deem necessary in addition to these measures.

14. The Arab foreign and economy ministers call on the Arab nation in all Arab countries to support the economic measures taken against the Zionist enemy and the Egyptian regime.

12. King Fahd of Saudi Arabia, Peace Plan, 6 August, 1981

1. Israeli evacuation of all Arab territories seized during the 1967 Middle East war, including the Arab sector of Jerusalem.

2. Dismantling the settlements set up by Israel on the occupied lands after

the 1967 war.

3. Guaranteeing freedom of religious practices for all religions in the Jerusalem holy shrines.

4. Asserting the rights of the Palestinian people and compensating those Palestinians who do not wish to return to their homeland.

5. Commencing a transitional period in the West Bank of Jordan and the Gaza Strip under United Nations supervision for a duration not exceeding a few months.

6. Setting up a Palestinian State with East Jerusalem as its capital.

7. Affirming the right of all countries of the region to live in peace.

8. Guaranteeing the implementation of these principles by the United Nations or some of its member states.

13. Arab League Summit Statement, Fez, Morocco, 6 September, 1982

I. The Arab-Israeli Conflict

The conference greeted the steadfastness of the Palestine revolutionary forces, the Lebanese and Palestinian peoples and the Syrian Arab Armed Forces and declared its support for the Palestinian people in their struggle for the retrieval of their established national rights.

Out of the conference's belief in the ability of the Arab nation to achieve its legitimate objectives and eliminate the aggression, and out of the principles and basis laid down by the Arab summit conferences, and out of the Arab countries' determination to continue to work by all means for the establishment of peace based on justice in the Middle East and using the plan of President Habib Bourguiba, which is based on international legitimacy, as the foundation for solving the Palestinian question and the plan of His Majesty King Fahd ibn 'Abd al-'Aziz which deals with peace in the Middle East, and in the light of the discussions and notes made by their majesties, excellencies and highnesses the kings, presidents and amirs, the conference has decided to adopt the following principles:

1. Israel's withdrawal from all Arab territories occupied in 1967, including Arab Jerusalem.

2. The removal of settlements set up by Israel in the Arab territories after 1967.

3. Guarantees of the freedom of worship and the performance of religious rites for all religions at the holy places.

4. Confirmation of the right of the Palestinian people to self-determination and to exercise their firm and inalienable national rights, under the leadership of the PLO, its sole legitimate representative, and compensation for those who do not wish to return.

5. The placing of the West Bank and Gaza Strip under UN supervision for a transitional period, not longer than several months.

6. The creation of an independent Palestinian State with Jerusalem as its capital.

7. The drawing up by the Security Council of guarantees for peace for all the states of the region, including the independent Palestinian State.

8. Security Council guarantees for the implementation of these principles.

14. Joint Jordanian — Palestinian Committee Communique, Amman, Jordan, 14 December, 1982

The joint Palestinian-Jordanian Committee ended a round of talks at noon today. Committee talks were conducted over the past two days. The committee issued the following communique to the press after the meetings:

"The Jordanian and Palestinian sides met with an understanding of the requirements of the current stage and for the effects that this stage will have on the Palestinian cause. The two sides met with a commitment to save the occupied territories and to restore the inalienable rights of the Palestinian people. The two sides met with an understanding of the historic and national dimensions which places the Palestinian and Jordanian peoples in a position which is directly affected by the continuous Zionist aggression against the Palestinian people and their national homeland.

"Joint continuous meetings have taken place since the historic meeting between PLO Chairman Arafat and Hussein on October 9, 1982. The Jordanian side was headed by Prime Minister Mudar Badran and the Palestinian side was headed by PLO Chairman Yasser Arafat.

"As a result of intensive deliberations the two sides agreed in the spirit of common understanding to develop a special and distinguished relationship between Jordan and Liberated Palestine.

"The two sides agreed to continue joint political moves on all levels and in conformity with the Fez Summit resolutions and within the framework of joint Arab moves which will guarantee the mobilization of Arab potentials to restore Arab and Palestinian rights.

"The two sides also agreed that the joint committee will continue further discussion on the question of bilateral relations and new political developments."

15. Iraqi President Saddam Hussein's Statement on Israel's Right for a Secure State. (Interview with Stephen Solarez, Member of U.S. House of Representatives), 2 Jan, 1983

[Question] Mr. President, I do appreciate your frank answers. I would like to ask you the second question and I would like you to give, with all sincerity, your viewpoint: should Israel agree to return to the pre-1967 borders, but only within an objective framework, giving Jordan the primary responsibility for administrating the West Bank and Gaza Strip. (?Does) this represent an acceptable solution to the problem? Would it be sufficient for Israel to withdraw to the 1967 lines and to accept the establishment of a Palestinian State in the West Bank and Gaza Strip as a way to solve the conflict?

[Answer] I do not believe that forcing the Palestinians, under the current circumstances, to accept a constitutional formula with any Arab State is a sound action. However, I believe that the simultaneous existence of an independent Palestinian State acceptable to the Palestinians and the existence of a secure state for the Israelis are both necessary.

I believe that you will be committing a grave mistake, unacceptable of course to the Arabs and Iraq, if you think that Jordan is suitable as a Palestinian State. In other words, the state of Palestine would be on the east bank of the Jordan, as some Israeli officials have remarked. The Arabs would feel that their entire existence was threatened and that the political map of their national entity could be threatened any time by an international conspiracy or by the desire of this or that big power.

16. Jordanian Statement on End of Negotiations with the P.L.O, Amman, Jordan, 10 April, 1983

Ladies and gentlemen, the following is the full text of the communique issued today after the Jordanian Cabinet meeting presided over by His Majesty King Hussein:

Since the Israeli aggression of June, 1967 and through our awareness of the dangers and repercussions of the occupation, Jordan has accepted the political option as one of the basic options that may lead to the recovery of Arab territories occupied through military aggression. Consequently, Jordan accepted Security Council Resolution 242 of November 22, 1967. When the October 1973 war happened, it underlined the importance of continuing work on the political option while at the same time building our intrinsic strength. This war brought about Security Council Resolution 338 which put a stop to military operations and implicitly reemphasized Security Council Resolution 242.

Based on Security Council Resolution 338, disengagement agreements were concluded between Israel, on the one hand, and Egypt and Syria on the other. This process completed the Arab circle immediately concerned itself with the recovery of the occupied lands through political means. On this basis, Jordan, in cooperation with the Arab States, developed and adopted the concept of forming a United Arab delegation that would attend an international conference for the purpose of achieving a just and comprehensive peace settlement to the Middle East problem.

In 1974, the Rabat Arab summit conference designated the PLO the sole legitimate representative of the Palestinian people. Jordan went along with the Arab consensus, and has been committed to that decision ever since.

The ensuing period saw the disjointment of Arab unity as evidenced by the Camp David accords. Further disintegration in the overall Arab position followed, even between those directly affected by the Israeli occupation. All the while, Jordan kept sounding the alarm on the one hand, persevering in its course of action on the other. Jordan warned repeatedly of the dangers inherent in the continuation of the no-war and no-peace situation, and of the exploitation by Israel of this situation to perpetuate the status quo by creating new facts in the occupied Arab territories, to realize its declared ambitions, aided by Arab disunity and by its military superiority.

Jordan has also cautioned against letting time pass by without concluding a just and comprehensive peace settlement because time was, and still is, essential to Israel's aim of creating new facts and bringing about a fait accompli. Sixteen years have passed since the occupation, during which Israel established 146 colonies in the West Bank alone and has illegally expropriated more than 50 percent of that land.

Even today, Israel forges ahead, in defiance of all international conventions and of United Nations resolutions, with a systematic policy of evacuating the inhabitants of the West Bank to change the demographic composition of the occupied Arab territories, thus realizing its designs to establish the Zionist state in the whole of Palestine.

From the early days of the occupation, and through awareness of the Zionist aims, Jordan issued all these warnings and undertook the task of implementing all policies that may support the steadfastness of the Palestinian people and help them stay in their national soil.

With this objective in mind, we worked incessantly on all levels. Domestically, Jordan provides markets for the industrial and agricultural products of the West Bank and Gaza, and continues to extend support to the existing institutions in the West Bank. Also, we continue to attach great importance to building our intrinsic defense capability in cooperation with other Arab States, through the conviction held by all our nation of the danger posed by Zionist ambitions which threaten the Arab world and its future generations. Within this context, Jordan paid particular attention to building its Armed Forces, looked for new sources of arms within the available financial means, and enacted the military service law to mobilize all its national resources for self-defense and for the defense of the Arab world, because Jordan remains, by virtue of its geographic location, a constant target for Israeli aggression, and the first line of defense on the east flank of the Arab world.

On the Arab level, Jordan sought to provide financial support for the steadfastness of the Palestinian people, and formed a joint Jordanian-Palestinian Committee which continues to implement the policy of supporting our people in the occupied lands.

On the international level, Jordan worked to mobilize world opinion to bring pressure to bear on Israel, and in the United Nations, through cooperation with Arab and friendly countries, Jordan succeeded in passing resolutions condemning, isolating, and putting pressure on Israel. All the while, Israel continued with its expansionist colonization program, evicting the Arab inhabitants of Palestine and replacing them by Jewish immigrants. We strive to confront this program which stands to affect Jordan more than any other country, which threatens Jordan's identity and national security.

In June 1982, Israel launched its aggression on Lebanon, which resulted in that country joining the list of occupied Arab territories. Lebanon was not excluded from the ambitions of Israel, which had already annexed de facto the West Bank and Gaza.

Last September, United States President Ronald Reagan declared his peace initiative to solve the Middle East crisis, and shortly after the Fez Arab summit conference resumed its proceedings where the Arab peace plan was formulated. It was evident that both peace proposals were inspired by the provisions of Security Council Resolution 242 and by the United Nations resolutions that followed. Jordan, as well as other Arab and friendly countries, found that the Reagan plan lacked some of the principles of the Fez peace plan but at the same time, it contained a number of positive elements. Given the realities of the international situation, on the other hand, the Arab peace plan lacked the mechanism that would enable it to make effective progress. The Reagan peace plan presented the vehicle that could propel the Fez peace plan forward, and Jordan proceeded to explore this possibility.

We believe, and continue to believe, that this aim can be achieved through an agreement between Jordan and the PLO, on the establishment of a confederal relationship that would govern and regulate the future of the Jordanian and Palestinian peoples. This relationship would express itself, from the moment of its inception, through joint Jordanian-Palestinian action based on the Fez peace plan, Security Council Resolution 242, and the principles of the Reagan initiative. In addition, such a confederal relationship would be sought if only through the faith Arabs have in the joint Arab destiny, and in recognition of the bonds that have linked the peoples of Jordan and Palestine throughout history.

These concepts, and the ideas and assessments that follow from them, formed the subject of intensive discussions held over several meetings between His Majesty King Hussein and the PLO Chairman Yasser Arafat, as well as between the Government of Jordan and a number of senior members of the PLO, within the framework of a higher committee which was formed for this purpose and which held its deliberations over the 5 months between October 1982 and the recent PNC convention in 1982 [as heard]. In addition, a number of prominent Palestinians inside and outside the occupied territories took part in the discussions.

These deliberations resulted in the irrefutable conclusion that Jordan and Palestine are joined by undeniable objective considerations reflected by the common threat against them which united their interests and their goals. There also resulted a joint conviction in the soundness of our approach, and we agreed to form a joint stand capable of pursuing political action which, with Arab support, can take advantage of the available opportunity to liberate our people, land, and foremost of all, Arab Jerusalem.

Then, upon request of Mr. Yasser Arafat, we waited to see the results of the PNC meeting, where Mr. Arafat assured us he would act to secure the support of the council for the envisaged joint political action, on whose basic elements we agreed, pending their development in the PNC by declaring a confederate-union relationship between Jordan and Palestine.

In our latest meeting with Mr. Arafat, held in Amman between March 31 and April 5, we conducted a joint assessment of the realities of the Palestine problem in general, and in particular of the dilemma facing the Palestinian people under occupation. We also discussed political action in accordance with the Arab and international peace plans, including President Reagan's peace initiative, bearing in mind the resolutions of the PNC. We held intensive talks on the principles and the methods, and reemphasized the importance of a confederal relationship between Jordan and Palestine as being a practical conceptualization from which to work for the implementation of this initiative. We agreed to work together in this delicate and crucial time to form a united Arab stand that would enable us to deal with the practical aspects of these initiatives, in the hope of achieving a just, permanent, and comprehensive solution to the Middle East problem, especially the Palestinian problem.

We also agreed to start immediately joint political action on the Arab level to secure Arab support that would contribute enormously to the realization of the common goal of liberating the lands and people under occupation, thus fulfilling our duty to work in all possible ways and to take advantage of every possible opportunity to achieve our aims.

Together with PLO Chairman Yasser Arafat we laid the final draft of our agreement, which required us and Mr. Arafat to make immediate contacts with Arab leaders to inform them of its contents, seeking their blessing of and support for the agreement.

The PLO Executive Committee deliberated on this issue in the course of several meetings, and finally Mr. Arafat decided to discuss the agreement with other PLO leaders outside Jordan, and return to Amman after 2 days to conclude the joint steps necessary for the implementation of the agreement.

Five days later, a delegate was sent by the PLO Executive Committee chairman to Amman, to convey to us new ideas and to propose a new course of action that differed from our agreement and that did not give priority to saving the land, thus sending us back to where we were in October 1982.

In the light of this, it became evident that we cannot proceed with the course of political action which we had planned together, and to which we had agreed in principle and in detail, in answer to our historic responsibility to take the opportunities made available by Arab and international initiatives, and save our land and people.

In view of the results of the efforts we made with the PLO, and in compliance with the 1974 Rabat summit resolution, and through the strict observance of the independence of the Palestinian decision, we respect the decision of the PLO, it being the sole legitimate representative of the Palestinian people. Accordingly, we leave it to the PLO and to the Palestinian people to choose the ways and means for the salvation of themselves and their land, and for the realization of their declared aims in the manner they see fit.

We in Jordan, having refused from the beginning to negotiate on behalf of the Palestinians, will neither act separately nor in lieu of anybody in any Middle East peace negotiations. Jordan will work as a member of the Arab League, in compliance with its resolutions, to support the PLO within our capabilities, and in compliance with the requirements of our national security.

Being consistent with ourselves, and faithful to our principles, Arab Jerusalem, and holy shrines, we shall continue to provide support for our brothers in the occupied Palestinian territories, and make our pledge to them before the Almighty that we shall remain their faithful brother, and side with them in their ordeal.

As for us in Jordan, we are directly affected by the results of the continued occupation of the West Bank and the Gaza Strip through the accelerating colonization program and through the economic pressures systematically being brought on the Palestinian people to force them out of their land.

In the light of these facts, and in the no-war and no-peace situation that prevails, we find ourselves more concerned than anybody else to confront the de facto annexation of the West Bank and the Gaza Strip, which forces us to take all steps necessary to safeguard our national security in all its dimensions.

Both Jordanians and Palestinians shall remain one family that cares for its national unity to the same extent that it cares to stay on this beloved Arab land.

May God assist us in our aspirations.

Notes

I International Documents

1. *The Search for Peace in the Middle East. Documents and Statements 1967-1979.* Report prepared for the Subcommittee on Europe and the Middle East of the Committee on Foreign Affairs, US House of Representatives (Washington: US Government Printing Office, 1979), p. 93.
2. *Ibid.*, p. 97.
3. *Ibid.*
4. *Middle East Record, 1969-70,* Daniel Dishon (ed.), vol. 5 (Jerusalem: Israel Universities Press, 1971), pp. 13-15.
5. *Israel's Foreign Relations,* Meron Medzini (ed.) *Selected Documents 1947-1974,* (Jerusalem: Ministry of Foreign Affairs 1976), pp. 1064-1065.
6. *The Search for Peace, op. cit., p. 101.*
7. *Ibid.*, pp. 159-160.
8. *Ibid.*, p. 176.
9. *Documents and Statements on Middle East Peace, 1979-82.* Report prepared for the Subcommittee on Europe and the Middle East of the Committee on Foreign Affairs, US House of Representatives (Washington: US Government Printing Office, 1982), p. 58.
10. *The New York Times,* 14 June, 1980.
11. *F.B.I.S. USSR International Affairs, Middle East & North Africa,* 16 September, 1982.

II US Documents

1. *The Search for Peace, op. cit., pp. 288-9.*
2. *Ibid.*, p. 292.
3. Israel Ministry of Foreign Affairs, Information Division, Jerusalem, 1975.
4. *The Search for Peace, op. cit.,* pp. 305-7.
5. *Ibid.*, pp. 155-6.
6. *Ibid.*, pp. 309-310.
7. *Ibid.*, p. 311.
8. *Ibid.*, p. 316.
9. *United States Information Services,* Embassy of the United States of America.
10. Israel Government Press Office.

III Sadat's Visit and the Autonomy Negotiations

1. *Israel's Foreign Relations, op. cit.,* 1977-1979, pp. 182-190.
2. *Ibid.*, pp. 191-201.
3. *F.B.I.S. Middle East and North Africa,* 29 December, 1977.
4. *The Search for Peace, op. cit.,* pp. 20-3.
5. *Documents and Statements, op, cit.,* pp. 16-20.
6. *Ibid.*, pp. 38-42.

IV   Israeli Documents

1. *International Documents on Palestine, 1967,* Fuad A. Jabber (ed.), (Beirut: Institute on Palestine Studies. The University of Kuwait, Kuwait, 1972) p. 156.
2. *Israel's Foreign Relations, 1947-1977 op. cit.,* pp. 849-857.
3. *The Jerusalem Post,* 14 May, 1969.
4. *The Jerusalem Post,* 12 December, 1969.
5. *The Jerusalem Post,* 17 March, 1972.
6. *International Documents on Palestine, op. cit.,* 1973, pp. 269-271.
7. *International Documents on Palestine, op. cit.,* 1974, pp. 314-315.
8. *The Hashemite Kingdom of Jordan and the West Bank, a Handbook,* Anne Sinai and Allan Pollock (eds.), (New York: American Academic Association for Peace in the Middle East, 1971), pp. 352-353.
9. *International Documents on Palestine, op. cit.,* 1976, pp 323-328.
10. *International Documents on Palestine, op. cit.,* 1977, p. 256.
11. *International Documents on Palestine, op. cit.,* 1980, pp. 211-212.
12. *Beyond Lebabon* Hillel Schenker (ed.), (New York: The Pilgrim Press, 1983), pp. 496-498.
13. *Israel Government Press Office.*

V   Israeli Party and Extra Parliamentary Platforms

1. *Agudat Israel Party* Information Department, 1981.
2. *Hatehiya Party* Information Department, 1981.
3. *Israel Labour Party* Information Department, 1980.
4. *Liberal Party* Information Department, 1981.
5. *Likud Party* information Department, 1981.
6. *Mafdal Party* Information Department, 1977.
7. *Mapam Party* Information Department, 1981.
8. *Ratz Party* Information Department, 1981.
9. *Hadash Party* Information Department, 1981.
10. *Shinui Party* Information Department, 1983.
11. *Tami Party* Information Department, 1981.
12. *Peace Now* Information Department, 1983.
13. *Gush Emunim* Information Department, n.d.
14. *New Outlook* February/March 1976, Vol 19, No 2 (165) p. 69.

VI   Palestinian Documents

1. *International Documents on Palestine, op. cit.,* 1967, pp. 715-716.
2. *Middle East Record.* op. cit., pp. 432-436.
3. *International documents on Palestine op. cit.,* 1968, pp. 399-403.
4. *F.B.I.S. Daily Report, Middle East and North Africa,* 14 July, 1971.
5. *Journal of Palestine Studies,* Spring, 1973, pp. 169-172.
6. *International Documents on Palestine, op. cit.,* 1974, pp. 410-411.
7. *F.B.I.S. Daily Report,* 10 June, 1974.
8. *International Documents on Palestine, op. cit.,* 1974, pp. 500-503.
9. *Journal of Palestine Studies,* Winter, 1975, pp. 181-192.
10. *B.B.C. Summary of World Broadcasts,* 22 March, 1977.

11. *International Documents on Palestine, op. cit.,* 1977, p. 462.

12. *Journal of Palestine Studies,* Summer, 1978, pp. 195-196.

13. *Journal of Palestine Studies,* Winter, 1979, pp. 194-195.

14. *Journal of Palestine Studies,* Spring, 1979, pp. 165-169.

15. *Congressional Record,* 11 October, 1979, p. 267.

16. *International Documents on Palestine, op. cit.,* 1980, pp. 154-157.

17. *F.B.I.S. Daily Report, The Middle East and North africa,* 22 April, 1981.

18. *Ibid.*

19. *Al-Fajr,* (English Edition), 4 March, 1983.

VII   Arab Documents

1. *International Documents on Palestine op. cit.,* 1967, pp. 656-657.

2. *Middle East Record,* 1969-1970 *op. cit., 1970, p. 15.*

3. *Arabia and the Gulf,* 16 May, 1977, pp. 12-13.

4. *B.B.C. Summary of World Broadcasts,* 17 March, 1972.

5. *Documents on Israel's Foreign Relations, op. cit.,* 1974-1976, pp. 1076-1077.

6. *The Search for Peace..., op. cit.,* p. 273.

7. *International Documents on Palestine,* op. cit., 1976, p. 503.

8. *The Search for Peace...,* op. cit., pp. 274-276.

9. *Arab Report and Record,* 16-30 September, 1978, p. 700.

10. *F.B.I.S. Daily Report, The Middle East and North Africa,* 6 November, 1978.

11. *F.B.I.S. Daily Report, The Middle East and North Africa,* 2 April, 1979.

12. *Saudi Press Agency,* 1981.

13. *F.B.I.S. Daily Report, The Middle East and North Africa,* 7 September, 1982.

14. *American Arab Affairs,* Winter, 1982, No. 3.

15. F.B.I.S. *Daily Report, The Middle East and North Africa,* 4 January, 1983.

16. *F.B.I.S. Daily Report, The Middle East and North Africa,* 11 April, 1983.